1001 FAST EASY Recipes

Cookbook Resources, LLC
Highland Village, Texas

1001 Fast Easy Recipes

1st Printing - January 2007
2nd Printing - December 2008
3rd Printing - August 2009

International Standard Book Number: 978-1-59769-027-0

Library of Congress Control Number: 2009907018

Cover and illustrations by Nancy Bohanan

Edited, Designed, Published and Manufactured in the United States of America by
Cookbook Resources, LLC
541 Doubletree Drive
Highland Village, Texas 75077

Toll free 866-229-2665

www.cookbookresources.com

cookbook resources LLC

Bringing Family and Friends to the Table

Introduction

Believe it or not, there are still 24 hours in each day. However, these days we spend more time away from home and our families. However late we arrive home from our busy day, there are still meals to prepare, dishes to clean, lunches to make, homework to be done and laundry that will need folding.

We can't help with the laundry or homework. We can help you save time in the kitchen, by offering you *1001 Fast Easy Recipes*. Time saved is time earned!

And, with 1,001 different recipes, moms will never-again hear the dreaded moan of "We're having this again?".

Included in this book are timesaving recipes guaranteed to please even the most discriminating of palates (read: children). These delicious recipes use ingredients that can be found in your own pantry. No long grocery lists needed!

Whether you are putting together an impromptu party or feeding your family on a weeknight, *1001 Fast Easy Recipes* is your quick-look book for easy, affordable meal ideas.

With all the time you are saving, you can finally follow through on 1998's New Year's resolution or start on that honey-do list somebody's been nagging about. Better yet, take the time for yourself. It's okay, we won't tell.

Contents

Contents

Dedication

With a mission of helping you bring family and friends to the table, Cookbook Resources strives to make family meals and entertaining friends simple, easy and delicious.

We recognize the importance of sharing meals as a means of building family bonds with memories and traditions that will be treasured for a lifetime. It is an opportunity to sit down with each other and share more than food.

This cookbook is dedicated with gratitude and respect for all those who show their love with homecooked meals, bringing family and friends to the table.

More and more statistical studies are finding that family meals play a significant role in childhood development. Children who eat with their families four or more nights per week are healthier, make better grades, score higher on aptitude tests and are less likely to have problems with drugs.

Whiz-Bang Starters

Dips
Appetizers
Beverages

Creamy Onion Dip

2 (8 ounce) packages cream cheese, softened	2 (230 g)
3 tablespoons lemon juice	45 ml
1 (1 ounce) packet dry onion soup mix	30 g
1 (8 ounce) carton sour cream	230 g

- Beat cream cheese until smooth. Blend in lemon juice and onion soup mix. Gradually fold in sour cream until it blends well. Refrigerate.
- Serve with chips, crackers or fresh vegetables.

Cottage-Ham Dip

1 (16 ounce) carton small curd cottage cheese, drained	455 g
2 (6 ounce) cans deviled ham	2 (170 g)
1 (1 ounce) packet dry onion soup mix	30 g
½ cup sour cream	120 g

- Blend cottage cheese in blender or mixer.
- Add ham, soup mix and sour cream and mix well. Serve with crackers.

Crunchy Asparagus Dip

1 (15 ounce) can asparagus spears, drained, chopped	425 g
½ cup mayonnaise	110 g
¼ teaspoon hot sauce	1 ml
½ cup chopped pecans	55g

- Combine all ingredients in medium bowl and refrigerate. Serve with wheat crackers.

Hot Crab Dip

1 (8 ounce) package cream cheese, softened	230 g
3 tablespoons milk	45 ml
½ teaspoon Worcestershire	2 ml
½ teaspoon hot sauce	2 ml
2 teaspoons prepared horseradish	10 ml
1 tablespoon instant onion flakes	15 ml
2 (6 ounce) cans crab, drained, flaked	2 (170 g)

● Preheat oven to 375° (190° C). In mixing bowl, combine cream cheese, milk, Worcestershire, hot sauce and horseradish, beat on low speed until all ingredients are well blended. Stir in onion flakes and crab and spread in small, buttered ovenproof dish and bake for 15 minutes. Serve warm with crackers.

Hot, Rich Crab Dip

1 (10 ounce) can cheddar cheese soup	280 g
1 (16 ounce) package cubed Mexican processed cheese	455 g
2 (6 ounce) cans crabmeat, flaked, drained	2 (170 g)
1 (16 ounce) jar salsa	455 g

● In microwave-safe bowl, combine cheese soup and processed cheese. Microwave at 1-minute intervals until cheese melts. Add crabmeat and salsa and mix well. Serve hot with chips.

Elegant Crab Dip

1 (6 ounce) can white crabmeat, drained, flaked	170 g
1 (8 ounce) package cream cheese	230 g
½ cup (1 stick) butter	115 g

● In saucepan, combine crabmeat, cream cheese and butter. Heat and mix thoroughly. Transfer to hot chafing dish. Serve with chips.

Cucumber Dip

2 seedless cucumbers, peeled, shredded, drained	
1 (8 ounce) carton sour cream	230 g
2 teaspoons white vinegar	10 ml
2 teaspoons olive oil	10 ml
1 teaspoon minced garlic	5 ml

- After shredding cucumbers, drain well on several paper towels. Add sour cream, vinegar, olive oil, garlic and 1 teaspoon (5 ml) salt, mixing well and refrigerate. Serve with wheat crackers or pita wedges.

White Bean Dip

1 (3 ounce) package cream cheese, softened	85 g
2 (15 ounce) cans cannellini (or navy) beans, drained	2 (425 g)
1 heaping teaspoon prepared minced garlic	5 ml
¼ cup extra-virgin olive oil	60 ml
2 teaspoons fresh, minced rosemary	10 ml
Grated zest of 1 lemon	

- Place cream cheese, beans, garlic and salt to taste, in bowl of food processor. Turn machine on and add olive oil in a steady stream and process until smooth. Place mixture in bowl and stir in minced rosemary and lemon zest. Refrigerate.

Talking Tomato Dip

1 (10 ounce) can diced tomatoes and green chilies, drained	280 g
1 (8 ounce) carton sour cream	230 g
2 teaspoons horseradish	10 ml
Chips	

- Combine all ingredients and 1½ teaspoons (7 ml) salt. Refrigerate and serve with chips.

Warm Cheddar-Onion Dip

1 (3 ounce) package cream cheese, softened, cut into chunks	85 g
⅔ cup mayonnaise	150 g
1 sweet yellow onion (Vidalia if available), finely chopped	
1 (12 ounce) package shredded cheddar cheese	340 g
½ teaspoon dried thyme	2 ml

- Preheat oven to 350° (175° C). Beat together cream cheese and mayonnaise, until mixture blends well. Stir in onions.
- In bowl, combine onion-cream cheese mixture, cheddar cheese and dried thyme. Spoon into a shallow baking dish; cover and bake 20 minutes. Cool slightly and serve with round buttery crackers.

Whip-It-Up Dip

1 (2.5 ounce) jar dried beef, coarsely chopped	70 g
1 (8 ounce) package shredded cheddar cheese	230 g
⅔ cup mayonnaise	150 g
⅔ teaspoon garlic powder	3 ml

- Combine all ingredients and mix well. Serve with crackers.

Velvet Dip

2 (16 ounce) packages cubed Mexican processed cheese	2 (455 g)
2 cups mayonnaise	450 g
1 (4 ounce) jar chopped pimentos, drained	115 g
1 (7 ounce) can diced green chilies	200 g

- Place cheese in saucepan and melt over low heat. Add other ingredients and mix well. Serve with chips.

Speedy Cheese Dip

2 (10 ounce) cans cheddar cheese soup	2 (280 g)
1 (10 ounce) can diced tomatoes and green chilies	280 g
1 (10 ounce) can cream of chicken soup	280 g
Pinch of cayenne pepper	

- Mix all ingredients in saucepan. Add ½ teaspoon (2 ml) salt to taste. Serve hot. Serve with chips.

Five Minute Dip

1 (8 ounce) package cream cheese, softened	230 g
1 cup mayonnaise	225 g
1 (1 ounce) packet ranch-style salad dressing mix	30 g
½ onion, finely minced	

- Combine cream cheese and mayonnaise and beat until creamy. Stir in dressing mix and onion. Refrigerate and serve with fresh vegetables.

Egg and Cheese Dip

5 eggs, hard-boiled, mashed	
1 cup mayonnaise	225g
½ cup shredded Monterey Jack cheese	55 g
½ teaspoon prepared mustard	2 ml

- Combine all ingredients in bowl and mix well. Add salt to taste and refrigerate. Serve with wheat crackers.

Cottage Cheese Dip

1 cup small curd cottage cheese	225 g
½ cup crumbled feta cheese	70 g
1 teaspoon dried oregano	5 ml
¼ teaspoon lemon juice	1 ml

- Combine all ingredients in blender and process until smooth. Pour into small bowl and serve with celery sticks, fresh broccoli florets or baby carrots.

Beer and Cheese Dip

1 large onion, finely chopped	
2 tablespoons butter	30 g
1 cup beer	250 ml
1 (2 pound) box Mexican processed cheese	910 g

- In large saucepan, cook onion in butter, but do not brown; add beer. Cut cheese into large chunks and add to onion and cook on low heat, stirring constantly until all cheese is melted. Serve with tortilla chips.

Easy Cheesy Bean Dip

1 (15 ounce) can refried beans	425 g
1 teaspoon minced garlic	5 ml
1 cup milk	250 ml
1 (16 ounce) package cubed Mexican processed cheese	455 g

- In large saucepan, combine beans, garlic and milk and stir on low heat until smooth. Add cheese and stir on low heat until cheese melts. Serve warm with chips.

California Clam Dip

1 (1 ounce) packet dry onion soup mix	30 g
2 (8 ounce) cartons sour cream	2 (230 g)
1 (6 ounce) can minced clams, drained	170 g
2 tablespoons chili sauce	35 g

- Combine onion soup mix and sour cream and mix well.
- Add clams and chili sauce and refrigerate.

Velvet Clam Dip

1½ (8 ounces) packages cream cheese	1½ (230 g)
¼ cup (½ stick) butter	60 g
2 (6 ounce) cans minced clams, drained	2 (170 g)
½ teaspoon Worcestershire sauce	2 ml

- Melt cream cheese and butter in double boiler. Add drained minced clams and Worcestershire sauce. Serve hot.

Party Shrimp Dip

1 (8 ounce) package cream cheese, softened	230 g
½ cup mayonnaise	110 g
1 (6 ounce) can tiny, cooked shrimp, drained	170 g
¾ teaspoon Creole seasoning	4 ml

- Blend cream cheese and mayonnaise in mixer. Stir in shrimp and seasoning. Mix well and refrigerate. Serve with chips.

Hot Cheesy Bean Dip

1 (15 ounce) can Mexican stewed tomatoes	425 g
1 (15 ounce) can pinto beans, drained	425 g
1 (15 ounce) can refried beans	425 g
¼ teaspoon ground cumin	1 ml
¼ teaspoon oregano	1 ml
1 cup shredded cheddar cheese	115 g

- Preheat oven to 350° (175° C). In bowl, combine tomatoes, pinto beans, refried beans, cumin, oregano and ¼ teaspoon (1 ml) salt. Spoon into 7 x 11-inch (18 x 28 cm) baking dish, cover and bake for 15 minutes. Remove cover and sprinkle cheese over top of bean mixture. Return to oven to 5 minutes. Serve with tortilla chips.

Pep-Pep-Pepperoni Dip

2 (8 ounce) packages cream cheese, softened	2 (230 g)
1 (3.5 ounce) package pepperoni slices	100 g
1 (10 ounce) bottle chili sauce	280 g
1 bunch green onions with tops, chopped	

- In mixing bowl, beat cream cheese until creamy. Cut pepperoni slices into smaller pieces. Add pepperoni, chili sauce and green onions to cream cheese and mix well. Refrigerate and serve with chips.

Spinach-Feta Dip

1 (8 ounce) carton sour cream	230 g
1 (8 ounce) package cream cheese, softened	230 g
¾ cup crumbled feta cheese	100 g
1 (10 ounce) package frozen chopped spinach, thawed	280 g

- In mixing bowl, beat sour cream, cream cheese and 1 teaspoon (5 ml) salt. Fold in feta cheese. Using several paper towels, squeeze spinach until all liquid is drained. Stir into cheese mixture, adding 1 teaspoon (5 ml) minced garlic if you like.

Creamy Sausage Dip

1 (16 ounce) roll sausage	455 g
1 teaspoon minced garlic	5 ml
2 (8 ounce) packages cream cheese	2 (230 g)
1 (10 ounce) can diced tomatoes and green chilies	280 g

- In skillet cook sausage over medium heat until it is slightly brown. Drain well.
- Stir in garlic, cream cheese and tomatoes and green chilies. On medium heat, stir until cream cheese melts and dip is thoroughly hot. Serve with chips.

Black Bean Dip

2 (15 ounce) cans black beans, rinsed, drained	2 (425 g)
1 sweet onion, finely chopped	
1 green bell pepper, finely chopped	
1 (4 ounce) can chopped pimentos	115 g
3 tablespoons olive oil	45 ml
2 tablespoons red wine vinegar	30 ml
2 teaspoons minced garlic	10 ml
2 teaspoons sugar	10 ml

- Place 1 can of beans in bowl and mash second can with fork and add to whole beans. Add chopped onion, bell pepper and pimentos.
- In small bowl, combine olive oil, vinegar, garlic, sugar and salt to taste. Stir into bean mixture.
- Serve at room temperature with tortilla chips. Refrigerate any leftover dip.

Crab Dip Kick

1 (8 ounce) package cream cheese, softened	230 g
3 tablespoons picante sauce	50 g
2 tablespoons prepared horseradish	30 g
1 (6 ounce) can crabmeat, drained, flaked	170 g

- In mixing bowl, beat cream cheese until creamy; add picante and horseradish and mix well.
- Stir in crabmeat and refrigerate. Serve with assorted crackers.

Broccoli-Cheese Dip

1 (10 ounce) can broccoli-cheese soup	280 g
1 (10 ounce) package frozen chopped broccoli, thawed	280 g
½ cup sour cream	120 g
2 teaspoons dijon-style mustard	10 ml

- In saucepan, combine soup, broccoli, sour cream, mustard and ½ teaspoon (2 ml) salt and mix well. Heat and serve hot.

Broccoli Dip

1 (10 ounce) package frozen chopped broccoli, thawed	280 g
1 (10 ounce) can cream of chicken soup	280 g
1 (12 ounce) package shredded cheddar cheese	340 g
1 (7 ounce) can diced green chilies	200 g

- In saucepan, cook broccoli for 5 minutes in butter and about ½ teaspoon (2 ml) salt.
- Add soup, cheese and green chilies and heat until cheese melts. (If chilies are not hot enough, add several dashes of hot sauce.) Serve with tostados.

Red Pepper Artichoke Dip

1 (14 ounce) can artichoke hearts, drained, chopped	395 g
1 cup mayonnaise	225 g
1½ cups shredded mozzarella cheese	170 g
½ cup roasted red peppers, drained, chopped	130 g

- Preheat oven to 350° (175° C). Combine all ingredients and place in greased 8-inch (20 cm) baking dish. Bake 25 minutes or until thoroughly hot.

Steamy Hot Artichoke Dip

1 (14 ounce) can artichoke, drained, chopped	395 g
1¼ cups mayonnaise (not light)	280 g
1 cup grated parmesan cheese	100 g
2 teaspoons minced garlic	10 ml

- Preheat oven to 350° (175° C). In bowl, combine artichoke, mayonnaise, parmesan and garlic, mixing well.
- Spoon into an 8 or 9-inch (20 cm) glass pie pan and bake uncovered for 25 minutes. Serve hot with wheat crackers.

Artichoke Bean Dip

1 (14 ounce) jar marinated artichoke hearts	395 g
2 (15 ounce) cans garbanzo beans, rinsed, drained	2 (425 g)
4 fresh green onions, sliced	
⅓ cup mayonnaise	75 g

- Drain artichokes and set aside liquid. Coarsely chop artichoke and set aside. In blender, combine beans, green onions and reserved liquid; pulse until smooth.
- Combine artichokes with mixture from blender and stir in mayonnaise and a little salt and pepper. Serve with crackers.

Special Guacamole

4 medium avocados, peeled	
3 tablespoons sour cream	45 g
1 tablespoon hot sauce	15 ml
1½ teaspoons garlic salt	7 ml
2 teaspoons lemon juice	10 ml
2 tablespoons Italian salad dressing	30 ml

- In bowl, mash avocados to desired smoothness and stir in sour cream, hot sauce, garlic salt, lemon juice and Italian dressing. You may want to taste to determine if you need extra salt. Serve with chips.

2 (15 ounce) cans black beans, drained, mashed	2 (425 g)
1 (16 ounce) jar mild salsa	455 g
1 (8 ounce) package shredded Monterey Jack cheese	230 g
2 teaspoons ground cumin	10 ml
1 teaspoon garlic powder	5 ml
1 (4.3 ounce) package real crumbled bacon	115 g

- In saucepan combine beans and salsa (use hot salsa if you want more spice), stir in cheese, cumin and garlic powder.
- Heat on low-medium, stirring constantly until mixture is hot. Stir in crumbled bacon and transfer to serving bowl. Serve with chips.

Holy Guacamole

4 avocados, peeled, seeded
½ cup salsa   130 g
¼ cup sour cream   60 g
Tortilla chips

- Mash avocados with fork and mix with salsa, sour cream and 1 teaspoon (5 ml) salt. Serve with tortilla chips.

Dipping Sauce for Leftover Ham

¾ cup peanut butter   215 g
2 tablespoons soy sauce   30 ml
½ cup honey   170 g
3 tablespoons lime juice   45 ml

- In bowl, combine all dip ingredients, mixing well. Cut ham in bite-size chunks and use toothpicks for ham and dip-dip-dip!

Quickie Shrimp Dunk

1 (8 ounce) package cream cheese, softened   230 g
1 (10 ounce) bottle of cocktail sauce   280 g
1 teaspoon Italian herb seasoning   5 ml
1 (6 ounce) can tiny shrimp, drained   170 g

- Place cream cheese in mixing bowl and beat until smooth.
- Add remaining ingredients and refrigerate. Serve with crackers.

Cream-Cheese Dip for Apples

1 (8 ounce) package cream cheese, softened   230 g
2 tablespoons powdered sugar   15 g
3 tablespoons orange juice concentrate, thawed   45 ml
1 teaspoon ground cinnamon   5 ml

- In mixing bowl, combine all ingredients and mix until well blended.

Caramel-Apple Dip

1 (8 ounce) package cream cheese, softened	230 g
1 cup packed brown sugar	220 g
1 teaspoon vanilla	5 ml
½ cup chopped dry-roasted peanuts	75 g

- With mixer beat together cream cheese, brown sugar and vanilla until creamy. Stir in peanuts and refrigerate. Serve with crisp apple slices.

Peachy Fruit Dip

1 (15 ounce) can sliced peaches, drained	425 g
½ cup marshmallow cream	125 ml
1 (3 ounce) package cream cheese, cubed	85 g
⅛ teaspoon ground nutmeg	.5 ml

- In blender or food processor, combine all ingredients. Serve with assorted fresh fruit.

Curried Cheese Spread

2 (8 ounce) packages cream cheese, softened	2 (230 g)
1 (10 ounce) jar mango chutney	280 g
1 (5 ounce) package slivered almonds, toasted	140 g
2 teaspoons curry powder	10 ml

- In blender, combine cream cheese, chutney, almonds and curry powder until creamy. Cover and refrigerate. Shape into round balls. Serve with assorted crackers or apple slices.

Hot Artichoke Spread

1 (14 ounce) can artichoke hearts, drained, finely chopped	395 g
1 cup mayonnaise	225 g
1 cup grated parmesan cheese	100 g
1 (1 ounce) package Italian salad dressing mix	30 g

- Remove tough outer leaves and chop artichoke hearts. Combine all ingredients and mix thoroughly.
- Pour into 8-inch (20 cm) baking pan. Bake at 350° (175° C) for 20 minutes. Serve hot with assorted crackers.

Devil's Spread

1 (4 ounce) can deviled ham	115 g
¾ cup mayonnaise	170 g
1 tablespoon grated onion	15 ml
1 (4 ounce) can diced green chilies, drained	115 g

- Mix all ingredients. Spread on wheat crackers.

Black Olive Spread

1 (8 ounce) package cream cheese, softened	230 g
½ cup mayonnaise	110 g
1 (4 ounce) can chopped black olives	115 g
3 green onions with tops, finely chopped	

- Blend cream cheese and mayonnaise until smooth. Add olives and onions and refrigerate. Spread on slices of party rye bread.

Sweet Cheezy-Garlic Spread

2 (8 ounce) packages cream cheese, softened	2 (230 g)
¼ cup apricot preserves	80 g
1 teaspoon minced garlic	5 ml
¼ cup finely chopped walnuts	30 g
3 fresh green onions, finely chopped (only green portion)	

- In mixing bowl, combine cream cheese and apricot preserves and beat until well blended. Stir in garlic, walnuts and green onions. Refrigerate. Serve with assorted crackers.

Artichoke-Cheese Spread

2 (8 ounce) packages cream cheese, softened	2 (230 g)
1½ cups grated parmesan cheese	150 g
1 tablespoon lemon juice	15 ml
1 teaspoon garlic salt	5 ml
¼ cup finely chopped green onions	25 g
1 (14 ounce) can artichoke hearts, drained, chopped	395 g

- In mixing bowl, beat together cream cheese, parmesan cheese, lemon juice and garlic salt. Stir in green onion, artichoke hearts and mix well. Refrigerate and serve with wheat crackers.

Pineapple-Island Spread

2 (8 ounce) packages cream cheese, softened	2 (230 g)
1 (8 ounce) carton sour cream	230 g
1 (8 ounce) can crushed pineapple with juice	230 g
½ cup finely chopped pecans	55 g

- In mixing bowl, combine cream cheese and sour cream and beat until creamy. Fold in pineapple and pecans and mix well; refrigerate.

Shrimp Squares Deluxe

1 (6 ounce) can shrimp, drained, chopped	170 g
1 cup mayonnaise	225 g
1 cup shredded cheddar cheese	115 g
10 - 12 slices white bread, trimmed, cut in 4 squares	

- Combine shrimp, mayonnaise and cheese. Spread shrimp mixture on bread squares and broil until bubbly.

Avocado Olé

3 large ripe avocados, mashed	
1 tablespoon fresh lemon juice	15 ml
1 (1 ounce) packet dry onion soup mix	30 g
1 (8 ounce) carton sour cream	230 g

- Mix avocados with lemon juice and blend in soup mix, sour cream and salt to taste. Serve with chips or crackers.

Chili-Cheese Bites

6 slices white sandwich bread	
1 (14 ounce) package shredded cheddar cheese	395 g
½ cup (1 stick) butter, softened	115 g
¾ teaspoon chili powder	4 ml

- Trim bread crusts and cut each slice into 4 squares. Combine cheese, butter and chili powder and mix well. Place heaping teaspoonful (5 ml) of mixture on each bread square and place on baking sheet. Bake at 375° (190° C) for 10 minutes or until puffy and light brown.

Olive-Cheese Empanadas

1 cup pimento-stuffed green olives or black olives, chopped, divided	95 g
1 cup finely shredded cheddar cheese	115 g
¼ cup mayonnaise	55 g
1 (15 ounce) package of 2 refrigerated piecrusts	425 g

- Preheat oven to 450° (230° C). Combine olives, cheese and mayonnaise.
- Use 3-inch (8 cm) biscuit cutter to cut each piecrust into 12 rounds. Place 1 teaspoon (5 ml) olive mixture in center of pastry round. Fold side of pastry to other side and press edges together.
- Crimp edge with thumb and forefinger or use tines of fork to seal edges. If pastry begins to dry it will not seal properly. Dip finger in water and lightly brush edges and seal.
- Place on baking sheet and bake for about 10 minutes or until golden brown.

Bacon-Wrapped Water Chestnuts

1 (8 ounce) can whole water chestnuts, drained	230 g
¼ cup soy sauce	60 ml
¼ teaspoon cayenne pepper	1 ml
½ pound bacon, cut in thirds	230 g

- Marinate water chestnuts for 1 hour in soy sauce and cayenne pepper. Wrap bacon around water chestnuts and secure with toothpick. Bake at 375° (190° C) for 20 minutes or until bacon is done. Drain and serve hot.

Olive-Cheese Appetizers

1 cup chopped pimento-stuffed olives	95 g
2 fresh green onions, finely chopped	
1½ cups shredded Monterey Jack cheese	170 g
½ cup mayonnaise	110 g
6 English muffins, cut in half	

- In large bowl, combine olives, onions, cheese and mayonnaise; mix well. Spread on muffins and bake at 375° (190° C) until bubbly.
- Cut muffins into quarters and serve hot.

Artichoke Bites

1½ cups mayonnaise	335 g
¾ cup freshly grated parmesan cheese	25 g
1 (4 ounce) can diced green chilies	115 g
1 (14 ounce) jar artichoke hearts, chopped	395 g

- Combine mayonnaise, parmesan cheese, green chilies and artichoke hearts. (Remove any spikes or tough leaves from artichokes.) Place 1 teaspoon (5 ml) mixture on bite-size toast rounds. Broil until light brown.

Baked Cheese Snacks

1½ cups biscuit mix	180 g
2 eggs, slightly beaten	
1 (4 ounce) can diced green chilies	115 g
1 cup shredded cheddar cheese	115 g

- Preheat oven to 375° (190° C). Blend together baking mix, eggs and green chilies and stir in cheese. Drop dough by teaspoonfuls about 2 inches (5 cm) apart on sprayed baking sheet. Bake for 12 minutes or until golden brown. Serve warm.

Sausage Cheese Balls

1 pound hot sausage	455 g
1 pound regular sausage	455 g
1½ cups biscuit mix	180 g
1 (16 ounce) package shredded sharp cheddar cheese	455 g
½ cup finely chopped celery	50 g
½ cup finely chopped onion	80 g
½ teaspoon garlic powder, optional	2 ml

- Preheat oven to 375° (190° C). Combine all ingredients and form into 1-inch (2.5 cm) balls. Place balls on ungreased cookie sheet. Bake about 15 minutes. Balls can be made and frozen; then baked at a later time.

Sausage Rounds

1 (8 ounce) package crescent dinner rolls	230 g
½ teaspoon garlic powder	2 ml
½ cup grated cheddar cheese	55 g
1 pound sausage	455 g

- Open package of rolls, smooth out dough with rolling pin and seal seams. Sprinkle dough with garlic powder and cheese.
- Break up sausage with hands and spread thin layer sausage over rolls. Roll into a log. Wrap in wax paper and freeze for several hours.
- Slice into ¼-inch (6 mm) rounds. Place on baking sheet and bake at 350° (175° C) for 20 minutes or until light brown.

Bits of Frank

1 (8 count) package frankfurters	
1 (8 ounce) package cornbread-muffin mix	230 g
½ teaspoon chili powder	2 ml
½ cup milk	125 ml
1 (10 ounce) bottle chili sauce	280 g

- Cut franks into 1-inch (2.5 cm) slices. Combine corn-muffin mix, chili powder and milk. Add frankfurters slices to corn-muffin mix and stir well to coat each piece. Drop one at a time into hot oil in deep fryer. Fry for 2 minutes or until brown; drain. Serve warm with chili sauce for dipping.

Bubbly Franks

1 (10 count) package wieners	
½ cup chili sauce	135 g
½ cup packed brown sugar	110 g
½ cup bourbon	125 ml

- Cut wieners into half inch slices. Combine chili sauce, sugar and bourbon in saucepan. Add wieners to sauce and simmer for 30 minutes. Serve in chafing dish.

Need a Snack Fix, Quick

Large tortilla chips	
1 (15 ounce) can refried beans	425 g
1 (8 ounce) package cheddar cheese	230 g
1 (16 ounce) jar chunky salsa	455 g

- Spread large tortilla chips on microwave-safe plate. Top each chip with dab of refried beans and sprinkle of cheese. Top with heaping teaspoon (5 ml) of salsa. Microwave on HIGH just until cheese melts.

Make Your Own Cajun Chips

2 teaspoons Cajun seasoning	10 ml
1 teaspoon paprika	5 ml
¼ teaspoon sugar	1 ml
½ teaspoon dried thyme	2 ml
½ teaspoon garlic powder	2 ml
10 (6-inch) flour tortillas	10 (15 cm)

- Preheat oven to 375° (190° C). Combine Cajun seasoning, paprika, sugar, thyme, garlic powder and ½ teaspoon (2 ml) salt. Spread tortillas on 2 baking sheets and coat with cooking spray and sprinkle Cajun seasoning over tortillas. Cut tortillas into wedges. Bake for 6 minutes or until crispy. Cool and store in airtight resealable bags.

Cheese Drops

2 cups biscuit mix	240 g
⅓ cup sour cream	80 g
1 egg	
1 (4 ounce) can diced green chilies, drained	115 g
1½ cups shredded sharp cheddar cheese	170 g

- Preheat oven to 375° (190° C). In bowl, combine biscuit mix, sour cream, egg and green chilies and mix until well blended. Stir in cheese, mixture will be thick. Drop by heaping teaspoons onto a greased baking sheet. Bake 10 minutes or until golden brown. Serve warm.

Cucumber Squares

1 (8 ounce) package cream cheese, softened	230 g
½ teaspoon dillweed	2 ml
3 medium cucumbers, peeled, grated	
1 (1 ounce) packet dry ranch-style salad dressing mix	30 g

- In mixing bowl, combine cream cheese and dillweed and beat until creamy. Fold in grated cucumbers and ranch dressing mix. Spread on pumpernickel or rye bread slices.

Deviled Ham Roll-Ups

1 (8 count) package refrigerated crescent dinner rolls	
1 (2 ounce) can deviled ham	55 g
½ cup sour cream	120 g
1 teaspoon dijon-style mustard	5 ml

- Preheat oven to 350° (175° C). Unroll crescent rolls on sheet of wax paper and form triangles. In bowl, combine deviled ham, sour cream and mustard and spoon heaping teaspoon (5 ml) mixture on each roll.
- Spread filling and leave ½-inch (1.2 cm) at edge. Roll each crescent from wide end to point. Place point-side down on sprayed baking pan and bake 15 minutes or until light brown. Serve warm.

Mexican Fudge

1 (16 ounce) package shredded American cheese, divided	455 g
4 eggs, beaten	
⅔ cup jalapeno green sauce	175 g
1 teaspoon Worcestershire sauce	5 ml

- Spread half cheese in sprayed 9 x 13-inch (23 x 33 cm) baking dish. Combine eggs with green sauce and Worcestershire and pour over cheese in dish. Add remaining cheese.
- Bake at 350° (175° C) for 30 minutes. Cut into squares to serve. May be served hot or room temperature.

English Muffin Pizza

English muffins, halved
Canned or bottled pizza sauce
Sliced salami or pepperoni
Grated mozzarella or cheddar cheese

- Split muffins in half. Spread pizza sauce on muffins. Add salami or pepperoni. Top with grated cheese and place under broiler until cheese melts and begins to bubble.

Puffy Taco Balls

½ pound pork sausage	455 g
1 (8 ounce) package shredded cheddar cheese	230 g
⅓ cup mild taco sauce	75 ml
1½ cups biscuit mix	180 g

- Preheat oven to 375° (190° C). In skillet, brown sausage, drain and crumble; allow to cool. In mixing bowl, combine sausage, cheese, taco sauce and biscuit mix, mixing well. Form into 1-inch (2.5 cm) balls and place on baking sheet.
- Bake about 18 minutes or until balls are light brown.

Shrimp-Stuffed Eggs

8 eggs, hard-boiled	
¼ cup mayonnaise	55 g
1 (6 ounce) can tiny shrimp, drained	170 g
2 tablespoons sweet pickle relish, drained	30 g

- Cut eggs in half lengthwise and set aside egg whites. In small bowl, mash egg yolks with mayonnaise. Add shrimp and pickle relish and mix well. Refill egg whites and refrigerate.

Spicy Cheese Bites

1 cup flour	120 g
½ teaspoon cayenne pepper	2 ml
1 (8 ounce) package finely shredded sharp cheddar cheese	230 g
½ cup (1 stick) butter, softened	115 g

- Preheat oven to 375° (190° C). In bowl, combine flour, cayenne pepper, a little salt, cheese and butter. Mixture will be hard to combine, so the easiest way is to work with your hands until dough forms a ball. Place dough on large piece of wax paper and form into log. Roll tightly in paper and refrigerate.
- Slice dough into ¼-inch (6 mm) rounds and place on baking sheet 1-inch (2.5 cm) apart. Bake about 17 to 18 minutes or until edges are golden. Cool before serving.

Border Queso

2 canned jalapeno peppers	
1 (16 ounce) package cubed processed cheese	455 g
1 (4 ounce) jar pimentos, drained, chopped	115 g
3 green onions with tops, chopped	

- Seed and chop jalapeno peppers; set aside 1 tablespoon (15 ml) liquid. Combine peppers, cheese, pimentos and onions in saucepan. Heat on low and stir constantly, until cheese melts. Stir in set aside jalapeno liquid. Serve with tortilla chips.

Spinach Pinwheels

1 (8 ounce) can crescent dinner rolls	230 g
1 (8 ounce) package garlic-herb spreadable cheese, softened	230 g
6 thin slices cooked deli ham	
30 fresh spinach leaves, stems removed	

- Preheat oven to 350° (175° C). Separate crescent dough into 4 rectangles and press perforations to seal. Generously spread rectangles with cheese, leaving ¼-inch (6 mm) around edge without cheese. Top with ham slices and spinach leaves.
- Starting at short side of dough, roll each rectangle and press edges to seal. Refrigerate rolls for at least 30 minutes and slice each roll into 6 slices. Place slices on ungreased baking sheet and bake about 15 minutes or until lightly brown.

Tuna Melt Appetizer

1 (10 ounce) package frozen spinach, drained	280 g
2 (6 ounce) cans white tuna in water, drained, flaked	2 (170 g)
¾ cup mayonnaise	170 g
1½ cups shredded mozzarella cheese, divided	170 g

- Drain spinach well with several paper towels. In large bowl, combine spinach, tuna, mayonnaise and 1 cup (115 g) cheese and mix well.
- Spoon into buttered, pie plate and bake at 350° (175° C) for 15 minutes. Remove from oven and sprinkle remaining cheese over top. Bake another 5 minutes. Serve with crackers.

Stuffed Jalapenos

12 - 15 medium jalapeno chiles with stems attached	
1 (8 ounce) package cream cheese, softened	230 g
¾ cup finely shredded Monterey Jack cheese	85 g
3 slices cooked ham, chopped very fine	
1 tablespoon lime juice	15 ml
1 tablespoon garlic powder	15 ml

- Preheat oven to 325° (165° C). Cut (using rubber gloves) each jalapeno lengthwise through stem and remove ribs and seeds.
- In bowl, combine cream cheese, Jack cheese, ham, lime juice and garlic powder, beat until well blended. Fill each jalapeno half with cheese mixture. Place on foil lined baking sheet. Bake 15 minutes. Cool slightly before serving.

Cheese Straws

1 (5 ounce) package piecrust mix	140 g
¾ cup shredded cheddar cheese	85 g
Cayenne pepper	
¼ teaspoon garlic powder	1 ml

- Prepare piecrust according to package directions. Roll into rectangular shape. Press cheese into dough and sprinkle cayenne pepper and garlic powder over cheese. Fold dough over once to cover cheese. Roll to make ¼-inch (.6 cm) thickness.
- Cut dough into 3 x ½-inch (8 x 1.2 cm) strips and place on lightly sprayed baking sheet. Bake at 350° (175° C) for 12 to 15 minutes.

Turkey Pizza

4 (8-inch) flour tortillas	4 (20 cm)

Topping:

2 cups deli smoked turkey, diced	280 g
1 (11 ounce) can Mexicorn®, drained	310 g
1 (15 ounce) can black beans, rinsed, drained	425 g
2 tablespoons lemon juice	30 ml
1 cup Monterey Jack cheese with jalapeno peppers	115 g

- Preheat oven to 350° (175° C). Place tortillas on greased baking sheet and bake 10 minutes or until edges are light brown. Remove from oven, stack and press down to flatten.
- In skillet with a little oil, combine diced turkey, corn and black beans. Heat, stirring constantly until mixture is thoroughly hot; stir in lime juice.
- Place tortillas on baking sheet and spoon about ¾ cup (175 ml) turkey-corn mixture on each tortilla. Sprinkle cheese on top of each pizza and return to oven for 2 minutes or just until cheese melts.

Skillet Nachos

½ (16 ounce) package tortilla chips	½ (455 g)
1 (8 ounce) can whole kernel corn, drained	230 g
1 cup chili beans (from 15 ounce can)	255 g/425 g
½ cup thick-and-chunky salsa plus extra salsa for garnish	130 g
1 (8 ounce) package shredded 4-cheese blend	230 g
1 (4 ounce) can ripe olives, sliced	115 g

- Arrange tortilla chips in single layer in large 12-inch (32 cm) skillet (use a skillet that you can take to the table). In saucepan, combine corn, beans and salsa and heat just until hot and bubbly.
- Spoon salsa mixture over tortilla chips, then sprinkle on about three-fourths cheese. Cover skillet and cook on medium high heat about 5 minutes or until cheese melts. To serve, sprinkle ripe olives and remaining cheese over top. You may want to serve with more salsa.

Cheesy Quick Broccoli Quesadillas

1 (8 ounce) package shredded cheddar cheese	230 g
1 (10 ounce) package frozen chopped broccoli, well drained	280 g
⅓ cup salsa	90 g
8 (6 inch) flour tortillas	8 (15 cm)

- In bowl, combine cheese, broccoli and salsa and mix well. Spoon about ¼ cup (60 ml) cheese-broccoli mixture onto 1 side of each tortilla and fold tortilla over filling.
- Spray large non-stick skillet with cooking spray and cook 2 quesadillas at a time on medium heat. Cook about 3 minutes on both sides or until tortillas are light brown.

Taste-Tempting Hot Squares

1 cup grated parmesan cheese	100 g
1 cup shredded mozzarella cheese	115 g
2 (14 ounce) cans artichoke hearts, drained, chopped	2 (395 g)
1 (8 ounce) carton chive and onion cream cheese	230 g
2 (8 ounce) tubes refrigerated crescent rolls	2 (230 g)

- Preheat oven to 350° (175° C). In mixing bowl, combine both cheeses, chopped artichokes and cream cheese and beat until well blended.
- Unroll both tubes of dough and press into greased 10 x 15-inch (25 x 38 cm) baking pan, making it rectangle shape and sealing seams and perforations. Spread with artichoke mixture. Bake for 20 minutes or until crust is light golden brown. Cut into squares to serve.

Cinnamon Pecans

1 pound pecan halves	455 g
1 egg white, slightly beaten	
2 tablespoons ground cinnamon	30 ml
¾ cup sugar	150 g

- Combine pecans and egg white and mix well. Sprinkle with mixture of cinnamon and sugar. Stir until all pecans are well coated.
- Spread on baking sheet and bake at 325° (165° C) for about 20 minutes. Cool and store in covered container.

Crispy-Crunchy Treats

2 (10 ounce) packages marshmallows	2 (280 g)
½ cup (1 stick) butter	115 g
12 cups crispy rice cereal	310 g
1 cup coarsely chopped walnuts, toasted	130 g

- In large saucepan, combine marshmallows and butter; cook on low-medium heat, stirring several times until marshmallows are melted. Stir in half cereal and walnuts until well combined. Stir in remaining cereal and walnuts

- Transfer mixture to well-buttered 9 x 13-inch (23 x 33 cm) baking dish, spreading evenly with back of large buttered spoon or spatula. Cool completely. Cut into large squares and then into triangles.

Barbecued Walnuts

3 tablespoons butter, melted	45 g
¼ cup Worcestershire sauce	60 ml
3 dashes hot sauce	
2 tablespoons ketchup	35 g
5 cups walnut halves	600 g

- Preheat oven to 400° (205° C). In bowl, combine butter, Worcestershire sauce, hot sauce ketchup and a little touch of salt, mixing well. Pour over walnut halves and stir until all walnuts are well coated.

- Bake uncovered in a 9 x 13-inch (23 x 33 cm) baking pan, stirring every 5 minutes, for 20 minutes. Remove from oven and pour walnuts out onto 2 layers of paper towels. Cool to room temperature.

Sweet Nibblers

1 (6 ounce) package semi-sweet chocolate chips	170 g
⅓ cup peanut butter	95 g
1 cup chopped peanuts	150 g
7 cups Crispix® cereal	205 g
1½ cups powdered sugar	180 g

- In heavy saucepan over low heat, melt chocolate, stirring constantly. When melted, stir in peanut butter and peanuts until well mixed. Add cereal, stirring until evenly coated.
- Place powdered sugar in a large resealable bag and add coated cereal; close bag. Toss cereal gently until cereal is evenly coated with powdered sugar. Store in airtight container in refrigerator.

Creamy Strawberry Punch

1 (10 ounce) package frozen strawberries, thawed	280 g
½ gallon strawberry ice cream, softened	1.9 L
2 (2 liter) bottles ginger ale, chilled	2 (2 L)
Fresh strawberries	

- Process frozen strawberries through blender. Combine strawberries, chunks of ice cream and ginger ale in punch bowl.
- Stir and serve immediately with fresh strawberries.

Apple Party Punch

3 cups sparkling apple cider	750 ml
2 cups apple juice	500 ml
1 cup pineapple juice	250 ml
½ cup brandy	125 ml

- Combine all ingredients and freeze. Remove punch from freezer 30 minutes before serving. Place in small punch bowl and break into chunks. Stir until slushy.

Pina Colada Punch

1 (46 ounce) can pineapple juice, chilled	1.4 L
1 (20 ounce) can crushed pineapple with juice	570 g
1 (15 ounce) can cream of coconut	425 g
1 (2 liter) bottle lemon-lime carbonated drink, chilled	2 L

● Combine all ingredients. Serve over ice cubes.

Perfect Party Punch

1 (12 ounce) can frozen limeade concentrate	355 ml
1 (46 ounce) can pineapple juice, chilled	1.4 L
1 (46 ounce) apricot nectar, chilled	1.4 L
1 quart ginger ale, chilled	945 ml

● Dilute limeade concentrate according to directions on can. Add pineapple juice and apricot nectar and stir well. When ready to serve, add ginger ale.

Cranberry Punch

2 (28 ounce) bottles ginger ale, chilled	2 (825 ml)
1 (48 ounce) can pineapple juice, chilled	1.4 L
1 quart cranberry juice, chilled	945 ml
1 quart pineapple sherbet, broken up	945 ml

● Pour all ingredients in punch bowl. Serve.

Cranberry-Lemon Punch

2 quarts cranberry juice	1.9 L
1 (6 ounce) can lemonade concentrate, thawed	175 ml
⅔ cup maraschino cherry juice	150 ml
1 (2 liter) lemon-lime soda, chilled	2 L

● Combine all ingredients and mix well.

Best Tropical Punch

1 (46 ounce) can pineapple juice	1.4 L
1 (46 ounce) can apricot nectar	1.4 L
3 (6 ounce) cans frozen limeade concentrate, thawed	3 (175 ml)
3 quarts ginger ale, chilled	2.8 L

● Combine all ingredients except ginger ale. Stir in ginger ale just before serving.

Apricot Punch

1 (12 ounce) can apricot nectar	340 g
1 (6 ounce) can frozen orange juice concentrate, thawed	170 g
2 tablespoons lemon juice	30 ml
1 (2 liter) bottle ginger ale, chilled	2 L

● Combine apricot nectar, orange juice concentrate, lemon juice and 1 cup (250 ml) water. Refrigerate. When ready to serve stir in ginger ale.

Tropical Fruit Smoothie

2 (8 ounce) cartons vanilla yogurt	2 (230 g)
1 cup frozen blueberries	155 g
1 cup frozen peach slices	250 g
1 (8 ounce) can pineapple chunks, drained	230 g

● Process all ingredients in blender until smooth.

Banana-Peach Smoothie

3 ripe bananas, sliced	
2 cups frozen (or fresh) peaches	250 g
1 cup buttermilk	250 ml
¼ cup orange juice	60 ml
2 tablespoons honey	45 g

● Place all ingredients in blender and process until smooth, stopping to scrape down sides. Serve immediately.

Watermelon Smoothie

About 2 cups watermelon cubes, seeded	310 g
2 tablespoons honey	45 g
Dash of ground cinnamon	
1 (8 ounce) carton lemon yogurt	230 g

- With blender puree watermelon, honey and cinnamon quickly, being careful not to over blend. Pulse in lemon yogurt and serve immediately.

Fruit Smoothies

2 cups apple juice	500 ml
1 cup frozen strawberries and raspberries, thawed	230 g
1 large banana, sliced	
2 cups raspberry sherbet	295 g

- In blender, combine apple juice, strawberries, raspberries and banana; process just 1 minute, then add raspberry sherbet and process until well blended. Serve immediately.

Strawberry Smoothie

2 bananas, peeled, sliced	
1 pint fresh strawberries, washed, quartered	355 g
1 (8 ounce) container strawberry yogurt	230 g
¼ cup orange juice	60 ml

- Place all ingredients in blender. Process until smooth.

Orange Slush

1 (20 ounce) can crushed pineapple with juice	570 g
½ cup frozen pina colada concentrate	125 ml
1 pint orange sherbet	295 g
½ cup orange juice	125 ml

- Combine all ingredients in blender. Cover and blend on high speed until smooth. Serve immediately in sherbet glasses.

Blue Moon Slushes

1 (8 ounce) carton blueberry yogurt	230 g
1 cup chilled grape juice	250 ml
½ cup milk	125 ml

- In blender, combine yogurt, grape juice and milk, cover and blend. Add ice cubes and blend until slushy. Serve immediately.

Peanut Power Shake

2 bananas, cut up	
½ cup frozen orange juice concentrate, thawed	125 ml
¼ cup peanut butter	70 g
¼ cup milk	60 ml

- Combine all ingredients in blender container. Cover and blend until smooth. Blend 1 cup (230 g) ice cubes until smooth.

Purple Shakes

1 (6 ounce) can frozen grape juice concentrate, thawed	175 ml
1 cup milk	250 ml
2½ cups vanilla ice cream	375 g
2 tablespoons sugar	25 g

- In blender, combine all ingredients. Cover and blend at high speed for 30 seconds. Serve immediately.

Breakfast Shake

1 banana, cut into 1-inch (2.5 cm) slices	
1 mango, peeled, cubed	
1½ cups pineapple juice or orange juice, chilled	375 ml
1 (8 ounce) container vanilla yogurt	230 g

- Process banana slices, mango, juice and yogurt in blender until smooth. Scrape sides of blender and mix. Serve immediately.

Banana-Strawberry Shake

1 (10 ounce) package frozen strawberries, partially thawed	280 g
2 bananas, sliced in 1-inch pieces	2.5 cm
1 cup half-and-half cream	250 ml
½ cup sugar	100 g
1 quart vanilla ice cream	945 ml

- In blender, combine fruit, cream and sugar. Cover and blend at high speed for about 30 seconds. Add ice cream and blend for about 45 seconds. Serve immediately.

Creamy Orange Drink

1¾ cups milk	425 ml
½ pint vanilla ice cream	235 ml
⅓ cup frozen orange juice concentrate	75 ml
1 teaspoon non-dairy creamer	5 ml

- In blender, combine all ingredients and blend until smooth.

Strawberry Cooler

1 cup sliced fresh strawberries	165 g
½ cup milk	125 ml
⅓ cup sugar (or equal of Splenda®)	65 g
1 pint frozen strawberry yogurt	455 g

- Place all ingredients in blender. Cover and blend on high speed until smooth, about 30 seconds.

Berry Delight

1 (8 ounce) carton vanilla yogurt	230 g
1 ripe banana, cut in 1-inch pieces	
1 cup fresh or frozen raspberries	150 g
1 pint raspberry sherbet	475 ml

- Place all ingredients in blender and process until thick and smooth. Serve immediately.

Banana Split Float

2 ripe bananas, mashed
3 cups milk   750 ml
1 (10 ounce) package frozen sweetened strawberries, thawed   280 g
1½ pints chocolate ice cream, divided   710 ml

● Place bananas in blender and add milk, strawberries and ½ pint (150 g) chocolate ice cream. Beat just until they blend. Pour into tall, chilled glasses and top each with scoop of chocolate ice cream.

Orange Ice Cream Soda

2 large scoop orange sherbet
1 large scoop vanilla ice cream
1 (12 ounce) can orange soda, chilled   355 ml
1 can Reddi-wip® whipped topping, thawed

● Place sherbet and ice cream in tall 16-inch (40 cm) glass, slowly pour some of orange soda into glass, mixing well with spoon. Top with dash of whipped topping. Serve with straw and long teaspoon.

Party Orange Sipper

2½ cups vodka   625 ml
4 cups orange juice   1 L
2 (12 ounce) cans lemon-lime soft drink   2 (355 ml)
⅓ cup maraschino cherry juice   75 ml

● In pitcher, combine vodka, orange juice and lemon-lime soft drink. Fill 8 glasses with crushed ice and pour vodka-orange juice mixture over ice. Spoon about 2 teaspoons (10 ml) cherry juice into each glass, but do not stir. Serve immediately.

Pineapple-Strawberry Cooler

2 cups milk   500 ml
1 (20 ounce) can crushed pineapple, chilled   570 g
½ pint vanilla ice cream   235 ml
1 pint strawberry ice cream   470 ml

● In mixing bowl, combine milk, pineapple and vanilla ice cream until they blend. Pour into tall glasses and top with scoop of strawberry ice cream.

Spiced Coffee

1 cup instant coffee granules	55 g
4 teaspoons grated lemon peel	20 ml
4 teaspoons ground cinnamon	20 ml
1 teaspoon ground cloves	5 ml

- In small jar, combine all ingredients and cover tightly.
- For each serving, spoon 2 teaspoons (10 ml) coffee mix into coffee cup and stir in ¾ cup (175 ml) boiling water. Sweeten to taste.

Strawberry Drink

¾ cup milk	175 ml
¾ cup applesauce	190 g
1 small ripe banana, halved	
¾ cup sliced strawberries	125 g
8 - 10 ice cubes	

- In blender, combine all ingredients, cover and process until smooth. Serve immediately in chilled glasses.

Sweet Orange Fluff

1¾ cups milk	425 ml
½ pint vanilla ice cream	235 ml
⅓ cup frozen orange juice concentrate	75 ml
1 teaspoon non-dairy creamer	5 ml

- In blender, combine all ingredients, and blend until smooth.

Strawberry Lemonade

1 (16 ounce) package frozen strawberries, thawed	455 g
1 (10 ounce) jar maraschino cherries (without stems)	280 g
2 cups sugar	400 g
1 cup lemon juice	250 ml

- Place strawberries, cherries (with juice), sugar and lemon juice in blender; blend until smooth, stopping to scrape down sides. Pour mixture through strainer and pour into pitcher, discarding solids.
- Stir in 3 cups (750 ml) cold water, mixing well and serve over chipped ice.

Limeade Cooler

1½ pints lime sherbet	710 ml
1 (6 ounce) can frozen limeade concentrate	175 ml
3 cups milk	750 ml
Lime slices to garnish, optional	

- Beat lime sherbet in mixing bowl and add concentrated limeade and milk. Blend all ingredients. Top each glass with lime sherbet. Serve immediately.

Lemonade Tea

2 family-size tea bags	
½ cup sugar	100 g
1 (12 ounce) can frozen lemonade concentrate	355 ml
1 quart ginger ale, chilled	945 ml

- Steep tea in 3 quarts (2.8 L) water and mix with sugar and lemonade. Add ginger ale just before serving.

Spiced Iced Tea

2 quarts tea	1.9 L
⅔ cup sugar	135 g
1 (12 ounce) can frozen lemonade concentrate, thawed	355 ml
1 (2 liter) ginger ale, chilled	2 L

- Combine tea, sugar and lemonade and refrigerate. Just before serving, add chilled ginger ale.

Alamo Splash

¼ cup tequila	60 ml
¼ cup orange juice	60 ml
¼ cup pineapple juice	60 ml
Splash lemon-lime soda	

- Mix with cracked ice and pour into Collins glass.

White Sangria

1 (1 liter) bottle dry white wine	1 L
1 cup silver rum	250 ml
½ cup orange liqueur	125 ml
Thin slices of lemon and limes	
2 cups club soda, chilled	500 ml
Ice cubes	

- In 3-quart (3 L) pitcher, combine wine, rum and orange liqueur and add lemon and lime slices. Cover and refrigerate. When ready to serve, stir in club soda and about 2 cups (640 g) ice cubes.

Holiday Eggnog

1 gallon refrigerated eggnog	3.8 L
1 pint whipping cream	500 ml
1 quart brandy	945 ml
½ gallon vanilla ice cream, softened	1.9 L

- Mix all ingredients. Serve in individual cups, sprinkle with nutmeg and serve immediately.

Southwest Pina Colada

1 (8 ounce) can crushed pineapple with juice	230 g
1 (7 ounce) can cream of coconut	205 ml
1 cup rum	250 ml
Ice cubes	

- Combine all ingredients in blender, except ice and mix. Add enough ice for desired consistency and process until liquid is "slushy".

Chocolate-Mint Fizz

¼ cup creme de menthe liqueur	60 ml
¼ cup creme de cacao liqueur	60 ml
1 pint vanilla ice cream	475 ml
1 pint chocolate ice cream	475 ml

- Place liqueurs into blender container. Add ice creams gradually and blend until smooth after each addition.

Peach Delight

¾ cup pink lemonade concentrate, thawed	175 ml
¾ cup vodka	175 ml
3 - 4 peaches, pitted, peeled	

- Place all ingredients in blender. Mix well. Add crushed ice and blend until smooth.

Easy Frozen Strawberry Margarita

1 (10 ounce) package frozen strawberries	280 g
1 (6 ounce) can frozen limeade concentrate, thawed	175 ml
1 (6 ounce) can tequila	175 ml

- Pour all ingredients and ice into blender and process until smooth. Pour into margarita glasses.

Kahlua Frosty

1 cup coffee liqueur	250 ml
1 pint vanilla ice cream	475 ml
1 cup half-and-half cream	250 ml
¼ teaspoon almond extract	1 ml

- In blender combine all ingredients and 1 heaping cup (230 g) ice cubes. Blend until smooth. Serve immediately.

Coffee Liqueur

1 cup instant coffee granules	55 g
4 cups sugar	800 g
1 quart vodka	945 ml
3 tablespoons Mexican vanilla	45 ml

- In large saucepan combine 3 cups (750 ml) hot water and coffee, mix well. Add sugar. Boil 2 minutes, turn off heat and cool. Add vodka and vanilla. Shake in bottle or jar before serving.

Amaretto Cooler

1¼ cups amaretto liqueur	310 ml
2 quarts orange juice	1.9 L
1 (15 ounce) bottle club soda, chilled	445 ml
Orange slices	

- Combine all ingredients and stir well. Serve over crushed ice.

Amaretto

3 cups sugar	600 g
1 pint vodka	475 ml
3 tablespoons almond extract	45 ml
1 tablespoon vanilla (not imitation)	15 ml

- Combine sugar and 2¼ cups (560 ml) water in large pan. Bring to a boil. Reduce heat. Simmer for 5 minutes and stir occasionally. Remove from stove. Stir in remaining ingredients. Store in airtight jar.

Mexican Coffee

1 ounce coffee liqueur	30 ml
1 cup hot, black brewed coffee	250 ml
Ground cinnamon	
Sweetened whipped cream	

- Pour liqueur and coffee into tall mug. Top with cinnamon and whipped cream.

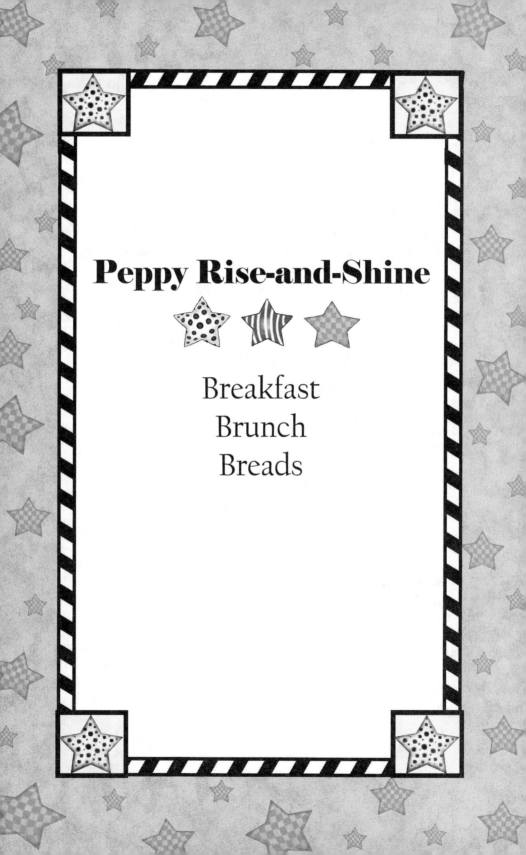

Peppy Rise-and-Shine

Breakfast
Brunch
Breads

Baked Eggs

4 eggs	
¼ cup cream, divided	60 ml
¼ cup cracker crumbs, divided	15 g
¼ cup shredded cheddar cheese, divided	30 g

- Grease 4 muffin cups and place 1 egg in each.
- Add one-fourth cream, one-fourth crumbs and one-fourth cheese on top of each egg. Sprinkle with a little salt and pepper.
- Bake at 325° (165° C) for 12 to 20 minutes until eggs are set.

Bacon and Egg Burrito

2 slices bacon, cooked, chopped	
2 eggs, scrambled	
¼ cup shredded cheddar cheese	30 g
1 flour tortilla	

- Sprinkle bacon, eggs and cheese in middle of tortilla. Fold tortilla sides over and place seam-side down on dinner plate. Microwave for 30 seconds or just until mixture heats thoroughly.

A Better Scramble

1 (10 ounce) can cheddar cheese soup	280 g
8 eggs, lightly beaten	
2 tablespoons butter	30 g
Snipped chives	

- Pour soup into bowl and stir until smooth. Add eggs and a little pepper and mix well.
- In skillet, melt butter. Pour in egg mixture and scramble over low heat until set. Sprinkle with chives.

Easy Omelet

2 tablespoons butter   30 g
4 - 5 eggs
⅓ cup shredded cheddar cheese   40 g

- Melt butter in 10-inch (25 cm) skillet over medium heat. While butter melts, whisk together eggs and ¼ teaspoon (1 ml) salt. Pour eggs into skillet and stir gently until they begin to set.

- Spread eggs evenly in pan and sprinkle with cheese. Reduce heat and cook until omelet just sets. Hold skillet over serving plate, tilt skillet until omelet slides out and almost half touches plate. Immediately turn skillet upside down to make omelet fold over itself. Serve immediately.

Cheesy Scrambled Eggs

2 tablespoons butter   30 g
8 eggs
1 (4 ounce) can diced green chilies   115 g
½ cup grated cheddar cheese   55 g

- Melt butter in skillet. Beat remaining ingredients well and add a little salt and pepper and pour into skillet; stirring until set.

Creamy Eggs on Toast

¼ cup (½ stick) butter   60 g
¼ cup flour   30 g
2 cups milk   500 ml
6 eggs, hard-boiled, sliced

- Melt butter in skillet, stir in flour and add milk. Cook over medium heat and stir constantly until sauce thickens.

- Gently fold in egg slices. Serve over 6 slices toasted bread.

Eggs in a Basket

2 (15 ounce) cans corned beef hash	2 (425 g)
6 eggs	
¼ cup seasoned breadcrumbs	30 g
Butter	

- Preheat oven to 325° (165° C). Grease 7 x 11-inch (18 x 28 cm) baking dish and spread hash evenly in dish. Press bottom of ½ cup measuring cup into hash to make 6 impressions.
- Break 1 egg into each impression. Sprinkle spoonful of breadcrumbs over each egg and top with dot of butter. Bake for 20 to 25 minutes or until eggs are as firm as desired.

Mexican Eggs

4 corn tortillas	
4 eggs	
1 cup green chile salsa	265 g
4 ounces grated longhorn cheese	115 g

- Dip tortillas in heated oil in skillet and remove quickly. Set tortillas in baking pan to keep warm.
- In skillet, fry eggs in a little butter until whites set. Place fried egg on each tortilla. Heat salsa and spoon over each egg. Sprinkle grated cheese on top.
- Place baking pan under broiler until cheese melts.

Heavenly Eggs

Bread and Butter
Eggs
Mozzarella cheese slices
Cooked bacon strips

- Preheat oven to 350° (175° C). Butter slice of bread for each person to be served and place butter side down in baking dish. Place cheese slice over bread.
- Separate an egg for each slice of bread; add a pinch of salt to whites and beat until stiff. Pile egg whites on cheese, making a nest in the top. Slip an egg yolk into each nest and bake for 20 minutes and serve immediately. Place cooked bacon slice over top of each egg.

Sunrise Tacos

4 eggs, scrambled, divided
½ cup shredded cheddar cheese, divided   55 g
½ cup salsa, divided   130 g
2 flour tortillas, divided

- For each taco, spread half scrambled eggs, half cheese and half salsa on tortilla and roll.

Breakfast Tacos

4 eggs
4 flour tortillas
1 cup chopped, cooked ham   140 g
1 cup grated cheddar cheese   115 g

- Scramble eggs in skillet. Lay tortillas flat and spoon eggs over 4 tortillas. Sprinkle with ham and cheese and roll to enclose filling. Place tacos in microwave-safe dish. Microwave for about 30 seconds or until cheese melts. Serve immediately.

Spicy Oven Omelet

4 eggs
¼ cup mayonnaise   55 g
¼ cup milk   60 ml
2 tablespoons flour   15 g
1 cup shredded cheddar cheese   115 g
½ cup chopped ham   70 g

- Preheat oven to 350° (175° C). In blender, combine eggs, mayonnaise, milk and flour and blend 15 seconds. Immediately after blending, pour mixture into sprayed 2-quart (2 L) glass baking dish.
- Stir in cheese and ham and bake 30 minutes or until omelet is firm when you shake the baking dish.

Corned Beef Hash Bake

2 (15 ounce) cans corned beef hash, slightly warmed   2 (425 g)
Butter
6 - 8 eggs
⅓ cup half-and-half cream   75 ml

- Spread corned beef hash in greased 9 x 13-inch (23 x 33 cm) pan. Pat down with back of spoon and make 6 to 8 deep hollows in hash large enough for egg to fit.
- Fill hollows with tiny dab of butter. Pour eggs into each hollow and cover with about 1 tablespoon (15 ml) of cream.
- Bake uncovered at 350° (175° C) for 15 to 20 minutes or until eggs set as desired. Divide into squares to serve.

English Muffin Breakfast Sandwich

4 - 6 eggs
1 (16 ounce) package precooked bacon slices, halved   455 g
1 (12 ounce) package English muffins, halved, toasted   340 g
1 (16 ounce) package cheese slices   455 g

- Preheat oven to 325° (165° C).
- Lightly scramble eggs in skillet over medium heat and stir often. Season according to taste. Heat bacon in microwave according to package directions. Spoon egg mixture onto bottom of muffin, add cheese slice, bacon and muffin top. Place on baking sheet and bake about 10 minutes or just until cheese begins to melt.

Sausage Gravy

½ pound pork sausage   230 g
¼ cup flour   30 g
2½ cups milk   625 ml

- Cook sausage in large skillet over medium heat, stirring until it crumbles. Remove sausage, but reserve about 2 tablespoons (30 ml) drippings in skillet.
- Stir flour into drippings and cook, stirring constantly until flour is slightly brown. Gradually stir in milk and cook, stirring constantly until gravy thickens. Stir in ¾ teaspoon (4 ml) black pepper, a little salt and cooked sausages.

Sausage Bites

¾ - 1 pound bacon slices	340 - 455 g
2 (8 ounce) sausage links	2 (230 g)
1 cup packed brown sugar	220 g
½ teaspoon cinnamon	2 ml

- Preheat oven to 350° (175° C).
- Cut each bacon strip in half and cut each sausage link in half. Wrap piece of bacon around each sausage half and secure with toothpick.
- Place brown sugar in shallow bowl and mix in cinnamon. Roll sausage rolls in brown sugar (you will have some brown sugar left).
- Place each sausage roll in large, foil-lined baking dish. Cover and refrigerate until ready to bake. Sprinkle brown sugar over each roll and bake for 30 minutes, turning once.

Glazed Bacon

1 pound bacon	455 g
⅓ cup packed brown sugar	75 g
1 teaspoon flour	5 ml
½ cup finely chopped pecans	55 g

- Arrange bacon slices close together, but not overlapping, on wire rack over drip pan. In bowl, combine brown sugar, flour and pecans and sprinkle evenly over bacon.
- Bake at 350° (175° C) for about 30 minutes. Drain on paper towels.

Easy Way to Cook Bacon

1 pound bacon	455 g

- Preheat oven to 400° (205° C).
- Bake on rack of roasting pan 20 to 30 minutes or until crisp. Remove bacon with tongs and discard bacon drippings.

Hot Tamale-Cheese Fiesta

2 (15 ounce) jars beef tamales with sauce	2 (425 g)
1 (8 ounce) package shredded Mexican 4-cheese blend, divided	230 g
1 (10 ounce) can cream of mushroom soup	280 g
2 teaspoons taco seasoning	10 ml

- Drain sauce from tamales into cup and set aside. Remove wrappers from tamales.
- Place tamales, side by side, in 9 x 13-inch (23 x 33 cm) baking dish. Sprinkle one-fourth cheese over top of tamales.
- Combine ½ cup (125 ml) sauce from tamales, mushroom soup and taco seasoning and mix well. Pour sauce mixture over tamales.
- Bake at 350° (175° C) for 5 to 10 minutes. Sprinkle remaining cheese over top and continue to heat until cheese melts.

Bacon-Cheese Stromboli

1 (10 ounce) tube refrigerated pizza dough	280 g
¾ cup shredded cheddar cheese	85 g
¾ cup shredded mozzarella cheese	85 g
6 bacon strips, cooked, crumbled	

- On ungreased baking sheet, roll dough into 12-inch (32 cm) circle. On one-half of dough, sprinkle cheeses and bacon to within ½ inch (1.2 cm) of edge.
- Fold dough over filling and pinch edges to seal.
- Bake at 400° (205° C) for about 10 minutes or until golden. Serve with salsa. Cut in pie slices.

Cheese Enchiladas

1 dozen corn tortillas	
1 (8 ounce) package shredded cheddar cheese, divided	230 g
½ cup chopped onion, divided	80 g
2 (10 ounce) cans enchilada sauce	2 (280 g)

- Wrap tortillas in slightly damp paper towel. Place between 2 salad plates and microwave on high for 45 seconds.
- Sprinkle ⅓ cup (40 g) cheese and ⅓ cup (55 g) onions on each tortilla and roll. Place seam-side down in 9 x 13-inch (23 x 33 cm) baking dish.
- Pour sauce over enchiladas. Sprinkle with remaining cheese and onions. Cover and microwave on MEDIUM HIGH for 5 to 6 minutes.

Chile Rellenos

2 (7 ounce) cans diced green chilies, drained	2 (200 g)
1 (16 ounce) package shredded Monterey Jack cheese	455 g
4 eggs, beaten	
½ cup milk	125 ml

- In 7 x 11-inch (18 x 28 cm) baking dish, layer half green chilies, half cheese, then remaining chilies and cheese.
- Combine eggs, milk and a little salt and pepper in small bowl and mix well. Pour over layers and bake uncovered at 350° (175° C) for 30 minutes or until light brown and set. Cool for 5 minutes before cutting into squares.

Rellenos Quiche

1 (9- inch) frozen pie shell (½ of 15 ounce package)	23 cm/425 g
1 (8 ounce) package shredded Monterey Jack cheese	230 g
1 (7 ounce) can diced green chilies, drained	200 g
4 large eggs, lightly beaten	
1¼ cups half-and-half cream	310 ml

- Preheat oven to 425° (220° C). Bake pie shell for 5 minutes. Remove from oven and reduce heat to 350° (175° C). Sprinkle half cheese and half green chilies over partially baked pie shell. Repeat both layers.
- Combine beaten eggs and cream, adding an ample amount of pepper and pour over cheese mixture. Bake 30 minutes.

Creamy Grits

3 pints half-and-half cream	1.4 L
½ teaspoon garlic powder	2 ml
½ teaspoon hot sauce	2 ml
1½ cups grits	235 g
2 (3 ounce) packages cream cheese	2 (85 g)

- In large saucepan combine half-and-half, garlic powder, hot sauce and 1 teaspoon (5 ml) salt. Bring to a boil and gradually stir in grits.
- Reduce heat and simmer for 6 minutes or until it thickens, stir occasionally.
- Stir in cream cheese, stirring until cream cheese melts.

Quick Cheese Grits

1⅔ cups quick-cooking grits	260 g
1 (8 ounce) package shredded sharp cheddar cheese	230 g
¾ cup shredded Monterey Jack cheese	85 g
⅔ cup half-and-half cream	150 ml
2 tablespoons butter	30 g

- In saucepan on medium-high heat, bring 6 cups (1.4 L) water, adding a little salt, to a boil and gradually add grits. Reduce heat to low-medium and simmer for 10 minutes, stirring occasionally or until mixture has thickened.
- Stir in both cheeses, half-and-half cream and butter, mixing until well blended. Serve immediately.

Cherry-Pecan Oatmeal

2 cups cooked oatmeal	470 g
½ cup dried cherries, chopped	60 g
½ cup packed brown sugar	110 g
2 tablespoons butter, softened	30 g
½ teaspoon ground cinnamon	5 ml
½ cup chopped toasted pecans	55 g

- While oatmeal is cooking, combine cherries, brown sugar, butter and cinnamon. Stir into cooked oatmeal.
- Sprinkle toasted pecans over top of each serving.

Breakfast Ready Oatmeal

1½ cups oats	120 g
3½ cups milk	875 ml
½ cup chopped pecans	55 g
⅓ cup packed brown sugar	75 g

- In saucepan over medium heat, combine and cook oats, milk, pecans, brown sugar and a dash of salt. Bring to a boil, lower heat and simmer for 6 minutes, stirring occasionally. Let stand several minutes before serving.

Light and Crispy Waffles

2 cups biscuit mix	240 g
1 egg	
½ cup oil	125 ml
1⅓ cups club soda	310 ml

- Preheat waffle iron. Combine all ingredients in mixing bowl and stir by hand. Pour just enough batter to cover waffle iron.

Waffle Flash

2 eggs	
1 cup milk	250 ml
½ teaspoon vanilla	2 ml
8 slices stale bread	

- Heat waffle iron according to directions. Beat eggs, slowly add milk and vanilla and beat well. Remove crust from bread and butter both sides of bread. When waffle iron is ready, dip bread in egg mixture and place in waffle iron. Close lid and grill until light brown.

Pecan Waffles

2 cups self-rising flour	250 g
½ cup oil	125 ml
½ cup milk	125 ml
⅔ cup finely chopped pecans	75 g

- Preheat waffle iron. In bowl, combine flour, oil and milk. Beat until they mix well. Stir in chopped pecans.
- Pour approximately ¾ cup (175 ml) batter into hot waffle iron and bake until brown and crispy.

No-Mess Oven Pancakes

⅔ cup flour	80 g
⅔ cup milk	150 ml
¼ cup sugar	50 g
5 large eggs, beaten	

- Preheat oven to 425° (220° C). Combine flour, milk, sugar and beaten eggs in mixing bowl. Place a little oil on large baking sheet and rub oil to cover whole surface of pan. Place in oven for 5 minutes. Pour pancake mixture onto pan to make several pancakes. Bake about 18 minutes or until puffy and golden.

Croissant French Toast with Strawberry Syrup

4 large day-old croissants
¾ cup half-and-half cream   175 ml
2 large eggs
1 teaspoon vanilla   5 ml
¼ cup (½ stick) butter, divided   60 g

- Slice croissants in half lengthwise. In shallow bowl, whisk together half-and-half cream, eggs and vanilla. Heat 1 tablespoon (15 ml) butter at a time in large skillet.

- Dip croissant halves into egg mixture and coat well. Cook 4 croissant halves about 2 minutes each time. Turn and cook on both sides until light brown. Repeat with remaining butter and croissant halves.

Strawberry Syrup:
¾ cup sugar   150 g
1 quart fresh strawberries, slices   665 g
¼ cup orange juice   60 ml

- In saucepan, combine all ingredients and let stand 30 minutes. Cook over low heat, and stir occasionally for 5 to 8 minutes. Serve warm over croissant toast.

French Toast

4 eggs
1 cup whipping cream   250 ml
2 thick slices bread, cut into 3 strips
Powdered sugar

- Place a little oil in skillet. Beat eggs, cream and pinch of salt. Dip bread into batter and allow batter to soak in.

- Fry bread in skillet until brown, turn and fry on other side.

- Transfer to baking sheet. Bake at 325° (165° C) for about 4 minutes or until they puff. Sprinkle with powdered sugar.

Orange-French Toast

1 egg, beaten	
½ cup orange juice	125 ml
5 slices raisin bread	
1 cup crushed graham crackers	105 g
2 tablespoons butter, more if needed for frying	30 g

- Combine egg and orange juice and dip each slice of bread in egg mixture and then in graham cracker crumbs. Fry in batches in butter until light brown.

Praline Toast

½ cup (1 stick) butter, softened	115 g
1 cup packed brown sugar	220 g
½ cup finely chopped pecans	55 g

- Combine all ingredients. Spread on bread slices. Toast in broiler until brown and bubbly.

Cinnamon Toast

⅔ cup sugar	135 g
1 heaping tablespoon ground cinnamon	15 ml
Bread	
Butter, softened	

- Mix sugar with cinnamon. Place in large salt or sugar shaker. Place bread on baking sheet and toast top by broiling in oven until light brown.
- Remove baking sheet and spread softened butter on toasted side. Sprinkle with cinnamon mixture.
- Return to oven and broil until tops are bubbly. Watch closely.

Berry Cream for Waffles

1 (8 ounce) carton whipping cream	250 ml
½ cup powdered sugar	60 g
2 cups sliced strawberries, well drained	330 g
½ cup blueberries	75 g

- Whip cream with powdered sugar until very stiff and fold in strawberries and blueberries. This will be enough berry cream to serve over 6 prepared frozen waffles.

Pumpkin and Apple Butter
for Toast or Waffles

1 (15 ounce) can pumpkin	425 g
1 (24 ounce) jar applesauce	680 g
1½ cups packed light brown sugar	330 g
¼ teaspoon ground ginger	1 ml
¼ teaspoon ground cinnamon	2 ml
¼ teaspoon ground nutmeg	2 ml

- In large, heavy saucepan, on high heat, combine all ingredients, stirring constantly. Reduce heat to low and simmer, uncovered for about 20 minutes, stirring occasionally or until mixture is very thick.
- Cool and spoon into pint jars or ½-pint (230 g) jelly jars; cover and refrigerate.

Cherry-Raspberry Syrup for Waffles

2 cups pitted, chopped sweet fresh cherries	310 g
2 cups raspberries, divided	245 g
1 cup sugar	200 g
2 cinnamon sticks	
¼ cup brandy	60 ml

- Place cherries, half raspberries, sugar and cinnamon sticks in saucepan and bring to a boil, reduce heat and simmer, stirring occasionally, about 20 minutes.
- Remove from heat and stir in brandy and remaining raspberries.

Nutty Apple Syrup for Pancakes

1 cup sugar	200 g
1½ cups packed brown sugar	330 g
½ cup apple jelly	160 g
¼ cup finely chopped pecans	30 g
1 teaspoon maple flavoring	5 ml

- In saucepan, combine both sugars and ⅓ cup (75 ml) water. Bring to a boil and cook and stir for 2 minutes. Remove from heat and stir in jelly, pecans and maple flavoring.

Strawberry Butter

1 (10 ounce) package frozen strawberries	280 g
1 cup (2 sticks) unsalted butter, softened	230 g
1 cup powdered sugar	120 g

- Mix all ingredients in food processor or mixer.

Honey Butter

½ cup (1 stick) butter, softened	125 ml
¼ cup honey	60 ml
2 tablespoons lemon juice	30 ml
1 tablespoon brown sugar	15 ml

- With hand mixer, cream butter until fluffy and add honey in fine stream. Add lemon juice and brown sugar and stir until all ingredients blend evenly. Refrigerate until ready to serve.

Orange Butter

⅔ cup butter (1⅓ sticks), room temperature	150 g
¼ cup frozen orange juice concentrate, thawed	60 ml
1 (16 ounce) box powdered sugar	455 g
1 teaspoon dried orange peel	5 ml

- Blend all ingredients in mixer. Store in refrigerator.

Peach Bake

2 (15 ounce) cans peach halves, drained	2 (425 g)
1 cup packed brown sugar	220 g
1 cup round, buttery cracker crumbs	60 g
½ cup (1 stick) butter, melted	115 g

- Butter 2-quart (2 L) casserole and layer peaches, sugar and cracker crumbs until all ingredients are used.
- Pour melted butter over casserole. Bake at 325° (165° C) for 30 minutes or until cracker crumbs are slightly brown. Serve hot or at room temperature.

Mini-Apricot Bake

2 (15 ounce) cans apricot halves, drained	2 (425 g)
¾ cup packed brown sugar	145 g
1 cup round, buttery cracker crumbs	60
½ cup (1 stick) butter, melted	115 g

- Butter 2-quart (2 L) casserole and layer apricots, sugar and cracker crumbs until all ingredients are gone.
- Pour melted butter over casserole.
- Bake at 325° (165° C) for 30 minutes or until cracker crumbs are slightly brown. Serve hot or room temperature.

Melon Boats

2 cantaloupes, chilled	
4 cups red and green seedless grapes, chilled	605 g
1 cup mayonnaise	225 g
⅓ cup frozen concentrated orange juice, thawed	75 ml

- Cut each melon in 6 lengthwise sections and remove seeds and peel. Place on lettuce leaves on separate salad plates.
- Heap grapes over and around each cantaloupe slice.
- Combine mayonnaise and juice concentrate and mix well. Ladle over fruit.

Ambrosia Spread

1 (11 ounce) can mandarin orange sections, drained	310 g
1 (8 ounce) container soft cream cheese with pineapple, softened	230 g
¼ cup flaked coconut, toasted	20 g
¼ cup slivered almonds, chopped, toasted	40 g

- Chop orange sections and set aside.
- Combine cheese, coconut and almonds and blend well. Gently fold in orange sections and refrigerate.

Cheese Bread

1 (16 ounce) package shredded, sharp cheddar cheese	455 g
1 cup mayonnaise	225 g
1 (1 ounce) package ranch-style dressing mix	30 g
10 (1-inch) slices French bread	10 (2.5 cm)

- Preheat oven to 300° (148° C).
- Combine cheese, mayonnaise and dressing mix.
- Spread on bread slices and heat in oven until brown.

Bacon-Cheese French Bread

1 (16 ounce) loaf unsliced French bread	455 g
5 slices bacon, cooked, crumbled	
1 (8 ounce) package shredded mozzarella cheese	230 g
½ cup (1 stick) butter, melted	115 g

- Slice bread at 1-inch (2.5 cm) intervals, cutting to, but not through, bottom of loaf. Place sliced loaf on large piece of foil. Combine bacon and cheese. Sprinkle bacon and cheese in between slices of bread.
- Drizzle butter over loaf and let some drip in between slices. Wrap loaf tightly in foil. Bake at 350° (175° C) for 20 minutes or until thoroughly hot. Serve immediately.

French Cheese Loaf

1 (16 ounce) loaf unsliced French bread	455 g
½ cup (1 stick) butter, softened	115 g
1 teaspoon prepared minced garlic	5 ml
1 (4 ounce) package crumbled blue cheese	115 g

- Preheat oven to 375° (190° C). Slice bread at 1-inch (2.5 cm) intervals, cutting to, but not through, bottom of loaf.
- In bowl, combine softened butter, garlic and blue cheese and spread evenly on both sides of each bread slice. Wrap loaf in foil and place on large baking pan. Bake 10 to 12 minutes or until bread is thoroughly hot.

Poppy Seed-Onion Loaf

2 tablespoons instant minced onions	7 g
1 tablespoon poppy seeds	15 ml
½ cup (1 stick) butter, melted	115 g
2 packages refrigerated butter flake biscuits	

- Combine onions and poppy seeds with butter.
- Separate each biscuit into 2 or 3 rolls.
- Dip each piece in butter mixture and turn to coat.
- Place rolls on edge in loaf pan and arrange rolls into 2 rows. Pour any remaining butter mixture over top of loaf.
- Bake at 325° (165° C) for 30 minutes. Serve warm.

Ranch-French Bread

1 loaf unsliced French bread
½ cup (1 stick) butter, softened   115 g
1 tablespoon ranch-style dressing mix   15 ml

- Cut loaf in half horizontally. Blend butter and dressing mix.
- Spread butter mixture on bread. Wrap bread in foil. Bake at 350° (175° C) for 15 minutes.

Toasted French Bread

1 unsliced loaf French bread
½ cup (1 stick) butter, softened   115 g
¾ cup parmesan cheese   75 g
1½ teaspoons hot sauce   7 ml

- Slice bread in half lengthwise and quarter. Combine butter, parmesan cheese and hot sauce. Spread entire mixture on top of slices. Place on baking sheet.
- Bake at 325° (165° C) for 25 minutes or until thoroughly hot and brown on top.

Cheese Biscuits

2 cups biscuit mix   240 g
⅔ cup milk   150 ml
⅔ cup grated sharp cheddar cheese   75 g
¼ cup (½ stick) butter, melted   60 g

- Mix biscuit mix, milk and cheese. Drop 1 heaping tablespoon (15 ml) dough for each biscuit onto sprayed baking sheet. Bake at 400° (205° C) for 10 minutes or until slightly brown. While hot, brush tops of biscuits with melted butter.

Speedy Biscuits

6 tablespoons shortening	70 g
3 cups flour	360 g
1 cup milk	250 ml

- Cut shortening into flour with pastry cutter or by hand. Add milk and mix until dough forms a ball. Knead until dough is smooth.
- Place on floured surface and flatten slightly. Cut with floured biscuit cutter, place in well-greased pan and turn to grease both sides of biscuits. Bake at 400° (205° C) for 10 to 12 minutes.

Sausage-Cheese Biscuits

1 (8 ounce) package grated cheddar cheese	230 g
1 pound hot bulk pork sausage	455 g
2 cups biscuit mix	240 g
¾ cup milk	175 ml

- Combine all ingredients. Drop on ungreased baking sheet.
- Bake at 400° (205° C) until light brown.

French-Onion Biscuits

2 cups biscuit mix	240 g
¼ cup milk	60 ml
1 (8 ounce) container French-onion dip	230 g
2 tablespoons finely minced green onion	12 g

- Mix all ingredients until soft dough forms. Drop dough onto greased baking sheet. Bake at 400° (205° C) for 10 minutes or until light golden brown.

Quick Sour Cream Biscuits

⅓ cup club soda	75 ml
⅓ cup sour cream	80 g
½ tablespoon sugar	7 ml
2 cups biscuit mix	240 g

- In mixing bowl, combine all ingredients with fork just until dry ingredients are moist. Turn dough out onto lightly floured board and knead gently several times.
- Roll dough into 1-inch (2.5 cm) thickness and cut with biscuit cutter. Place dough in sprayed 9 x 13-inch (23 x 33 cm) baking pan.
- Bake at 400° (205° C) for 12 to 14 minutes or until golden brown.

Maple Syrup Biscuits

2¼ cups baking mix	270 g
⅔ cup milk	150 ml
1½ cups maple syrup	375 ml

- Combine baking mix and milk. Stir just until moist. On floured surface, roll dough into ½-inch (1.2 cm) thickness. Cut with 2-inch (5 cm) biscuit cutter.
- Pour syrup into 7 x 11-inch (18 x 28 cm) baking dish. Place biscuits on top of syrup.
- Bake at 425° (220° C) for 13 to 15 minutes or until biscuits are golden brown. Serve with butter.

Come and Get 'em Biscuits

2 cups flour	240 g
¼ cup mayonnaise	55 g
1 cup milk	250 ml
Butter	

- Mix all ingredients and drop by teaspoonfuls on baking sheet.
- Bake at 425° (220° C) until biscuits are golden brown.
- Serve with plain or flavored butters.

Best Ever Biscuits

5 cups biscuit mix	600 g
¾ cup buttermilk	175 ml
½ cup (1 stick) butter, softened	115 g
¼ cup club soda	60 ml
1 large egg, beaten	
2 tablespoons sugar	25 g

- Preheat oven to 425° (220° C).
- Prepare baking sheet with a little oil. In large bowl, stir together all ingredients and 1 teaspoon (5 ml) salt. Knead dough by hand until smooth.
- With flour on your hands and on wax paper, pat dough flat to ¾-inch (1.8 cm) thickness. Cut out biscuits with 3-inch (8 cm) biscuit cutter. Place biscuits on prepared baking sheet and bake for 12 minutes or until golden brown.

Strawberry Topping for Biscuits

3½ cups sugar	700 g
1 (10 ounce) package frozen strawberries, thawed	280 g
1 (6 ounce) can frozen orange juice concentrate, thawed	175 ml
2 tablespoons lemon juice	30 ml

- Combine sugar and strawberries in large saucepan and mix well. Over high heat bring to full rolling boil. Boil 1 minute, stirring constantly.
- Remove from heat and stir in orange juice concentrate and lemon juice. Return to heat and bring to boil for 1 minute, stirring constantly. Skim foam off top. Add red food coloring, if you like. Pour into jelly glasses and seal with hot paraffin.

Parmesan-Bread Deluxe

1 (16 ounce) loaf unsliced Italian bread	455 g
½ cup refrigerated creamy Caesar dressing and dip	125 ml
⅓ cup grated parmesan cheese	35 g
3 tablespoons finely chopped green onions	20 g

- Preheat broiler.
- Cut 24 (½-inch /1.2 cm) thick slices from bread. Reserve remaining bread for other use.
- In small bowl, combine dressing, cheese and onions. Spread 1 teaspoon (5 ml) dressing mixture on each bread slice.
- Place bread on baking sheet. Broil 4 inches (10 cm) from heat until golden brown. Serve warm.

Parmesan Ring

2 (10 ounce) cans refrigerated flaky biscuits	2 (280 g)
¼ cup (½ stick) butter, melted	60 g
⅔ cup grated parmesan cheese	65 g
1 tablespoon sesame seeds	15 ml

- Preheat oven to 375° (190° C).
- Dip each biscuit lightly in melted butter, then parmesan cheese; place on greased baking pan in a circle, each biscuit overlapping slightly, making a ring. Sprinkle with sesame seeds and bake for 15 minutes or until golden brown.

Garlic Rounds

2 teaspoons minced garlic	10 ml
2 teaspoons dried parsley flakes	10 ml
2 tablespoons olive oil	30 ml
½ teaspoon dried oregano	2 ml
1 (13 ounce) package refrigerated pizza crust	370 g

- Preheat oven to 400° (205° C). In small bowl, combine garlic, parsley flakes, olive oil and oregano.
- On flat surface, unroll pizza dough and brush with garlic-oil mixture and reroll dough. Using a serrated knife, cut into 1-inch (2.5 cm) pieces and place each piece in greased muffin pan. Brush any remaining garlic mixture over top of rounds. Bake 15 minutes or until golden brown.

Cheese Sticks

1 loaf thick-sliced bread	
½ cup (1 stick) butter, melted	115 g
1 cup grated parmesan cheese	100 g
1½ teaspoons paprika	7 ml

- Remove crust from bread and slice into sticks. Brush or roll in melted butter. Place on baking sheet. Sprinkle parmesan and paprika. Bake at 325° (165° C) for 20 minutes.

Breadsticks

1½ cups shredded Monterey Jack cheese	170 g
¼ cup poppy seeds	35 g
2 tablespoons dry onion soup mix	30 ml
2 (11 ounce) cans breadstick dough	2 (310 g)

- Spread cheese evenly in 9 x 13-inch (23 x 33 cm) baking dish. Sprinkle poppy seeds and soup mix evenly over cheese. Separate breadstick dough into sticks. Stretch strips slightly. Roll strips 1 at a time in cheese mixture and coat all sides. Cut into 3 or 4-inch (8 cm) strips. Place on cookie sheet and bake at 375° (190° C) for 12 minutes.

Seasoned Breadsticks

1 (11 ounce) package refrigerated breadsticks	310 g
¼ cup (½ stick) butter, melted	60 g
2 tablespoons prepared pesto	30 ml
¼ teaspoon garlic powder	1 ml
3 tablespoons grated parmesan cheese	20 g

- Preheat oven to 375° (190° C). Unroll and separate breadsticks and place on ungreased baking pan. Combine melted butter, pesto and garlic powder and brush over breadsticks. Twist each breadstick 3 times. Sprinkle with parmesan cheese.
- Bake for about 12 minutes or until golden brown.

Texas Cornbread

1 cup yellow cornmeal	160 g
⅔ cup flour	80 g
¼ teaspoon baking soda	1 ml
1¼ cups buttermilk	310 ml
1 large egg, beaten	

- Preheat oven to 400° (205° C). Combine cornmeal, flour and baking soda and stir in buttermilk and egg, until moistened.
- Pour into a buttered 7 x 11-inch (18 x 28 cm) baking pan and bake for 15 minutes, until golden brown.

Sausage Cornbread

1 (10 ounce) can cream of celery soup	280 g
2 eggs	
1 (8 ounce) package corn muffin mix	230 g
⅓ pound pork sausage, crumbled, cooked	150 g

- In medium bowl combine soup, eggs, and ¼ cup (60 ml) water or milk. Stir in corn muffin mix just until it blends. Fold in sausage. Pour mixture into greased 9-inch (23 cm) baking pan.
- Bake at 375° (190° C) for 25 minutes or until golden brown.

Mexican Cornbread

1 (16 ounce) package Mexican cubed cheese	455 g
¼ cup milk	60 ml
2 (8 ounce) packages corn muffin mix	2 (230 g)
2 eggs, beaten	

- In saucepan, melt cheese with milk over low heat. Combine corn muffin mix and eggs in bowl. Fold in cheese and mix until moist. Pour into greased 9 x 13-inch (23 x 33 cm) baking pan. Bake at 375° (190° C) for 25 minutes.

Corn Sticks

2 cups biscuit mix	240 g
2 tablespoons minced green onions	15 g
1 (8 ounce) can cream-style corn	230 g
Melted butter	

- Combine biscuit mix, green onions and cream-style corn. Place dough on floured surface and cut into 3 x 1-inch (8 x 2.5 cm) strips. Roll in melted butter. Bake at 400° (205° C) for 15 to 16 minutes.

Green Chili-Cheese Bread

1 loaf unsliced Italian bread	
½ cup (1 stick) butter, melted	15 g
1 (4 ounce) can diced green chilies, drained	115 g
¾ cup grated Monterey Jack cheese	85 g

- Slice bread almost all the way through. Combine melted butter, chilies and cheese. Spread between bread slices.
- Cover loaf with foil. Bake at 350° (175° C) for 25 minutes.

Hot-Water Cornbread

2 cups yellow cornmeal	320 g
¼ teaspoon baking powder	1 ml
1 teaspoon sugar	5 ml
¼ cup half-and-half cream	60 ml

- In bowl combine cornmeal, baking powder, 1 teaspoon (5 ml) salt and sugar, mixing well. Stir in cream and gradually add about 1 cup (250 ml) boiling water, stirring until batter is consistency of grits.
- In heavy skillet, pour enough oil for depth of ½-inch (1.2 cm) and heat on medium-high heat. Scoop batter into ¼ cup (60 ml) measure and drop in hot oil. Fry in batches for about 3 minutes on both sides; drain. Serve immediately.

Broccoli-Cheddar Corn Bread

1 (8 ounce) box corn muffin mix	230 g
1 egg	
⅓ cup milk	75 ml
½ cup frozen chopped broccoli, thawed, drained	80 g
½ cup shredded cheddar cheese	55 g

- Preheat oven to 375° (190° C).
- In bowl, combine muffin mix, egg and milk (the egg and milk are ingredients the mix calls for). Gently stir in chopped broccoli and cheese.
- Batter can be placed in muffin pan (with paper cupcake liners) or in greased 8-inch (20 cm) baking pan. If using muffin pan, bake for 18 minutes or 20 to 25 minutes if using baking pan.

Filled Muffins

1 (16 ounce) box blueberry muffin mix with blueberries	455 g
1 egg	
⅓ cup red raspberry jam	105 g
¼ cup sliced almonds	45 g

- Rinse blueberries and drain; set aside. In bowl, combine muffin mix, egg and ½ cup (125 ml) water. Stir until moist and break up lumps in mix.
- Place paper liners in 8 muffin cups. Fill cups halfway.
- Combine raspberry jam with blueberries. Spoon mixture on top of batter. Cover with remaining batter and sprinkle almonds over batter.
- Bake at 375° (190° C) for about 18 minutes or until light brown.

Quick Cinnamon Rolls

2¾ cups biscuit mix, divided	330 g
1 egg	
⅓ cup milk	75 ml
¼ cup (½ stick) butter, softened	60 g
⅔ cup sugar	135 g
2 teaspoons ground cinnamon	10 ml

- Preheat oven to 375° (190° C).
- In bowl, combine 2½ cups (300 g) baking mix, egg and milk, mixing until soft dough forms. Place dough on wax paper sprinkled with ¼ cup (30 g) baking mix. Shape into ball and knead gently just until smooth.
- Pat dough into 8 x 10-inch (20 x 25 cm) rectangle and spread with softened butter. Mix sugar and cinnamon and sprinkle over dough. Roll tightly and pinch edge of dough into roll to seal. Place sealed side down on ungreased baking sheet. With kitchen scissors, cut roll at 1-inch (2.5 cm) sections almost through to bottom.
- Bake 25 minutes or until light brown. Serve warm and, if you like, sprinkle with powdered sugar.

Blueberry-Orange Muffins

1 (16 ounce) package blueberry muffin mix with blueberries	455 g
2 egg whites	
½ cup orange juice	125 ml
Orange marmalade	

- Wash blueberries with cold water and drain.
- Stir muffin mix, egg whites and orange juice and break up any lumps.
- Fold blueberries gently into batter.
- Pour into muffin tins (with paper liners) about half full.
- Bake at 375° (190°) for 18 to 20 minutes or until toothpick inserted in center comes out clean.
- Spoon orange marmalade over top of hot muffins.

Banana-Gingerbread Muffins

1 (14 ounce) package gingerbread cookie mix	395 g
1 large ripe bananas, mashed	
2 eggs	
¾ cup oats	55 g
1 (16 ounce) can caramel frosting	455 g

- Preheat oven to 350° (175° C). Line bottoms of 16 muffin cups with paper liners.
- Combine cookie mix, bananas, eggs and oats in bowl, mix well. Divide batter evenly among muffin cups. Bake 18 minutes and immediately remove from pan. Cool before frosting muffins.

Easy Cinnamon Crisps

Flour tortillas
Vegetable oil
Sugar
Ground cinnamon

- Cut tortillas into wedges and carefully place in large skillet with hot oil. Fry until golden brown, remove from skillet and drain on paper towels. Sprinkle both sides of tortilla wedges heavily with sugar and cinnamon.

Honey-Cinnamon Butter

1 cup (2 sticks) butter	230 g
½ cup honey	170 g
1 teaspoon ground cinnamon	5 ml
Breakfast breads	

- Combine all ingredients in small mixing bowl and beat until smooth.

Topping for English Muffins

½ pound bacon slices, cooked, crumbled	230 g
¼ (½ stick) butter, softened	60 g
1 (5 ounce) jar sharp processed cheese spread	140 g
2 green onions, finely minced	
4 English muffins	

- Preheat oven to 325° (165° C). In bowl, combine all ingredients, mixing well and spread on each half (8) of 4 English muffins.
- Bake for 15 minutes or until each slice is light golden brown.

Breakfast Cinnamon Cake

⅔ cup packed brown sugar	145 g
1 tablespoon grated orange peel	15 ml
2 (12.4 ounce each) refrigerated cinnamon rolls	2 (350 g)

- Preheat oven to 375° (190° C).
- In small bowl, combine brown sugar and orange peel.
- Open cans of rolls (save frosting) and cut each in quarters and coat each quarter with cooking spray. Dip in sugar-orange mixture and arrange evenly in sprayed 10-inch (25 cm) bundt pan; gently pressing down. Bake for 30 minutes until light brown and about double in size. Cool slightly in pan.
- Invert serving plate on top of pan and with oven mitts, hold plate and pan together and invert. Remove pan. Spread frosting unevenly over top of cake and serve warm.

Crunchy Breadsticks

1 (8 count) package hot dog buns
1 cup (2 sticks) butter, melted   230 g
Garlic powder
Paprika

- Preheat oven to 225º (110° C).
- Slice each bun in half lengthwise. Use pastry brush to butter all breadsticks and sprinkle a little garlic powder and a couple sprinkles of paprika on each
- Place on baking sheet and bake for 45 minutes. Serves 8.

Ginger-Raisin Muffins

1 (18 ounce) box gingerbread mix   510 g
1 egg
2 (1.5 ounce) boxes seedless raisins   2 (45 g)

- Preheat oven to 350° (175° C).
- Combine gingerbread mix, 1¼ cups (310 ml) lukewarm water and egg in bowl and mix well. Stir in raisins. Fill sprayed or paper-lined muffin cups half full.
- Bake for 20 minutes or until toothpick inserted in center comes out clean. Serves 16.

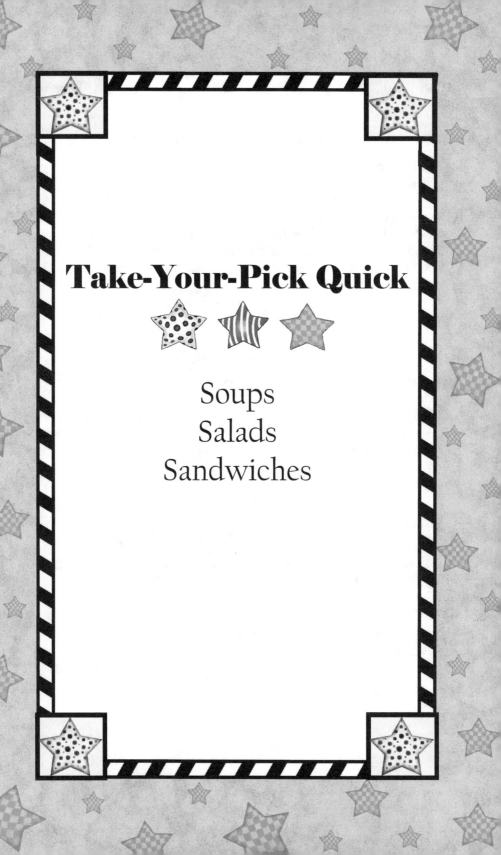

Take-Your-Pick Quick

Soups
Salads
Sandwiches

Easy Gazpacho

2 (28 ounce) cans diced tomatoes	2 (795 g)
1 unpeeled seedless cucumber, cut in chunks	
1 cup red onion, cut in chunks	160 g
1 cup celery, cut in chunks	100 g
2 serrano chile peppers, seeded, coarsely chopped	

- Working in batches, combine all ingredients plus a little salt and pepper, in food processor and pulse until mixture is a thick soup. Refrigerate. Serve chilled in individual bowls.

Swiss-Vegetable Soup

1 (1 ounce) packet dry vegetable soup mix	30 g
1 cup half-and-half cream	250 ml
1½ cups shredded Swiss cheese	160 g

- In saucepan, combine soup mix and 3 cups (750 ml) water and bring to a boil. Lower heat and simmer about 10 minutes. Add half-and-half cream and cheese and serve hot.

Tomato-French Onion Soup

1 (10 ounce) can tomato-bisque soup	280 g
2 (10 ounce) cans French-onion soup	2 (280 g)
Croutons	
Grated parmesan cheese	

- In saucepan, combine soups and 2 soup cans water. Heat thoroughly.
- Serve in bowls topped with croutons and a sprinkle of cheese.

Tortellini Soup

3 (14 ounce) cans chicken broth	3 (395 g)
2 (9 ounce) packages refrigerated cheese tortellini	2 (255 g)
1 (15 ounce) can cannellini beans, rinsed, drained	425 g
1 (4 ounce) jar chopped pimento	115 g
1 teaspoon dried basil	5 ml
1 tablespoon balsamic vinegar	15 ml

- In large saucepan, bring chicken broth to a boil; add tortellini and cook about 6 minutes or until tender.
- Stir in beans, pimento, basil, vinegar and salt and pepper to taste. Simmer for 8 to 10 minutes.

Zesty Black Bean Soup

2 onions, finely chopped	
1 tablespoon chili powder	15 ml
2 teaspoons cumin	10 ml
3 (15 ounce) cans black beans	3 (425 g)
2 (14 ounce) cans beef broth	2 (395 g)

- Saute onions in soup pot with a little oil for 5 minutes and stir in chili powder and cumin.
- Puree one can of beans and add to onion mixture. Add remaining beans and beef broth. Bring to a boil; reduce heat and simmer for 10 minutes. Garnish with shredded cheese or salsa.

Spinach Soup

2 (10 ounce) packages frozen chopped spinach, cooked	2 (280 g)
2 (10 ounce) can cream of mushroom soup	2 (280 g)
1 cup half-and-half cream	250 ml
1 (14 ounce) can chicken broth	395 g

- Place spinach, soup and half-and-half cream in blender; puree until smooth.
- Place spinach mixture and chicken broth in saucepan and heat on medium heat until well heated. Reduce heat to low and simmer for 20 minutes. Serve hot or cold.

Mexican-Style Minestrone Soup

1 (16 ounce) package frozen garlic-seasoned pasta and vegetables	455 g
1 (16 ounce) jar thick-and-chunky salsa	455 g
1 (15 ounce) can pinto beans with liquid	425 g
1 teaspoon chili powder	5 ml
1 teaspoon cumin	5 ml
1 (8 ounce) package shredded Mexican 4-cheese blend	230 g

- In large saucepan, combine pasta and vegetables, salsa, pinto beans, chili powder, cumin and 1 cup (250 ml) water. Heat to a boil; reduce heat to low-medium and simmer for about 15 minutes, stirring occasionally or until vegetables are tender.
- When ready to serve; top each serving with cheese.

Speedy Taco Soup

1 (12 ounce) can chicken	340 g
1 (14 ounce) can chicken broth	395 g
1 (16 ounce) jar mild thick-and-chunky salsa	455 g
1 (15 ounce) can chili beans	425 g

- In large saucepan, combine chicken, broth, salsa and beans.
- Bring to boil, reduce heat and simmer for 15 minutes.

TIP: A 15-ounce (425 g) can whole kernel corn may also be added.

Homemade Tomato Soup

3 (15 ounce) cans whole tomatoes	3 (425 g)
1 (14 ounce) can chicken broth	395 g
1 tablespoon sugar	15 ml
1 tablespoon minced garlic	15 ml
1 tablespoon balsamic vinegar	15 ml
¾ cup heavy cream	175 ml

- With blender, puree tomatoes (in batches) and pour into large saucepan. Add chicken broth, sugar, garlic, balsamic vinegar and a little salt and bring to a boil. Reduce heat and stir in heavy cream, cook stirring constantly for 2 to 3 minutes or until soup is thoroughly hot.

Fiesta Vegetable Soup

1 (15 ounce) can Mexican-style stewed tomatoes	425 g
1 (15 ounce) can whole kernel corn	425 g
1 (15 ounce) can pinto beans	425 g
2 (14 ounce) cans chicken broth	2 (395 g)
1 (10 ounce) can fiesta nacho cheese soup	280 g

- In soup pot, on high heat, combine tomatoes, corn, pinto beans, chicken broth and a little salt, mixing well.
- Stir in soup and heat until hot.

Easy Spinach Soup

2 (10 ounce) packages frozen chopped spinach, cooked	2 (280 g)
2 (10 ounce) cans cream of mushroom soup	2 (280 g)
1 cup half-and-half cream	250 ml
1 (14 ounce) can chicken broth	395 g

- Place spinach, mushroom soup and half-and-half in blender and puree until smooth. Place spinach mixture and chicken broth in saucepan and heat on medium heat until hot.
- Simmer on low for 20 minutes.

Crunchy Peanut Soup

2 (10 ounce) cans cream of chicken soup	2 (280 g)
2 soup cans milk	
1¼ cups crunchy peanut butter	360 g
½ teaspoon celery salt	2 ml

- In saucepan on medium heat, blend soup and milk.
- Stir in peanut butter and celery salt and heat until they blend well.

Easy Potato Soup

1 (20 ounce) package frozen hash-brown potatoes with	
onions and peppers	570 g
1 sweet red bell pepper, seeded, chopped	
2 (14 ounce) cans chicken broth	2 (395 g)
1 (10 ounce) can cream of celery soup	280 g
1 (10 ounce) can cream of chicken soup	280 g
1 (8 ounce) carton whipping cream	230 g
4 fresh green onions, chopped, for garnish	

- Combine potatoes, bell pepper, chicken broth and 1 cup (250 ml) water in large saucepan and bring to a boil. Cover, reduce heat and simmer 25 minutes.
- Stir in both soups and whipping cream and stirring well, heat until thoroughly hot. Garnish with green onions.

Avocado-Cream Soup

4 ripe avocados, peeled, diced	
1½ cups whipping cream	375 ml
2 (14 ounce) cans chicken broth	2 (395 g)
¼ cup dry sherry	60 ml

- Blend half avocados and half cream. Repeat with remaining avocados and cream. In saucepan, bring broth to boil, reduce heat and stir in avocado puree. Add 1 teaspoon (5 ml) salt and sherry and refrigerate thoroughly.

At Home Black Bean Soup

2 onions, finely chopped	
3 teaspoons minced garlic	15 ml
3 (15 ounce) cans black beans, rinsed, drained, divided	3 (425 g)
2 (14 ounce) cans beef broth, divided	2 (395 g)
1½ teaspoons dried cumin	7 ml
2 teaspoons chili powder	10 ml

- Saute onions and garlic in soup pot with little oil and cook on medium heat for 5 minutes.
- Place one can of beans and about ½ cup (125 ml) broth in food processor and process until beans are smooth.
- Transfer to soup pot with stir in remaining beans, remaining broth, cumin, chili powder and salt and pepper to taste and bring to a boil, reduce heat and simmer 15 minutes.

Creamy Broccoli and Rice Soup

1 (6 ounce) package chicken and wild rice mix	170 g
1 (10 ounce) package frozen chopped broccoli	280 g
2 (10 ounce) cans cream of chicken soup	2 (280 g)
1 (12 ounce) can chicken breast chunks	340 g

- In soup pot, combine rice mix, contents of seasoning packet and 5 cups (1.2 L) water. Bring to a boil, reduce heat and simmer for 15 minutes. Stir in broccoli, chicken soup and chicken; cover and simmer for another 5 minutes.

Fiesta-Veggie-Chicken Soup

1 (15 ounce) can Mexican-style stewed tomatoes	425 g
1 (15 ounce) can whole kernel corn	425 g
1 (15 ounce) can pinto beans	425 g
2 (14 ounce) cans chicken broth	2 (395 g)
1 (10 ounce) can fiesta nacho cheese soup	280 g
1 (12 ounce) can chicken breasts	340 g

- Combine tomatoes, corn, beans, broth and soup in large soup pot and heat 10 minutes over medium-high heat, mixing well. Stir in chicken and liquid and heat until thoroughly hot.

Cheesy Chicken Soup

1 (10 ounce) can fiesta nacho cheese soup	280 g
1 (10 ounce) can cream of chicken soup	280 g
1 (10 ounce) soup can of milk	280 g
1 chicken bouillon cube or 1 teaspoon bouillon granules	5 ml

- Mix soups, milk and bouillon cube in saucepan and stir until smooth. Serve hot.

Chicken-Noodle Soup

1 (14 ounce) can chicken broth	395 g
2 tablespoons butter	30 g
1 (3 ounce) package chicken-flavored ramen noodles, broken	85 g
1 (10 ounce) package frozen green peas, thawed	280 g
1 (4 ounce) jar sliced mushrooms	115 g
3 cups cooked, cubed chicken or deli turkey	420 g

- In large saucepan, boil 2 cups (500 ml) water. Add broth, butter, ramen noodles, contents of seasoning packet and peas.
- Heat to boiling, reduce heat to medium and cook about 5 minutes. Stir in mushrooms and chicken and continue cooking over medium heat until all ingredients are heated thoroughly.

Tasty Turkey Soup

1 (16 ounce) package frozen chopped onions and bell peppers	455 g
2 (3 ounce) packages chicken-flavored ramen noodles	2 (85 g)
2 (10 ounce) cans cream of chicken soup	2 (280 g)
1 cup cubed turkey	140 g

- In soup pot with a little oil, cook onions and peppers just until tender but not brown. Add ramen noodles, seasoning packet and 2 cups (500 ml) water. Cook 5 minutes or until noodles are tender. Stir in chicken soup and cubed turkey. Stir until hot.

Cream of Turkey Soup

1 (10 ounce) can cream of celery soup	280 g
1 (10 ounce) can cream of chicken soup	280 g
2 (10 ounce) cans milk or cream	2 (280 g)
1 cup finely diced turkey	140 g

- Combine all ingredients in large saucepan. Serve hot.

Hearty 15-Minute Turkey Soup

1 (14 ounce) can chicken broth	395 g
3 (15 ounce) cans navy beans	3 (425 g)
1 (28 ounce) can stewed tomatoes	795 g
3 cups small chunk white turkey meat	420 g
2 teaspoons minced garlic	10 ml
¼ teaspoon cayenne pepper	1 ml
1 (6 ounce) package baby spinach, stems removed	170 g

Freshly grated parmesan cheese for garnish

- In soup pot, combine broth, beans, stewed tomatoes, turkey chunks, garlic, cayenne pepper and salt and pepper to taste. Bring to a boil; reduce heat and simmer on medium heat for about 10 minutes.
- Stir in baby spinach; bring to a boil and cook, stirring constantly for 5 minutes. When ready to serve, sprinkle each serving with grated parmesan cheese.

Chili-Soup Warmer

1 (10 ounce) can tomato-bisque soup	280 g
1 (10 ounce) can chili	280 g
1 (10 ounce) can fiesta nacho cheese soup	280 g
1(15 ounce) can chicken broth	425 g

- In saucepan, combine all soups and broth. Add amount of water to produce desired thickness of soup.
- Heat and serve hot with crackers.

Spaghetti Soup

1 (7 ounce) package spaghetti	200 g
1 (18 ounce) package frozen, cooked meatballs, thawed	510 g
1 (28 ounce) jar spaghetti sauce	795 g
1 (15 ounce) can Mexican stewed tomatoes	425 g

- In soup pot with 3 quarts (3 L) boiling water and a little salt, cook spaghetti about 6 minutes (no need to drain).
- When spaghetti is done, add meatballs, spaghetti sauce and stewed tomatoes and cook until mixture is thoroughly hot.

Bacon-Potato Soup

2 (14 ounce) cans chicken broth seasoned with garlic   2 (395 g)
2 potatoes, peeled, cubed
1 onion finely chopped
6 strips bacon, cooked, crumbled

- In large saucepan, combine broth, potatoes and onion. Bring to boil, reduce
  heat to medium-high and boil about 10 minutes or until potatoes are tender.
  Season with a little pepper and sprinkle bacon on servings.

Spicy Tomato Soup

2 (10 ounce) cans tomato soup   2 (280 g)
1 (15 ounce) can Mexican stewed tomatoes   425 g
Sour cream
½ pound bacon, fried, drained, crumbled   230 g

- Combine soup and stewed tomatoes in saucepan and heat.

- To serve, place dollop of sour cream on top of soup and sprinkle crumbed bacon
  over sour cream.

Lucky Pea Soup

1 onion, chopped
1 cup cooked, cubed ham   140 g
1 (15 ounce) cans black-eyed peas with jalapeno peppers   425 g
1 (14 ounce) can chicken broth   395 g
1 teaspoon minced garlic   5 ml
1 teaspoon rubbed sage   5 ml

- In a large saucepan, saute onion in a little oil. On high heat, add ham, black-
  eyed peas, broth, garlic and sage. Bring to a boil, reduce heat and simmer,
  stirring occasionally, for 20 minutes.

Italian Garbanzo Soup

1 (16 ounce) package frozen diced onion and bell peppers	455 g
1 pound Italian sausages, sliced	455 g
1 (14 ounce) can beef broth	395 g
1 (15 ounce) can Italian stewed tomatoes	425 g
2 (15 ounce) cans garbanzo beans, rinsed, drained	2 (425 g)

- Saute onion and bell peppers in soup pot with a little oil. Add Italian sausage and cook until brown. Stir in broth, stewed tomatoes and garbanzo beans.
- Bring mixture to a boil; reduce heat and simmer about 30 minutes.

Easy Meaty Minestrone

2 (20 ounce) cans minestrone soup	2 (570 g)
1 (15 ounce) can pinto beans	425 g
1 (18 ounce) package frozen Italian meatballs, thawed	510 g
1 (5 ounce) package grated parmesan cheese	140 g

- In large saucepan, combine soups, beans, meatballs and ½ cup (125 ml) water. Bring to a boil, reduce heat to low and simmer about 15 minutes. Sprinkle each serving with parmesan cheese.

Italian Vegetable Soup

1 pound bulk Italian sausage	455 g
2 onions, chopped	
2 teaspoons minced garlic	10 ml
1 (1 ounce) packet beefy recipe soup mix	30 g
1 (15 ounce) can sliced carrots, drained	425 g
2 (15 ounce) cans Italian stewed tomatoes	2 (425 g)
2 (15 ounce) cans garbanzo beans, drained	2 (425 g)
1 cup elbow macaroni	105 g

- In large soup pot, brown sausage, onions and garlic. Pour off fat and add 4 cups (1 L) water, soup mix, carrots, tomatoes, garbanzo beans. Bring to a boil, reduce heat to low-medium and simmer for 15 minutes.
- Add elbow macaroni and continue cooking another 15 minutes or until macaroni is tender.

Potato-Sausage Soup

1 pound pork sausage link	455 g
1 cup chopped celery	100g
1 cup chopped onion	160 g
2 (10 ounce) cans potato soup	2 (280 g)
1 (14 ounce) can chicken broth	395 g

- Cut pork sausage in 1-inch (2.5 cm) diagonal slices. In large heavy skillet, brown sausage slices, drain and remove to separate bowl. Leave about 2 tablespoons (30 ml) sausage drippings in skillet and saute celery and onion.
- Add potato soup, ¾ cup (175 ml) water, chicken broth and cooked sausage slices. Bring to a boil, reduce heat and simmer for 20 minutes.

Easy Pork Stew

1 (1 pound) pork tenderloin, cut into small chunks	455 g
2 (12 ounce) jars pork gravy	2 (340 g)
½ cup chili sauce	135 g
1 (16 ounce) package frozen stew vegetables, thawed	455 g

- In greased soup pot on medium-high heat, cook pork pieces for 10 minutes, stirring frequently.
- Stir in gravy, chili sauce and stew vegetables and bring to a boil. Reduce heat and simmer for 15 minutes or until vegetables are tender.

Meatball Stew

1 (18 ounce) package frozen, cooked Italian meatballs	510 g
1 (14 ounce) cans beef broth	395 g
2 (15 ounce) cans Italian stewed tomatoes	2 (425 g)
1 (16 ounce) package frozen stew vegetables	455 g

- Place meatballs, beef broth and stewed tomatoes in large saucepan. Bring to boiling, reduce heat and simmer for 10 minutes or until meatballs are thoroughly hot.
- Add vegetables and cook on medium heat for 10 minutes. Mixture will be fairly thin. For thicker stew, mix 2 tablespoons (15 g) cornstarch in ¼ cup (60 ml) water and stir into stew. Bring to a boil and stir constantly until stew thickens.

Southern Turnip Greens Stew

2 (16 ounce) packages frozen chopped turnip greens	2 (455 g)
1 (10 ounce) package frozen diced onion and bell peppers	280 g
2 cups chopped, cooked ham	280 g
2 (15 ounce) cans chicken broth	2 (425 g)

- In soup pot, combine all ingredients and 1 teaspoon (5 ml) pepper. Bring mixture to a boil, reduce heat, cover and simmer for 30 minutes.

Easy Pork Tenderloin Stew

2 - 3 cups cubed, cooked pork	280 - 420 g
1 (12 ounce) jar pork gravy	340 g
¼ cup chili sauce	70 g
1 (16 ounce) package frozen stew vegetables	455 g

- In soup pot, combine all ingredients and ½ cup (125 ml) water.
- Boil 2 minutes; reduce heat and simmer for 10 minutes. Serve with cornbread or hot biscuits.

Quick Brunswick Stew

1 (15 ounce) can beef stew	425 g
1 (15 ounce) can chicken stew	425 g
1 (15 ounce) can lima beans	425 g
2 (15 ounce) cans stewed tomatoes	2 (425 g)
1 (15 ounce) can whole kernel corn	425 g
½ teaspoon hot sauce, optional	2 ml

- In large stew pot, combine beef stew, chicken stew, beans, tomatoes and corn. On medium-high heat, bring stew to boiling, reduce heat and simmer for 20 minutes.
- Brunswick stew needs to be a little spicy, so stir in ¼ teaspoon (1 ml) hot sauce, taste and add more if needed. If you don't want spicy, add 1 tablespoon (15 ml) Worcestershire sauce to stew.

Bean and Chicken Chili

3 (15 ounce) cans navy beans with liquid	3 (425 g)
2 (14 ounce) cans chicken broth	2 (395 g)
¼ cup (½ stick) butter	60 g
1 large onion, chopped	
3 cups cooked, chopped chicken	420 g
1 (7 ounce) can diced green chilies	200 g
2 teaspoons ground cumin	10 ml
½ teaspoon dried oregano	2 ml
Shredded Monterey Jack cheese	

- In large saucepan, combine beans, broth, butter and onion. Bring to a boil; reduce heat and simmer 15 minutes, stirring occasionally.
- With potato masher, mash bean mixture several times so that about half the beans are mashed. Add chicken, green chilies and seasoning. Bring to a boil, reduce heat, cover and simmer for another 15 minutes.
- To serve, spoon into soup bowls and top with a heaping tablespoon of cheese.

A Different Chili

2 onions, coarsely chopped	
3 (15 ounce) cans great northern beans, drained	3 (425 g)
2 (14 ounce) cans chicken broth	2 (395 g)
2 tablespoons minced garlic	30 ml
1 (7 ounce) can diced green chilies	200 g
1 tablespoon ground cumin	15 ml
3 cups cooked, finely chopped chicken breasts	420 g
1 (8 ounce) package shredded Monterey Jack cheese	230 g

- In large, heavy pot with a little oil, cook onions, about 5 minutes, but do not brown. Place 1 can beans in shallow bowl and mash with fork.
- Add mashed beans, 2 remaining cans of beans, chicken broth, garlic, green chilies and cumin. Bring to a boil, reduce heat, cover and simmer 30 minutes.
- Add chopped chicken (or deli turkey), stirring to blend well and heat until chili is thoroughly hot. When serving, top each bowl with 3 tablespoons (20 g) of cheese.

Black Bean Stew Supper

1 pound pork sausage ring, thinly sliced	455 g
2 onions, chopped	
3 ribs celery, sliced	
3 (15 ounce) cans black beans, drained, rinsed	3 (425 g)
2 (10 ounce) cans diced tomatoes and green chilies	2 (280 g)
2 (14 ounce) cans chicken broth	2 (395 g)

- Place sausage slices, onion and celery in soup pot with a little oil and cook until sausage is slightly brown and onion is soft. Drain fat off. Add beans, tomatoes and green chilies and broth.
- Bring mixture to a boil, reduce heat and simmer for 25 minutes. Take out about 2 cups (500 ml) soup mixture and place in food processor and pulse until almost smooth. Return mixture to soup pot and stir; this will thicken stew. Return heat to high until stew is thoroughly hot.

Supper Gumbo

1 (10 ounce) can pepper pot soup	280 g
1 (10 ounce) can chicken gumbo soup	280 g
1 (6 ounce) can white crabmeat, flaked	170 g
1 (6 ounce) can tiny shrimp	170 g

- In saucepan, combine all ingredients with 1½ soup cans water.
- Cover and simmer for 15 minutes.

Potato and Ham Chowder

1 grated carrot	
2 ribs celery, sliced	
1 onion, chopped	
1 (4.5 ounce) package julienne potato mix	128 g
3 cups milk	750 ml
2 cups cooked, cubed ham	280 g

- In soup pot, combine 2¾ cups (675 ml) water with carrot, celery, onion and potato mix. Bring to a boil, reduce heat, cover and simmer 20 minutes.
- Stir in milk and packet of sauce mix (from potatoes), mix well and return to boiling. Simmer 2 minutes and stir in ham.

Crab and Corn Chowder

1 (1.8 ounce) package Knorr's® leek soup mix	60 g
2 cups milk	500 ml
1 (8 ounce) can whole kernel corn	230 g
½ (8 ounce) package cubed processed cheese	½ (230 g)
1 (7 ounce) can crabmeat	200 g

- In large saucepan, combine soup mix and milk and cook over medium heat, stirring constantly until soup begins to thicken. While still on medium heat, stir in corn and cheese. Just before serving, add crab and stir until thoroughly hot.

Crunchy Sweet Onion-Jicama Salad

1 supersweet onion, thinly sliced
1 medium jicama, peeled, julienned
Roasted garlic-vinaigrette salad dressing
Red leaf lettuce

- Combine onion and jicama in large bowl, pour enough salad dressing to partially cover. Toss and refrigerate.
- Arrange lettuce leaves on individual salad plates and mound onion-jicama mixture onto lettuce.

Sesame-Romaine Salad

1 large head romaine lettuce	
2 tablespoons sesame seeds, toasted	15 g
6 strips bacon, fried, crumbled	
½ cup grated Swiss cheese	55 g
1 (8 ounce) bottle creamy Italian salad dressing	230 g

- Wash and dry lettuce. Tear into bite-size pieces.
- When ready to serve, sprinkle sesame seeds, bacon and cheese over lettuce and toss with about ½ cup (125 ml) salad dressing, adding more if needed.

Orange-Almond Salad

1 head green leaf lettuce	
4 slices bacon, fried, crumbled	
⅓ cup slivered almonds, toasted	55 g
1 (11 ounce) can mandarin oranges, drained, chilled	310 g

- Combine all ingredients in salad bowl.
- When ready to serve toss with vinaigrette dressing.

Greens and Fruit

1 (10 ounce) package spring salad greens	280 g
1 (11 ounce) can mandarin oranges, drained	310 g
¼ cup sliced almonds	45 g
1 cup halved green seedless grapes	150 g
¼ cup precooked bacon bits	30 g

- In salad bowl, combine salad greens, oranges, almonds and grapes. Toss with raspberry vinaigrette salad dressing. Sprinkle with bacon bits.

Pear and Goat Cheese Salad

1 (10 ounce) package baby salad greens	280 g
¾ cup crumbled goat cheese	100 g
2 pears, peeled, sliced	
½ cup balsamic vinaigrette	125 ml
½ cup coarsely chopped walnuts	65 g

- In salad bowl, combine salad greens, cheese and pear slices and toss with vinaigrette. Sprinkle walnuts over top of salad to serve.

Harmony Salad

2 heads red leaf lettuce, torn	
2 (11 ounce) cans mandarin oranges, drained	2 (310 g)
2 avocados, peeled, cut into chunks	
1 red onion, sliced	
¼ cup sunflower seeds	30 g

Dressing:

3 tablespoons red wine vinegar	45 ml
1 teaspoon ground cumin	5 ml
¼ cup extra-virgin olive oil	60 ml
2 tablespoons honey	45 g

- In salad bowl, place lettuce, oranges, avocados and onion slices. Refrigerate. Using 16-ounce (500 ml) jar with lid, combine all dressing ingredients and shake well to mix. When ready to serve, shake dressing again and drizzle over salad and toss. Sprinkle sunflower seeds over top of salad.

Italian Salad

1 (10 ounce) package mixed salad greens	280 g
1 cup shredded mozzarella cheese	115 g
1 (2 ounce) can sliced ripe black olives	60 g
1 (15 ounce) can cannellini beans, rinsed, drained	425 g

- In salad bowl, combine greens, cheese, olives and well drained cannellini beans. Toss with zesty Italian salad dressing.

Swiss Salad

1 large head romaine lettuce	
1 bunch fresh green onions with tops, chopped	
1 (8 ounce) package shredded Swiss cheese	230 g
½ cup toasted sunflower seeds	65 g

- Tear lettuce into bite-size pieces. Add onions, cheese, sunflower seeds and toss. Serve with vinaigrette dressing.

Vinaigrette for Swiss Salad:

⅔ cup salad oil	150 ml
⅓ cup red wine vinegar	75 ml

- Mix all ingredients with 1 teaspoon (5 ml) salt and refrigerate.

Crunchy Salad

¼ cup sesame seeds	30 g
½ cup sunflower seeds	65 g
½ cup slivered almonds	85 g
1 head red leaf lettuce	

- Toast sesame seeds, sunflower seeds and almonds at 300° (150° C) for about 10 minutes or until light brown.
- Tear lettuce into bite-size pieces and add seed mixture.
- Toss with creamy Italian dressing.

Mandarin Salad

1 head red-tipped lettuce	
2 (11 ounce) cans mandarin oranges, drained	2 (310 g)
2 avocados, peeled, diced	
1 small red onion, sliced	
1 (8 ounce) bottle poppy seed dressing	235 ml

- Combine all ingredients. When ready to serve, toss with ½ cup (125 ml) salad dressing, using more if needed.

Berry Delicious Salad

1 (10 ounce) package mixed salad greens	280 g
2 cups fresh blueberries	295 g
⅔ cup crumbled gorgonzola cheese	115 g
⅓ cup chopped pecans, toasted	35 g
1 (8 ounce) bottle raspberry-vinaigrette salad dressing	235 ml

- In salad bowl, combine salad greens, blueberries, cheese and pecans. Toss salad with about half the dressing, adding more if needed. Refrigerate.

Luscious Papaya-Chicken Salad

1 (10 ounce) package torn romaine lettuce leaves	280 g
2 ripe papayas, peeled, seeded, cubed	
1 large red bell pepper, seeded, chopped	
2 cups cooked, cubed chicken breast	280 g
½ cup toasted, chopped pecans	55 g

Dressing:

¼ cup lime juice	60 ml
⅓ cup honey	15 g
2 teaspoons minced garlic	10 ml
3 tablespoons extra-virgin olive oil	45 ml

- In large salad bowl, combine lettuce, papayas and bell pepper. In small bowl, whisk together lime juice, honey, garlic and a little salt to taste. Slowly add olive oil in thin stream and whisk dressing until well blended.
- Pour dressing over salad, add cubed chicken and toss. To serve, sprinkle pecans over top of salad.

Raspberry-Orange Tossed Salad

Dressing:

½ cup seedless raspberry preserves	160 g
¼ cup white wine vinegar	60 ml
¼ cup honey	85 g
¼ cup canola oil	60 ml

Salad:

1 (10 ounce) package torn romaine	280 g
1 cup fresh raspberries	125 g
1 (11 ounce) can mandarin oranges	310 g

- In bowl, combine all dressing ingredients and refrigerate until ready to use. In salad bowl, combine romaine, raspberries and oranges and toss with raspberry dressing.

Grandmother's Wilted Lettuce

6 cups leaf lettuce	210 g

Dressing:

3 slices bacon	
½ cup white vinegar	125 ml
1 tablespoon prepared mustard	15 ml
2 hard-boiled egg yolks, mashed, discard whites	

- Place lettuce in salad bowl. Fry bacon until crisp in skillet; remove bacon and drain. Crumble bacon. With bacon drippings remaining in skillet, add vinegar, mustard and egg yolks and cook until hot. While very hot, add crumbed bacon and pour over leaf lettuce and toss until thoroughly mixed. Serve immediately.

Spring Pear Salad Supper

1 (10 ounce) package spring salad mix	280 g
1 pound deli turkey, cut into thin strips	455 g
2 pears, cored, sliced	
1 cup Craisins® (dried cranberries)	120 g
⅔ cup honey roasted slivered almonds	85 g

Dressing:

1 (8 ounce) bottle wild berry vinaigrette	230 g
2 tablespoons olive oil	30 ml

- In salad bowl, combine salad mix, turkey strips, pears and Craisins® and refrigerate. When ready to serve, spoon vinaigrette and olive oil over salad and toss. Sprinkle almonds over top of salad.

Toss the Greens

1 (10 ounce) package mixed salad greens	280 g
1½ cups cherry tomato halves	225 g
1 sliced cucumber	
1 sliced red onion, separated into rings	
1 pound seasoned, cooked chicken breasts, cut into strips	455 g

Dressing:

1 (8 ounce) bottle Italian salad dressing	235 ml
Seasoned pepper	
¼ teaspoon cayenne pepper	1 ml

- In large salad bowl, combine greens, tomatoes, cucumber and onion rings and toss.
- When ready to serve, toss with salad dressing. Arrange salad on individual salad plates and top with strips of chicken and sprinkle with seasoned pepper and cayenne pepper.

Green-Rice Salad

1 (10 ounce) package mixed baby salad greens	280 g
2 cups cooked rice, chilled	315 g
2 (11 ounce) cans mandarin oranges, well drained, chilled	2 (310 g)
½ cup thinly sliced scallions, chilled	80 g

Dressing:

1 (8 ounce) bottle Italian salad dressing	235 ml
1 teaspoon ground cumin	5 ml
1 avocado, peeled and well mashed	

- In salad bowl, combine salad greens, rice, oranges and scallions.
- In jar with lid, combine salad dressing, cumin, avocado, ½ teaspoon (2 ml) each of salt and pepper. Pour about half dressing over salad and toss; adding more as needed.

Colorful Salad Toss

2 (8 ounce) packages baby spinach, stems removed	2 (230 g)
1 small head cauliflower, cut into small florets	
1 red bell pepper, seeded, chopped	
¾ cup walnut halves	90 g
½ cup roasted sunflower seeds	65 g
1 (8 ounce) bottle wild berry vinaigrette salad dressing	235 ml

- In large salad bowl, combine spinach, cauliflower, bell pepper strips, walnuts, sunflower seeds and a generous amount of salt and refrigerate. Pour about half salad dressing over salad and toss. Add more dressing if needed.

Wilted Spinach-Walnut Salad

2 (8 ounce) packages baby spinach, stems removed	2 (230 g)
1 teaspoon minced garlic	5 ml
2 tablespoons olive oil	30 ml
½ cup walnut halves, toasted	60 g

- In skillet, saute spinach and garlic in hot oil on medium-high heat for about 5 minutes or until spinach is wilted. Sprinkle a little salt over spinach and mix. Toss with whole toasted walnuts.

Wilted Spinach Salad

1 (10 ounce) package fresh baby spinach	280 g
1 (15 ounce) can cannellini beans, rinsed, drained	425 g
¾ cup zesty Italian salad dressing	175 ml
¾ cup shredded Monterey Jack cheese	85 g

- Remove large stems from spinach and place in salad bowl and add cannellini beans, toss. In saucepan, heat Italian salad dressing to boiling and pour over spinach-bean mixture and toss. Sprinkle cheese over salad and serve immediately.

Strawberry-Spinach Salad

1 (10 ounce) package fresh spinach, washed, stemmed	280 g
1 small jicama, peeled, julienne	
1 pint fresh strawberries, stemmed, halved	355 g
2½ cups fresh bean sprouts	260 g
1 (8 ounce) bottle poppy seed dressing	235 ml

- Combine spinach, jicama, strawberries and bean sprouts in large bowl. Toss with half the dressing, using more if needed.

Spinach and Apple Salad

1 (10 ounce) package fresh spinach	280 g
⅓ cup frozen orange juice concentrate, thawed	75 ml
¼ cup mayonnaise	55 g
1 red apple, unpeeled, diced	
5 slices bacon, fried, crumbled	

- Tear spinach into small pieces. Mix orange juice and mayonnaise. Mix spinach and apple (cut apple at the last minute); pour dressing over salad and top with bacon.

Spinach-Orange Salad

1 (10 ounce) package spinach, stems removed	280 g
2 (10 ounce) cans mandarin oranges, drained	2 (280 g)
⅓ small jicama, peeled, julienned	
⅓ cup slivered almonds, toasted	55 g

- Combine all ingredients in bowl. Toss with vinaigrette dressing.

Special Spinach Salad

1 (10 ounce) package fresh spinach	280 g
1 (16 ounce) can bean sprouts, drained	455 g
8 slices bacon, cooked crisp	
1 (11 ounce) can water chestnuts, chopped	310 g

- Combine spinach and bean sprouts.
- When ready to serve, add crumbled bacon and water chestnuts. Toss with vinaigrette salad dressing made from 3 parts olive oil and 1 part red wine vinegar.

Spinach Pecan Salad

1 (10 ounce) package baby spinach	280 g
2 eggs, hard-boiled, sliced	
½ cup toasted pecans	55 g
1 (6 ounce) package cooked, crumbled bacon	170 g
¼ cup crumbled blue cheese	45 g
Italian salad dressing	

- In salad bowl, combine spinach, sliced eggs, pecans, bacon and blue cheese; toss. Drizzle with a prepared Italian salad dressing.

Spinach and Chicken Salad

1 (10 ounce) package baby spinach	280 g
1 seedless cucumber, sliced	
1 red delicious apple, unpeeled, thinly sliced	
1 bunch fresh green onions, sliced	
3 cups coarsely shredded rotisserie chicken meat	420 g

Dressing:

⅓ cup red wine vinegar	75 ml
3 tablespoons olive oil	45 ml
1 tablespoon dijon-style mustard	15 ml
½ teaspoon dried thyme	2 ml
1 tablespoon sugar	15 ml

- In salad bowl, combine spinach, cucumber, apple slices, green onions and chicken; toss to mix well.
- In saucepan, combine all dressing ingredients and heat just until thoroughly hot. Pour over salad and toss until salad is evenly coated. Serve immediately.

Spinach and Turkey Salad Supper

2 (8 ounce) packages baby spinach, stems removed	2 (230 g)
½ cup walnut halves	60 g
½ cup Craisins® (dried cranberries)	60 g
2 red delicious apples, unpeeled, sliced	
1 pound deli smoked turkey, julienned	455 g
½ (15 ounce) bottle refrigerated honey-mustard dressing	½ (445 ml)

- In large salad bowl, combine spinach, walnuts, cranberries, apples and turkey. Toss salad with half honey-mustard dressing and add more if needed.

Spinach Salad

1 (10 ounce) bag baby spinach	280 g
1 cup fresh sliced strawberries	165 g
1 (3 ounce) package silvered almonds, toasted	85 g
½ cup crumbled feta cheese	70 g

- In salad bowl, combine all ingredients and toss with poppy seed vinaigrette dressing.

Poppy Seed Vinaigrette Dressing:

½ cup sugar	100 g
¼ cup white wine vinegar	60 ml
⅓ cup olive oil	75 ml
2 teaspoons poppy seeds	10 ml

- Combine all ingredients and toss with spinach mixture.

Salad Surprise

1 (10 ounce) bag fresh spinach, washed, stemmed	280 g
1 pint fresh strawberries, stemmed, halved	355 g
1 large banana, sliced	
⅔ cup chopped walnuts	85 g
Poppy seed dressing	

- In large bowl, combine all salad ingredients.
- When ready to serve, toss with prepared poppy seed dressing.

Spinach Salad Oriental

1 (10 ounce) package fresh spinach	280 g
2 eggs, hard-boiled, sliced	
1 (14 ounce) can bean sprouts, drained	395 g
1 (8 ounce) can water chestnuts, chopped	230 g

- Combine all 4 ingredients. Top with dressing.

Dressing for Spinach Salad Oriental:

¾ cup olive oil	175 ml
⅓ cup sugar	65 g
¼ cup ketchup	70 g
3 tablespoons red wine vinegar	45 ml

- Combine all ingredients and mix well. Use desired amount of dressing and refrigerate remaining salad dressing.

Warm Spinach Salad

1 (10 ounce) package fresh spinach, stems removed	280 g
1 (15 ounce) can cannellini beans, rinsed, drained	425 g
1 (11 ounce) can Mexicorn®, drained	310 g
1 cup shredded Monterey Jack cheese	115 g

Dressing:

1 (8 ounce) bottle zesty Italian salad dressing	235 ml
1 sweet red bell pepper, seeded and chopped	

- In salad bowl, combine spinach, cannellini beans and corn.
- In saucepan, combine salad dressing and chopped bell pepper. On high heat, bring to boiling, reduce heat to low and cook 2 minutes. Pour hot dressing over spinach-corn mixture and toss. Sprinkle with cheese and serve warm.

Spinach-Feta Cheese Salad

1 (10 ounce) bag baby spinach	280 g
1 cup fresh sliced strawberries	165 g
1 (3 ounce) package slivered almonds, toasted	85 g
½ cup crumbled feta cheese	70 g

Dressing:

½ cup sugar	100 g
¼ cup white wine vinegar	60 ml
⅓ cup olive oil	75 ml
2 teaspoons poppy seeds	10 ml

- Combine spinach, strawberries, almonds and feta cheese in salad bowl.
- Combine all dressing ingredients and toss with spinach mixture.

Tossed Zucchini Salad

¾ cup unpeeled, grated zucchini	95 g
1 (6 ounce) package shredded lettuce	170 g
½ cup sliced ripe olives	65 g
1 carrot, grated	
⅓ cup shredded mozzarella cheese	40 g
Zesty Italian salad dressing	

- In salad bowl, toss zucchini, lettuce, olives and grated carrot. Add cheese and toss with salad dressing.

Green Salad with Candied Pecans

Candied pecans:

1⅓ cups pecan halves	165 g
¼ cup honey	85 g
3 tablespoon light corn syrup	45 ml

Continued on following page

Continued from previous page

Salad:

1 (10 ounce) package baby spinach	280 g
4 cups young salad greens	170 g
1 tart apple, thinly sliced	
1 cup crumbled blue cheese	175 g
1 (8 ounce) bottle zesty Italian salad dressing	235 ml

- Preheat oven to 350° (175° C). Combine pecans, honey and corn syrup in bowl and stir until all pecans are well coated. Spread out to rimmed baking sheet and bake 12 minutes. Remove to piece of foil, separating clumps with fork; cool.

- In salad bowl, combine spinach, greens, apple slices and bleu cheese; toss with about half bottle of salad dressing. Top with candied pecans.

Red and Green Salad

3 small zucchini, thinly sliced	
2 red delicious apples with peel, chopped	
2 cups fresh broccoli florets	140 g
¾ cup coarsely chopped walnuts	100 g
1 (8 ounce) bottle creamy Italian salad dressing	235 ml

- In salad bowl, combine zucchini, apples, broccoli and walnutsand toss.

- Pour about ¾ bottle of salad dressing over salad and toss. Use more dressing if needed. Serve immediately.

Summer Cucumbers

2 seedless cucumbers, peeled, sliced	
1 (8 ounce) bottle zesty Italian salad dressing	235 ml
1 (8 ounce) carton sour cream	230 g
1 tablespoon chopped chives	15 ml

- Place cucumbers in bowl and pour salad dressing over cucumbers and marinate about 30 minutes, tossing once to distribute marinade. To serve, drain marinade from cucumbers and stir in sour cream and chives.

Sunshine Carrots

3 cups shredded carrots	330 g
1 (15 ounce) can crushed pineapple, drained	425 g
½ cup mayonnaise	110 g
½ cup sliced almonds	95 g
½ cup sunflower seeds	65 g

- In bowl, combine carrots and pineapple and stir in mayonnaise. Refrigerate until ready to serve. To serve, stir in almonds and sunflower seeds and toss to coat almonds and sunflower seeds.

Special Stuffed Celery

1 bunch celery	
1 (8 ounce) package cream cheese	230 g
¼ cup finely chopped pecans	30 g
¼ cup finely chopped bell pepper	35 g
1 (4 ounce) jar diced pimentos	115 g

- Cut celery into pieces convenient for handling.
- With mixer, beat cream cheese until creamy and stir in pecans, bell pepper, pimentos and a little salt. Fill celery hollows and serve with a relish plate.

Marinated Cucumbers

⅓ cup vinegar	75 ml
2 tablespoons sugar	25 g
1 teaspoon dried dillweed	5 ml
3 cucumbers, peeled, sliced	

- Combine vinegar, sugar, 1 teaspoon (5 ml) salt, dillweed and ¼ teaspoon (1 ml) pepper. Pour over cucumbers. Refrigerate.

Carrot Salad

3 cups finely grated carrots	330 g
1 (8 ounce) can crushed pineapple, drained	230 g
¼ cup flaked coconut	20 g
1 tablespoon sugar	15 ml
⅓ cup mayonnaise	75 g

- Combine all ingredients. Toss with mayonnaise and mix well. Refrigerate.

Sweet Corn Salad

2 (10 ounce) packages frozen whole kernel corn	2 (280 g)
2 ribs celery, sliced	
⅓ cup sweet pickle relish, drained	80 g
¾ cup diced apples	135 g
3 tablespoons lemon juice	45 ml

Dressing:

⅓ cup mayonnaise	75 g
1½ tablespoons mustard	22 ml
2 tablespoons sugar	25 g
1 teaspoon dried parsley	5 ml

- Cook corn as directed on package. Toss with celery, pickle relish and apples that have been covered with lemon juice.

- In small bowl, combine mayonnaise, mustard, sugar and parsley, mixing well. Spoon over corn mixture and toss; refrigerate.

Cucumber-Onion Salad

2 - 3 seedless cucumbers, sliced	
2 onions, sliced	
1 tablespoon white vinegar	15 ml
½ cup sour cream	120 g

- In mixing bowl, sprinkle ½ teaspoon (2 ml) salt over cucumbers and let stand 20 minutes; drain. Add onions and vinegar, toss. Refrigerate. When ready to serve, stir in sour cream.

Veggie Salad

1 (5.6 ounce) box toasted pine nut couscous	155 g
1 (15 ounce) can mixed vegetables, well drained	425 g
1 sweet red bell pepper, diced	
⅔ cup crumbled feta cheese	90 g
Cherry tomatoes for garnish	

Dressing:

⅓ cup olive oil	75 ml
2 tablespoons lemon juice	30 ml
2 teaspoons sugar	10 ml
1 teaspoon lemon pepper	5 ml

- Cook couscous as directed on box and cool. In bowl, combine couscous, mixed vegetables, bell pepper and cheese, mixing well.
- In jar with lid, combine oil, lemon juice, sugar and lemon pepper; shake well to blend ingredients. Pour over salad and toss. Serve on bed of lettuce and garnish with cherry tomatoes.

Green and White Salad

1 (16 ounce) package frozen green peas, thawed	455 g
1 head cauliflower, cut into bite-size pieces	
1 (8 ounce) carton sour cream	230 g
1 (1 ounce) package dry ranch-style salad dressing	30 g

- In large bowl, combine peas and cauliflower.
- Combine sour cream and salad dressing. Toss with vegetables and refrigerate.

Warm Bean Salad

1 small onion, diced	
2 large ribs celery, diced	
1 sweet red bell pepper, diced	
2 (15 ounce) cans cannellini beans, washed, drained	2 (425 g)

Dressing:

¼ cup olive oil	60 ml
2 teaspoons prepared minced garlic	10 ml
⅓ cup lemon juice	75 ml
1 teaspoon sugar	5 ml

Continued on following page

Continued from previous page

- In skillet with a little oil, cook onion and celery for 5 minutes or until onion is slightly brown and celery is tender-crisp. Add bell pepper and beans and toss.
- Combine dressing ingredients and 1 teaspoon (5 ml) salt, mixing well. Pour over bean mixture and toss. Serve warm.

Colorful English Pea Salad

2 (16 ounce) packages frozen green peas, thawed, drained	2 (455 g)
1 (12 ounce) package cubed mozzarella cheese	340 g
1 red bell pepper, chopped	
1 orange bell pepper, chopped	
1 onion, chopped	
1¼ cups mayonnaise	280 g

- In large salad bowl, combine peas (uncooked), cubed cheese, bell peppers and onion; toss to mix. Stir in mayonnaise, 1 teaspoon (5 ml) each of salt and pepper. Refrigerate.

Colorful Veggie Salad

4 cups fresh broccoli florets	285 g
4 cups cauliflower florets	400 g
1 red onion, sliced	
1 (4 ounce) can sliced ripe olives	115 g
3 small zucchini, sliced	

Dressing:

1 packet zesty Italian dry dressing mix	
1½ cups bottled zesty Italian salad dressing	375 ml
2 tablespoons extra-virgin olive oil	30 ml

- In large bowl, combine broccoli, cauliflower, onion, olives and zucchini and toss together.
- In small bowl, combine dry dressing mix, bottled dressing and olive oil, mixing well. Pour over vegetables and toss to coat. Refrigerate.

Cashew-Pea Salad

1 (16 ounce) package frozen green peas, thawed	455 g
¼ cup diced celery	25 g
1 bunch fresh green onions with tops, chopped	
1 cup cashew pieces	135 g
½ cup mayonnaise	110 g

- Combine peas, celery, onions and cashews.
- Toss with mayonnaise and seasoned with ½ teaspoon (2 ml) each of salt and pepper.

Cherry Tomato Salad

Dressing:

2 tablespoons red-wine vinegar	30 ml
2 tablespoons olive oil	30 ml

Salad:

2 pints cherry tomatoes, halved	595 g
1 bunch green onions, chopped	
1 small cucumber, peeled, chopped	

- Combine all dressing ingredients and 1 teaspoon (5 ml) salt and ½ teaspoon (2 ml) pepper, mixing well.
- In salad bowl, combine tomato halves, green onion and cucumber and toss with dressing. Refrigerate.

Black Bean and Mandarin Salad

1 (15 ounce) can black beans, rinsed, drained	425 g
1 (11 ounce) can mandarin oranges, well drained	310 g
1 cup diced jicama	130 g
¼ cup finely diced red onion	40 g
¼ cup finely diced jalapeno	40 g
½ (8 ounce) bottle zesty Italian dressing	½ (235 ml)

- In large bowl, combine all ingredients and refrigerate until ready to serve, tossing occasionally.

Carrot and Apple Salad

1 (16 ounce) package shredded carrots	455 g
1 green apple, unpeeled, chopped	
1 red apple, unpeeled, chopped	
½ cup golden raisins	75 g
1 tablespoon mayonnaise	15 ml
1 tablespoon lemon juice	15 ml

- In bowl, combine shredded carrots, apples and raisins. Add mayonnaise and lemon juice and toss. Refrigerate.

Festive Green and Yellow Veggie Salad

3 - 4 cups small broccoli florets	215 - 285 g
3 small yellow squash, seeded, cubed	
3 - 4 cups small cauliflower florets	300 - 400 g
1 cup chopped celery	100 g
1 cup chopped red bell pepper	150 g

Dressing:

½ cup mayonnaise	110 g
2 tablespoons white vinegar	30 ml
3 tablespoons sugar	35 g

- In large salad bowl (with lid) combine broccoli, squash, cauliflower florets, celery and bell pepper and mix.
- Combine all dressing ingredients with 1 teaspoon (5 ml) salt and mix well. Spoon over veggie ingredients and toss. Refrigerate for 30 minutes before serving.

Four Bean Salad and Extra

2 (15 ounce) cans garbanzo beans, rinsed, drained	2 (425 g)
1 (15 ounce) can cut green beans, drained	425 g
1 (15 ounce) can great northern beans, drained	425 g
1 (15 ounce) can black beans, drained	425 g
2 ribs celery, sliced	
1 red onion, thinly sliced	

Dressing:

⅓ cup red wine vinegar	75 ml
¼ cup extra-virgin olive oil	60 ml
2 teaspoons dijon-style mustard	10 ml
1 tablespoon sugar	15 ml

- In large bowl, combine all beans, celery and onion slices, mixing well.
- In pint jar with lid combine vinegar, olive oil, mustard, sugar and about 1 teaspoon (5 ml) of salt. Shake jar vigorously until all ingredients are mixed well. Pour over bean mixture, stirring well. Refrigerate.

Broccoli Salad

5 cups stemmed broccoli florets	355 g
1 red bell pepper, julienned	
1 cup chopped celery	100 g
8 - 12 ounces Monterey Jack cheese, cubed	230 - 340 g

- Combine all ingredients and mix well.
- Toss with dressing. Refrigerate.

Creamy Vegetable Salad

1 (10 ounce) package frozen green peas, thawed	280 g
1 cup chopped celery	100 g
1 cup diced carrots	130 g
1 (15 ounce) can Italian green beans, drained	425 g
1 cucumber, peeled and sliced	

Dressing:

1 (8 ounce) bottle French dressing	235 ml
½ cup mayonnaise	110 g
1 teaspoon minced garlic	5 ml

Continued on following page

Continued from previous page

- In bowl (with lid) combine peas, celery, carrots, green beans and cucumber. Combine French dressing, mayonnaise and garlic, mixing well and pour over vegetables; toss. Refrigerate for 30 minutes before serving.

Cheesy Vegetable Salad

2 seedless cucumbers coarsely chopped	
1 sweet red bell pepper, julienned	
1 sweet (Vidalia) onion, coarsely chopped	
1 cup crumbled feta cheese	135 g
⅔ cup vinaigrette salad dressing	150 ml

- In salad bowl, combine cucumbers, bell pepper, onion and feta cheese and toss with salad dressing.

Asparagus with Citrus Dressing

2 bunches fresh asparagus, ends trimmed

Citrus Dressing:

3 tablespoons extra-virgin olive oil	45 ml
⅔ cup fresh orange juice	150 ml
1 teaspoon orange zest	5 ml

- Place about 2 cups (500 ml) water and ½ teaspoon (2 ml) salt in large skillet (large enough to lay asparagus flat in skillet) and bring to a boil. Add asparagus and cook until tender, about 7 or 8 minutes.
- Drain asparagus on cloth towel and scatter some ice cubes over asparagus to cool.
- For dressing, combine oil, orange juice, orange zest and ½ teaspoon (2 ml) black pepper in small bowl, mix well.
- Refrigerate, but bring to room temperature before using. When serving, spoon dressing over asparagus and serve immediately.

Avocado-Corn Salad

2 ripe avocados, peeled, diced	
2 tablespoons fresh lime juice	30 ml
3 cups grape tomatoes, halved	445 g
2 (11 ounce) cans mexicorn, drained	2 (310 g)
1 (8 ounce) bottle zesty Italian salad dressing	235 ml

- Place avocados in salad bowl and spoon lime juice and a little salt over avocados. Add tomatoes and corn.
- Spoon about ½ cup (125 ml) of dressing over salad.

Green Beans with Tomatoes

2 pounds frozen, cut green beans	910 g
4 tomatoes, chopped, drained	
1 bunch green onions, chopped	
1 cup Italian salad dressing	250 ml

- Place beans in saucepan, cover with water and bring to boil.
- Cook uncovered for 8 to 10 minutes or until tender crisp, drain and refrigerate.
- Add tomatoes, green onions and salad dressing and toss to coat.

Cabbage-Carrot Slaw

1 (10 ounce) package slaw mix	280 g
1 (16 ounce) package shredded carrots	455 g
2 delicious apples, diced	
1 cup Craisins® (dried cranberries)	120 g
⅔ cup chopped walnuts	85 g
1 (8 ounce) bottle poppy seed salad dressing	235 ml

- In salad bowl, combine slaw mix, carrots, apples, cranberries and walnuts. Toss with poppy seed dressing and refrigerate

Jicama-Zucchini Slaw

Dressing:

½ cup olive oil	125 ml
⅓ cup red wine vinegar	75 ml
1 teaspoon dijon-style mustard	5 ml
2 tablespoon mayonnaise	30 g

Slaw:

1½ pounds jicama	680 g
3 small zucchini	
½ sweet red bell pepper, diced	

- Combine all dressing ingredients in bowl. Toss with jicama, zucchini and bell pepper. Refrigerate.

Red Cabbage Slaw

1 large head red cabbage	
2 onions, chopped	
½ cup coleslaw dressing	125 ml
½ cup French salad dressing	125 ml

- Slice cabbage and combine with onions.
- Combine dressings and toss with cabbage and onions and refrigerate.

Nutty Slaw

1 (16 ounce) package shredded carrots	455 g
3 cups shredded cabbage	210 g
2 red delicious apples, diced	
¾ cup raisins	120 g
¾ cup chopped walnuts	100 g
1 (8 ounce) bottle coleslaw dressing	235 ml

- In plastic bowl with lid, combine shredded carrots, shredded cabbage, apples, raisins and walnuts.
- Pour about three-fourths bottle of slaw dressing over mixture and increase dressing as needed. Cover and refrigerate.

Broccoli Slaw

1 (16 ounce) package broccoli slaw	455 g
1 cup very small fresh broccoli florets	70 g
¾ cup Craisins® (dried cranberries)	90 g
1 Granny Smith apple, unpeeled, diced	
1 (11 ounce) can mandarin oranges, well drained	310 g
1 (8 ounce) bottle poppy seed dressing	235 ml
½ cup toasted, slivered almonds	85 g

- In salad bowl, combine broccoli slaw, broccoli florets, cranberries, apple and oranges. Toss with poppy seed dressing. Sprinkle almonds on top of salad. Refrigerate 20 minutes before serving.

Coleslaw with Buttermilk Dressing

Slaw:

2 (10 ounce) packages finely shredded cabbage	2 (280 g)
1 carrot, shredded	

Dressing:

½ cup mayonnaise	110 g
½ cup sugar	100 g
½ cup buttermilk	125 ml
3 tablespoons lemon juice	45 ml

- Place cabbage and carrot in salad bowl.
- In small bowl, combine mayonnaise, sugar, buttermilk, lemon juice and 1 teaspoon (5 ml) salt. Pour over cabbage and carrot and toss. Cover and refrigerate at least 25 minutes.

Color-Coded Salad

1 (16 ounce) package tri-colored macaroni, cooked, drained	455 g
1 red bell pepper, julienned	
1 cup chopped zucchini	125 g
1 cup broccoli florets	70 g
1 (8 ounce) bottle Caesar salad dressing	235 ml

- Combine all ingredients. Toss with salad dressing. Refrigerate.

Sesame-Broccoli Salad

¼ cup sesame seeds	30 g
1 (16 ounce) package broccoli slaw	455 g
1 sweet red bell pepper, seeded, chopped	
2 (9 ounce) packages fresh tortellini, cooked	2 (255 g)

Dressing:

1 (8 ounce) bottle vinaigrette salad dressing	235 ml
2 tablespoons olive oil	30 ml

- In skillet, toast sesame seeds over low to medium heat in just a little oil and set aside.
- In salad bowl, combine broccoli slaw, bell pepper and cooked tortellini. Drizzle salad dressing and olive oil over salad and toss. Refrigerate and just before serving, sprinkle sesame seeds over salad.

Tri-Color Pasta Salad

1 (8 ounce) package tricolor spiral pasta	230 g
1 tablespoon olive oil	15 ml
1 (8 ounce) package cubed cheddar cheese	230 g
1 large bunch broccoli, cut into small florets	
1 cup celery, cubed	100 g
1 cup cucumber, peeled, cubed	120 g
Ranch salad dressing	

- Cook pasta according to package directions, drain well and add olive oil to keep pasta from sticking together. Transfer to large salad bowl and add cheese cubes, broccoli, celery, cucumber and ample amount of salt and pepper. Toss with ranch dressing.

Pronto Pasta Lunch

1 pound refrigerated fettuccine	455 g
1 cup diced zucchini	125 g
1 cup diced yellow squash	115 g
1 (10 ounce) package frozen peas and carrots, thawed	280 g
¼ cup pine nuts, toasted	30 g

Dressing:

½ cup ricotta cheese	245 g
1 cup chicken broth	250 ml
2 tablespoons butter	30 ml

- Cook fettuccine according to package directions, drain.
- While fettuccine is cooking, place all dressing ingredients with ½ teaspoon (2 ml) each of salt and pepper in saucepan and heat, mixing well. Add vegetables and cook about 3 minutes or until vegetables are tender-crisp.
- Stir into cooked fettuccine and add pine nuts; toss to serve.

TIP: *If you like, parmesan cheese can be sprinkled over tossed vegetables and pasta.*

Special Macaroni Salad

1 (16 ounce) carton deli macaroni salad	455 g
1 (8 ounce) can whole kernel corn, drained	230 g
2 small zucchini, diced	
⅔ cup chunky salsa	175 g

- In salad bowl with lid, combine macaroni salad, corn, zucchini and salsa, mixing well. Cover and refrigerate until ready to serve.

Quick Salad Supper

1 (12 ounce) package frozen precooked salad tortellini, thawed	340 g
1 (16 ounce) package frozen cooked salad shrimp	455 g
1 (4 ounce) can sliced ripe olives, drained	115 g
⅓ cup finely chopped red onion	55 g

Dressing:

1 (8 ounce) bottle zesty Italian salad dressing	235 ml
½ teaspoon paprika	2 ml

- In salad bowl, combine tortellini, shrimp, olives and onion and toss with about ½ cup (125 ml) of salad dressing. Before serving, sprinkle with ½ teaspoon (2 ml) pepper and paprika.

Pasta Salad Bowl

1 (16 ounce) package bow-tie pasta	455 g
1 (16 ounce) package frozen green peas	455 g
½ cup sliced scallions	80 g
1 seedless cucumber, thinly sliced	
2 cups deli (or leftover) ham, cut in strips	280 g

Dressing:

⅔ cup mayonnaise	150 g
¼ cup cider vinegar	60 ml
2 tablespoons sugar	25 g
2 teaspoons dried dill	10 ml

- Cook pasta according to package directions; drain and cool under cold running water and drain again. Transfer to serving bowl and add peas, scallions, cucumber slices and ham strips.
- In small bowl, combine all dressing ingredients and spoon over salad; toss to mix and coat well. Refrigerate.

Pasta Plus Salad

1 (16 ounce) package bow-tie pasta	455 g
1 (10 ounce) package frozen green peas, thawed	280 g
1 red bell pepper, seeded, cut in strips	
1 (8 ounce) package cubed Swiss cheese	230 g
1 small yellow summer squash, sliced	

Dressing:

¾ cup mayonnaise	170 g
2 tablespoons lemon juice	30 ml
1 tablespoon sugar	15 ml
½ cup heavy cream	125 ml

- Cook pasta according to package directions and add peas last 2 minutes of cooking time. Drain pasta and peas; rinse in cold water and drain again. Transfer to large salad bowl. Add bell pepper, cheese and squash.

- Combine dressing ingredients and mix well. Spoon over salad with a little salt and pepper to taste. Toss salad and refrigerate.

Nutty Rice Salad

1 (6 ounce) package long-grain and wild rice mix	170 g
1 (6 ounce) jar marinated artichoke hearts, drained, chopped	170 g
1 cup golden raisins	150 g
4 fresh green onions, chopped with tops	
¾ cup toasted pecan halves	85 g

Dressing:

⅓ cup orange juice	75 ml
¼ cup olive oil	60 ml
1 tablespoon lemon juice	15 ml
1 tablespoon sugar	15 ml

- Prepare rice mix according to package directions, drain and cool. Place in salad bowl and add artichoke hearts, raisins and green onions.

- For dressing, combine orange juice, oil, lemon juice, and sugar. Stir dressing until well blended and spoon over salad; toss. Cover and refrigerate at least 30 minutes; top with pecans before serving.

TIP: Pecans can be toasted in 300° (150° C) oven for 10 minutes.

Skillet Rice Salad

Dressing:

8 slices bacon	
1 tablespoon flour	15 ml
1 tablespoon sugar	15 ml
¼ cup white vinegar	60 ml

Salad:

1 (6 ounce) box long-grain, wild rice	170 g
1 cup chopped celery	100 g
1 cup chopped cucumbers	120 g
1 small onion, sliced, separated into rings	
3 cups romaine, broken into bite-size pieces	140 g

- In large skillet, fry bacon until crisp. Break into small chunks; set aside. With bacon drippings still in skillet, stir in flour, sugar, vinegar, and a little salt and stir in ¾ cup (175 ml) water. Cook over low-medium heat, stirring constantly until dressing is smooth.

- In saucepan, cook rice as directed on box. While rice is still hot, add rice, celery, cucumbers, onion rings and romaine to skillet and toss with dressing until all ingredients are well coated. Serve right from skillet with bacon pieces sprinkled over top.

Cool Couscous and Spinach Salad

1 (10 ounce) package chicken-flavored couscous	280 g
1 (8 ounce) package fresh baby spinach, torn	230 g
1 bunch green onions, sliced	
1 (5 ounce) package grated parmesan cheese	140 g

Dressing:

⅓ cup olive oil	80 ml
¼ cup lemon juice	60 ml
2 tablespoons snipped fresh dill	30 ml
2 tablespoons sugar	30 ml

- Cook couscous according to package directions and let stand 5 minutes, then fluff with fork. Cool. Stir in torn spinach and green onions. In small bowl, combine all dressing ingredients, mixing well.

- When ready to serve, place couscous, spinach and green onions in salad bowl and toss with dressing. Sprinkle with parmesan cheese and toss lightly.

Couscous Salad

1 (5.6 ounce) box parmesan couscous	155 g
¾ cup chopped fresh mushrooms	55 g
1 (4 ounce) can sliced ripe olives, drained	115 g
½ cup green bell pepper	75 g
½ cup red bell pepper	75 g
½ cup Italian salad dressing	125 ml

- Cook couscous according to package directions. Cover and let stand 5 minutes, then fluff with fork. In salad bowl, combine couscous, mushrooms, olives and bell peppers. Stir in salad dressing, cover and refrigerate before serving.

Gourmet Couscous Salad

1 (10 ounce) box chicken-flavored couscous	280 g
2 tomatoes, coarsely chopped	
2 zucchini, coarsely chopped	
4 green onions, sliced	
1 cup feta cheese, crumbled	135 g

Dressing:

1 tablespoon lemon juice	15 ml
¼ cup olive oil	60 ml
½ teaspoon dried basil	2 ml
½ teaspoon seasoned pepper	2 ml

- Cook couscous according to package directions, leaving out butter. In salad bowl combine tomatoes, zucchini, green onions and couscous. Combine dressing ingredients in pint jar with lid and shake until well blended. When ready to serve, add feta cheese to salad, pour dressing over salad and toss.

Cracker Salad

1 sleeve saltine crackers
1 tomato, chopped, drained
1 egg, hard-boiled, finely chopped
½ green bell pepper, chopped
4 green onions, chopped
1½ cups mayonnaise   335 g

- This salad must be made just before serving!
- In salad bowl, coarsely crush crackers with your hands (in large pieces). Add remaining ingredients, adding a little salt and pepper, if you like. Serve immediately; it will not keep.

Dilled Potato Salad

2 pounds small new (red) potatoes   910 g
1 sweet red bell pepper, chopped
1 bunch green onions, sliced
¾ cup crumbled feta cheese   100 g

Dressing:
½ cup olive oil   125 ml
⅓ cup red wine vinegar   75 ml
1 tablespoon dried dill   15 ml
1 teaspoon sugar   5 ml

- In saucepan, bring potatoes and about 2 cups (500 ml) water to a boil and cook about 25 minutes or until potatoes are tender; drain and bring to room temperature. Cut potatoes in quarters. Place in bowl and add bell pepper and green onions.
- For dressing, combine oil, vinegar, dill, sugar, 1 teaspoon (5 ml) pepper and liberal amount of salt. Pour over warm potatoes, bell pepper and onions and toss. Sprinkle cheese over top and gently stir to toss.

A Crunchy Potato Salad

10 - 12 small new (red) potatoes, cut in wedges
1 (10 ounce) package red-tip lettuce   280 g
6 ounces feta cheese, crumbled   170 g
½ cup pecan halves   55 g
3 eggs, hard-boiled, cut in wedges

Dressing:
⅓ cup very finely chopped shallots   55 g
⅓ cup honey   115 g
¼ cup lemon juice   60 ml
½ cup olive oil   125 ml

- In saucepan, cook potatoes in salted water about 15 minutes or until tender; drain and set aside to cool. In salad bowl, combine lettuce, feta cheese and pecans.
- For dressing, combine shallots, honey, lemon juice, olive oil and an ample amount of salt and pepper in pint jar with lid. Shake vigorously until well blended.
- When ready to serve, add potatoes to salad bowl mixture and toss. Shake dressing again and pour over salad and toss. Garnish with egg wedges.

Super Orzo-Veggie Salad

1 (8 ounce) package orzo pasta   230 g
1 (10 ounce) package frozen broccoli florets   280 g
1 (10 ounce) package frozen green peas   280 g
1 (12 ounce) jar baby corn nuggets, drained   340 g
3 cups cooked (deli or leftover) cubed ham   420 g

Dressing:
1 (8 ounce) jar sweet-and-sour sauce   230 g
2 tablespoon olive oil   30 ml

- In large saucepan, cook orzo according to package directions. Five minutes before orzo is done, stir in broccoli and peas; bring back to boiling and cook for 5 minutes. Drain well.
- Transfer pasta and vegetables to salad bowl and add corn and ham. Sprinkle salad with 1 teaspoon (5 ml) salt and add sweet-and-sour sauce and olive oil. Toss and serve immediately.

Sour Cream Potato Salad

12 medium red potatoes, unpeeled	
1¼ cups mayonnaise	280 g
1 cup sour cream	240 g
1 cup green onions with tops, chopped	95 g

- Boil red potatoes until tender about 20 minutes. Slice potatoes.
- Combine mayonnaise, sour cream and 1 teaspoon (5 ml) salt.
- When potatoes are cool toss with sour cream mixture. Add green onions.

Quick Potato Salad

3 - 4 baking potatoes	
½ cup diced dill or sweet pickles	80 g
3 eggs, hard-boiled, chopped	
¾ - 1 cup mayonnaise	170 -225 g

- Cook potatoes (potatoes can be cooked the night before using) in microwave and when cooled, peel and cut into 1-inch (2.5 cm) cubes. Place in large bowl.
- Add pickles (or pickle relish), chopped eggs and ample amount of salt and pepper. Stir in mayonnaise.

Potato Salad-German Style

2 pounds new (red) potatoes, cut in thin slices	910 g
½ pound bacon, cooked and crumbled (save drippings)	230 g
1 small onion, chopped	
¼ cup chopped fresh parsley	15 g
1 red bell pepper, chopped	
1 green bell pepper, chopped	

Dressing:

½ cup cider vinegar	125 ml
¼ cup sugar	50 g
Bacon drippings from cooked bacon	

- Steam potatoes, covered, for 10 to 12 minutes or until tender and transfer to bowl with lid. Add onion, parsley and bell peppers.
- For dressing, combine vinegar, sugar and 1 teaspoon (5 ml) each of salt and pepper, mix well and stir in bacon drippings. Spoon over potato-onion mixture and toss. Serve at room temperature.

Deviled Eggs

6 eggs, hard-boiled
2 tablespoons sweet pickle relish   30 g
3 tablespoons mayonnaise   40 g
½ teaspoon mustard   2 ml

- Peel eggs and cut in half lengthwise. Take yolks and mash with fork. Add relish, mayonnaise and mustard to yolks. Place this yolk mixture back into egg white halves.

Chunky Egg Salad

12 eggs, hard-boiled, quartered
⅓ cup sun-dried tomato GourMayo®   75 g
2 ribs celery, sliced
½ cup sliced, stuffed green olives   65 g

- Place all ingredients in salad bowl and add salt and pepper to taste.
- Gently toss and serve over bed of lettuce leaves with crackers.

A Different Deviled Egg

10 large eggs, hard-boiled, peeled
⅔ cup creamy dijon GourMayo®   150 g
2 tablespoons fresh snipped parsley   10 g
2 teaspoons dried dillweed   10 ml
2 teaspoons dried chives   10 ml

- Cut off tops (about ⅓-inch/8 mm) of each egg and scoop out yolks and place in mixing bowl. Cut thin slice from bottom of egg so egg will sit up.
- Mash yolks with fork and add GourMayo®, parsley, dillweed, chives and salt and pepper to taste. Carefully stuff each egg with yolk mixture and place on serving plate sitting up.

Basic Deviled Eggs

8 large eggs	
3 - 4 tablespoons mayonnaise	45 - 55 g
1 tablespoon prepared mustard	15 ml
3 tablespoons sweet pickle relish, drained	45 g

- In large saucepan place eggs adding water to cover. Bring to boil and cook 2 minutes. Cover and let stand about 15 minutes. Cool.
- Peel eggs under cold water and slice eggs in half lengthwise, carefully removing yolks. Mash yolks with mayonnaise, mustard, pickle relish and a little salt and pepper.
- Spoon yolk mixture into egg whites and refrigerate before serving.

Savory Chicken Salad

4 boneless skinless chicken breast halves, cooked	
1 cup chopped celery	100 g
1 red bell pepper, seeded, chopped	
⅔ cup slivered almonds, toasted	110 g
½ cup mayonnaise	110 g
1 tablespoon lime juice	15 ml

- Slice chicken breasts into long thin strips.
- Combine chicken, celery, bell pepper and almonds.
- Combine mayonnaise and lemon juice, stir into salad and toss.

Strawberry-Chicken Salad

1 pound boneless, skinless chicken breast halves	455 g
1 (10 ounce) package spring greens mix	280 g
1 pint fresh strawberries, sliced	355 g
½ cup chopped walnuts	65 g

Dressing:

¾ cup honey	255 g
⅔ cup red wine vinegar	150 ml
1 tablespoon soy sauce	15 ml
½ teaspoon ground ginger	2 ml

- Cut chicken into strips and place in large skillet with a little oil. Cook on medium-high heat for about 10 minutes and stir occasionally.
- While chicken cooks, combine all dressing ingredients and mix well. After chicken strips cook for 10 minutes, pour ½ cup (125 ml) dressing into skillet with chicken and cook 2 minutes longer or until liquid evaporates. In salad bowl, combine spring greens mix, strawberries and walnuts, pour on remaining dressing and toss. Top with chicken strips.

Broccoli-Chicken Salad

3 - 4 boneless skinless chicken breast halves, cooked, cubed	
2 cups fresh broccoli florets	140 g
1 red bell pepper, seeded, chopped	
1 cup chopped celery	100 g
1 (16 ounce) jar refrigerated honey-mustard salad dressing	475 ml

- Combine chicken, broccoli, bell pepper and celery. Toss with about half the dressing, using more if needed and refrigerate.

Tarragon-Chicken Salad

1 cup chopped, toasted pecans	110 g
3 - 4 boneless skinless chicken breast halves cooked, cubed	
1 cup chopped celery	100 g
¾ cup peeled, chopped cucumbers	80 g

- Place pecans in shallow pan and toast at 300° (150° C) for 10 minutes. Combine chicken, celery and cucumbers.

Dressing:

⅔ cup mayonnaise	150 g
1 tablespoon lemon juice	15 ml
2 tablespoons tarragon vinegar	30 ml
1¼ teaspoons crumbled, dried tarragon	6 ml

- Mix all dressing ingredients. When ready to serve, toss with chicken mixture and add pecans.

Chicken Caesar Salad

4 boneless, skinless chicken breast halves, grilled	
1 (10 ounce) package romaine salad greens	280 g
½ cup shredded parmesan cheese	50 g
1 cup seasoned croutons	40 g
1 (8 ounce) bottle Caesar salad dressing	235 ml

- Cut chicken breasts into strips.
- Combine chicken, salad greens, cheese and croutons in large bowl. When ready to serve, toss with salad dressing.

Bridge Club Luncheon

1 rotisserie-cooked chicken	
1 cup red grapes, halved	150 g
1 cup green grapes, halved	150 g
2 cups chopped celery	200 g
⅔ cup walnut halves	80 g
1 orange bell pepper, seeded, chopped	

Dressing:

½ cup mayonnaise	110 g
1 tablespoon orange juice	15 ml
2 tablespoons red wine vinegar	30 ml
1 tablespoon honey	15 ml
1 teaspoon paprika	5 ml

- Skin chicken and cut chicken breast in thin strips (reserve dark meat for another use) and place in bowl with lid. Add red and green grapes, celery, walnuts and bell pepper.
- Combine all dressing ingredients, adding salt and pepper to taste; mix well. Spoon over salad mixture and toss. Refrigerate.

Chicken-Artichoke Salad

4 cups cooked, chopped chicken breasts	560 g
1 (14 ounce) can artichoke hearts, drained, chopped	395 g
½ cup chopped walnuts	65 g
1 cup chopped red bell pepper	150 g
⅔ cup mayonnaise	150 g

- In bowl, combine all ingredients, adding salt and pepper to taste. Cover and refrigerate until ready to serve.

Derby Chicken Salad

3 - 4 boneless skinless chicken breast halves, cooked, cubed	
¼ pound bacon, cooked, crumbled	115 g
2 avocados, peeled, diced	
2 tomatoes, diced, drained	
1 (8 ounce) bottle Italian salad dressing	235 ml

- Combine all ingredients. When ready to serve, pour dressing over salad and toss. Refrigerate.

Chicken Waldorf Salad

1 pound boneless, skinless chicken breasts	455 g
1 red and 1 green apple, unpeeled and sliced	
1 cup sliced celery	100 g
½ cup chopped walnuts	65 g
1 (6 ounce) carton orange yogurt	170 g
½ cup mayonnaise	110 g
1 (6 ounce) package shredded lettuce	170 g

- Place chicken in large saucepan and cover with water. On high heat, cook about 15 minutes; drain and cool. Cut into 1-inch (2.5 cm) chunks and season with salt and pepper; place in large salad bowl.
- Add sliced apples, celery and walnuts. Stir in yogurt and mayonnaise; toss to mix well (may be served room temperature or refrigerated for several hours). Serve over shredded lettuce.

Hawaiian Chicken Salad

3 cups cooked, diced chicken breasts	420 g
1 (20 ounce) can pineapple tidbits, well drained	570 g
1 cup halved red grapes	150 g
3 ribs celery, sliced	
1 large ripe banana, sliced	

Dressing:

½ cup mayonnaise	110 g
¾ cup poppy seed dressing	175 ml
½ cup salted peanuts	75 g

- In bowl, combine diced chicken, pineapple, grapes and celery and toss. Cover and refrigerate.
- Combine mayonnaise, poppy seed dressing and a sprinkle of salt. When ready to serve, add bananas and top with mayonnaise-poppy seed dressing, toss and sprinkle peanuts over top.

Chicken-Grapefruit Salad Supper

1 (10 ounce) package romaine salad mix	280 g
1 (24 ounce) jar grapefruit sections, well drained	680 g
1 rotisserie chicken, boned, cubed	
½ red onion, sliced	

Dressing:

2 tablespoons orange juice	30 ml
2 tablespoons white wine vinegar	30 ml
2 tablespoons extra-virgin olive oil	30 ml

- Combine salad mix, well-drained grapefruit sections, chicken and onion in salad bowl.
- In small bowl combine all dressing ingredients with 1 teaspoon (5 ml) each of salt and pepper; pour over salad and toss.

Great Chicken 'n Greens Salad

2 cups skinned, diced rotisserie chicken	280 g
1 (10 ounce) package mixed salad greens	280 g
½ cup chopped sun-dried tomatoes	25 g
1 red bell pepper, seeded, chopped	
3 tablespoons toasted sunflower seeds	25 g

Dressing:

½ (8 ounce) bottle vinaigrette salad dressing	½ (235 ml)
2 tablespoons refrigerated honey-mustard salad dressing	30 ml

- In salad bowl, combine diced chicken, greens, tomatoes and bell pepper and toss.
- Combine vinaigrette dressing and honey-mustard dressing and pour over salad (using more vinaigrette dressing if needed) and toss. Sprinkle sunflower seeds over salad and serve.

Brown Rice Chicken Salad

1 (8.8 ounce) package whole-grain brown ready rice	255 g
1 (12 ounce) can premium chunk chicken breasts, drained	340 g
⅔ cup sun-dried tomatoes, chopped	35 g
2 ripe avocados, peeled, diced	
¾ cup dijon-style mustard vinaigrette dressing	175 ml

Continued on following page

Continued from previous page

- Prepare rice according to package directions (microwave in package). Combine rice, chicken, tomatoes, avocados and salt and pepper to taste. Spoon dressing over salad and gently toss to mix well. Served chilled.

Fruited Chicken Salad

1 (10 ounce) package spring salad mix	280 g
1 (6 ounce) package frozen, ready-to serve chicken strips, thawed	170 g
½ cup fresh strawberries, sliced	85 g
½ cup fresh raspberries	60 g
1 (8 ounce) bottle raspberry salad dressing	235 ml
Shredded lettuce	

- In salad bowl, combine salad mix, chicken strips and berries.
- Toss with just enough salad dressing to coat salad, adding more if needed. Serve on a bed of shredded lettuce with crackers.

Herbed Chicken Salad

1 rotisserie-cooked chicken	
¼ cup chopped fresh chives	10 g
½ cup chopped pecans	55 g
1 cup chopped celery	100 g
1 cup chopped sweet pickles	160 g

Dressing:

2 tablespoons honey	45 g
¼ cup extra-virgin olive oil	60 ml
3 tablespoons white wine vinegar	45 ml
1 teaspoon chopped fresh thyme	5 ml

- Skin chicken and cut meat from bones. Slice chicken pieces in thin strips and place in bowl. Add fresh chives, pecans, celery and sweet pickles, mixing well.
- In separate bowl, whisk together honey, olive oil, vinegar, thyme and salt and pepper to taste. Spoon over chicken salad and toss. Refrigerate.

Tri-Color Pasta-Turkey Salad Supper

1 (12 ounce) package tri-color spiral pasta	340 g
1 (4 ounce) can sliced ripe olives, drained	115 g
1 cup fresh broccoli florets	70 g
1 cup cauliflower florets	100 g
2 small yellow squash, sliced	
1 cup halved cherry tomatoes	150 g
1 (8 ounce) bottle cheddar and parmesan ranch dressing	235 ml
Slices from a 1½ pound hickory smoked cracked pepper	
turkey breast	680 g

- Cook pasta according to package directions; drain and rinse in cold water. Place in large salad bowl and add olives, broccoli, cauliflower, squash and tomatoes. Toss with dressing.
- Place thin slices of the turkey breast, arranged in a row, over salad. Serve immediately.

Noodle-Turkey Salad

1 (3 ounce) package oriental-flavor ramen noodle soup mix	85 g
1 (16 ounce) package finely shredded coleslaw mix	455 g
¾ pound deli smoked turkey, cut into strips	340 g
½ cup vinaigrette salad dressing	125 ml

- Coarsely crush noodles and place in bowl with lid. Add coleslaw mix and turkey strips. In small bowl, combine vinaigrette salad dressing and seasoning packet from noodle mix and pour over noodle-turkey mixture and toss to coat mixture well. Refrigerate.

Asian Turkey Salad

¾ pound deli turkey breasts, julienned	340 g
1 (9 ounce) package coleslaw mix	255 g
¼ cup chopped fresh cilantro	5 g
1 sweet red bell pepper, seeded, julienned	
1 bunch green onions, sliced in 1-inch slices	2.5 cm

Continued on following page

Continued from previous page

Dressing:

¼ cup olive oil	60 ml
2 tablespoons lime juice	30 ml
1 tablespoon sugar	15 ml
1 tablespoon peanut butter	15 ml
1 tablespoon soy sauce	15 ml

- In salad bowl, combine salad ingredients.
- In jar with lid, combine dressing ingredients. Seal jar and shake dressing until well blended. Spoon over salad and toss. Serve immediately.

Fiesta Holiday Salad

1 (10 ounce) package torn romaine lettuce	280 g
3 cups diced smoked turkey	420 g
1 (15 ounce) can black beans, rinsed, drained	425 g
2 tomatoes, quartered, drained	

Dressing:

⅔ cup mayonnaise	150 g
¾ cup salsa	175 g

- Combine salad ingredients in large salad bowl. Combine mayonnaise and salsa.
- When ready to serve, spoon dressing over salad and toss.

Friday After Thanksgiving Salad

2 (10 ounce) packages prepared romaine lettuce	2 (280 g)
3 cups cooked, sliced turkey	420 g
1 (8 ounce) jar baby corn, cut in fourths	230 g
2 tomatoes, chopped	
1 (8 ounce) package shredded Colby cheese	230 g

Dressing:

⅔ cup mayonnaise	150 g
⅔ cup salsa	175 g
¼ cup cider vinegar	60 ml
2 tablespoons sugar	25 g

- Combine salad ingredients in large bowl. Combine all dressing ingredients in separate bowl. When ready to serve, sprinkle on a little salt and pepper and then spoon dressing over salad and toss to coat well.

After Thanksgiving Day Salad

1 (10 ounce) package torn romaine lettuce	280 g
1 (15 ounce) can black beans, rinsed, drained	425 g
1 (8 ounce) package cubed cheddar cheese	230 g
2 - 3 cups cooked, leftover, diced turkey	280 - 420 g
⅓ cup precooked, crumbled bacon	35 g

Dressing:

½ cup mayonnaise	110 g
¾ cup salsa	175 g

- In salad bowl, combine lettuce, black beans, cheese and turkey (deli turkey can be used), mixing well.
- Combine mayonnaise, salsa and ¾ teaspoon (4 ml) pepper; spoon over salad and toss. Sprinkle crumbled bacon over top.

Beefy Green Salad

⅓ pound cooked deli roast beef	150 g
1 (15 ounce) can 3-bean salad, chilled, drained	425 g
½ pound mozzarella cheese, cubed	230 g
1 (8 ounce) bag mixed salad greens	230 g
1 (8 ounce) bottle Italian dressing	235 ml

- Cut beef in thin strips. In large salad bowl, lightly toss beef, 3-bean salad, cheese and greens. Pour in just enough salad dressing to moisten greens.

Supper Ready Beef and Bean Salad

¾ pound deli roast beef, cut in strips	340 g
2 (15 ounce) can kidney beans, rinsed, drained	2 (425 g)
1 cup chopped onion	160 g
1 cup chopped celery	100 g
3 eggs, hard-boiled, chopped	

Dressing:

⅓ cup mayonnaise	75 g
⅓ cup chipotle chili GourMayo®	75 g
¼ cup ketchup	70 g
¼ cup sweet pickle relish	60 g
2 tablespoons olive oil	30 ml

- Combine salad ingredients in salad bowl. In small bowl, combine dressing ingredients, mixing well. Spoon over beef-bean mixture and toss. Refrigerate.

Warm Cannellini Salad

4 slices prosciutto	
1 (19 ounce) can cannellini beans, rinsed, drained	538 g
3 green onions, chopped	
1 tablespoon dried parsley	15 ml
½ red bell pepper, finely chopped	
1 (10 ounce) package fresh arugula	280 g

Dressing:

¼ cup olive oil	60 ml
2 teaspoons minced garlic	10 ml
2 tablespoons lemon juice	15 ml
2 teaspoons snipped fresh sage	10 ml

- Preheat oven to 350° (175° C). Arrange prosciutto in single layer on large baking sheet and bake for 25 minutes. Set aside.
- Prepare dressing by heating oil in small saucepan and cook garlic until it begins to brown. Remove from heat and stir in lemon juice, sage, and salt and pepper to taste.
- Combine beans, green onions, parsley and bell pepper in bowl. Arrange arugula, bean mixture and prosciutto on individual plates. Drizzle with warm dressing and serve immediately.

Cauliflower-Bacon Salad

1 large head cauliflower, cut into florets	
1 red bell pepper, chopped	
1 green bell pepper, chopped	
1½ cups cubed mozzarella cheese	200 g
1 (6 ounce) package cooked, crumbled bacon	170 g
1 bunch fresh green onions, sliced	

Dressing:

1 cup mayonnaise	225 g
1 tablespoon sugar	15 ml
1 tablespoon lemon juice	15 ml

- In plastic bowl with lid, combine cauliflower, bell peppers, cheese, crumbled bacon and green onions.
- In small bowl, combine mayonnaise, sugar, lemon juice and 1 teaspoon (5 ml) salt, stirring to blend well. Spoon dressing over salad and toss to coat. Cover and refrigerate 20 minutes before serving.

Hot Bean Salad

6 slices bacon	
½ cup mild taco sauce	125 ml
2 (15 ounce) cans cut green beans, drained	2 (425 g)
2 (15 ounce) cans pinto beans with jalapenos, drained	2 (425 g)

- In skillet fry bacon until crisp; remove from skillet, reserving drippings. Crumble bacon and set aside.
- In saucepan, combine remaining ingredients and reserved bacon drippings. Heat until thoroughly hot, stirring occasionally. Place in serving bowl and sprinkle crumbled bacon on top.

Tuna-Tortellini Salad

1 (7 ounce) package cut spaghetti	200 g
¼ cup (½ stick) butter	60 g
1 (12 ounce) can tuna, drained	340 g
1 (4 ounce) can sliced ripe olives	115 g

Dressing:

¾ cup whipping cream	175 ml
1 teaspoon dried basil leaves	5 ml
2 tablespoons parmesan cheese	15 g

- Cook spaghetti according to package directions and drain. Add butter and stir until butter melts. Add tuna and olives.
- Combine whipping cream, basil, cheese and 1 teaspoon (5 ml) salt for dressing. Pour over spaghetti-tuna mixture and toss.

Supper Ready Shrimp Salad

1 (14 ounce) package frozen, cooked tortellini, thawed	395 g
1 (16 ounce) package frozen salad shrimp, thawed	455 g
½ cup sliced ripe olives	65 g
½ cup chopped celery	50 g
1 (8 ounce) bottle zesty Italian salad dressing, divided	235 ml

- In salad bowl, combine tortellini, shrimp, olives and celery. Pour about half salad dressing over salad and toss.

Fruit and Pork Salad Lunch

1 (10 ounce) package fresh green salad mix	280 g
2 cups halved seedless green grapes	300 g
1 cup fresh strawberries, halved	150 g
1 cup refrigerated red grapefruit sections,	
drained, set aside liquid	230 g
6 (leftover) slices cooked pork tenderloin, cut in strips	

Dressing:

¼ cup reserved grapefruit juice	60 ml
2 tablespoons red wine vinegar	30 ml
2 tablespoons olive oil	30 ml
2 tablespoons honey	45 g
1 tablespoon poppy seeds	15 ml

- In salad bowl, toss together salad mix, green grapes, strawberries and grapefruit sections. Arrange salad on individual plates and place tenderloin slices over top.

- Combine all dressing ingredients in jar with lid. Seal jar and shake ingredients until well blended. Pour dressing over top of individual salad plates.

Stained-Glass Fruit Salad

2 (20 ounce) cans peach pie filling, chilled	2 (570 g)
3 bananas, sliced, chilled	
1 (16 ounce) package frozen unsweetened strawberries, drained	455 g
1 (20 ounce) can pineapple tidbits, drained, chilled	570 g

- Mix fruits, place in crystal bowl and refrigerate.

Creamy Fruit Salad

2 (20 ounce) cans pineapple chunks	2 (570 g)
1 (3 ounce) package cook-and-serve coconut pudding	85 g
2 apples, sliced	
2 bananas, sliced	
¾ cup chopped pecans	85 g

- Drain pineapple and place liquid in saucepan. Add pudding and cook over low-medium heat until it thickens, stirring constantly. Refrigerate.
- Combine pineapple chunks, sliced apples, bananas and pecans. Stir in cooled pudding and refrigerate until ready to serve.

Zesty Fruit Salad

1 (24 ounce) jar refrigerated mixed fruit salad, drained	680 g
1 (24 ounce) jar refrigerated red grapefruit, drained	680 g
1 red delicious apple, with peel, thinly sliced	
¼ cup slivered almonds, toasted	35 g

Dressing:

⅔ cup honey	225 g
¼ cup frozen limeade concentrate, thawed	60 ml
2 teaspoons poppy seeds	10 ml

- In salad bowl, combine all fruits.
- In small bowl, combine honey, limeade concentrate and poppy seeds and toss with fruit. Sprinkle with almonds.

Sunday Special Apple Salad

Sauce:

1 (20 ounce) can crushed pineapple, drain and set aside liquid	570 g
⅔ cup sugar	135 g
1 tablespoon flour	15 ml
1 tablespoon white vinegar	15 ml

Continued on following page

Continued from previous page

Salad Ingredients:

1 (12 ounce) carton whipped topping, thawed	340 g
3 red delicious apples, with peel, diced	
1 (10 ounce) package miniature marshmallows	280 g
½ cup roasted peanuts	75 g

- In saucepan, combine sugar, flour, vinegar and reserved pineapple liquid, mixing well. Place on medium heat and cook, stirring constantly, until mixture thickens. Set aside to cool.
- After first mixture is completely cooled, place in large salad bowl and fold in whipped topping. Fold in pineapple, diced apples and marshmallows and refrigerate. When ready to serve, sprinkle peanuts over top of salad.

Snickers® Salad

6 large delicious apples, with peels, chopped	
6 (2 ounce) Snickers® candy bars, chopped	6 (60 g)
½ cup chopped pecans	55 g
1 (12 ounce) carton whipped topping, thawed	340 g

- In large bowl, combine apples, candy bars and pecans and mix well. Fold in whipped topping and refrigerate.

Citrus-Banana Salad

Dressing:

1 (6 ounce) carton plain yogurt	170 g
1 ripe banana, mashed	
¼ cup sugar	50 g
1 tablespoon lemon juice	15 ml

Salad:

1 (6 ounce) package shredded lettuce	170 g
1 (24 ounce) jar grapefruit sections, well drained	680 g
2 (11 ounce) cans mandarin oranges, well drained	2 (310 g)

- Whisk together yogurt, banana, sugar and lemon juice, mixing well. Refrigerate.
- Place shredded lettuce on 4 to 6 individual salad plates and arrange grapefruit sections and oranges on top. Drizzle dressing.

Nutty Grape-Pineapple Salad

1 pound seedless green grapes, halved	455 g
½ cup chopped pecans	55 g
⅔ cup shredded cheddar cheese	75 g
1 (15 ounce) can pineapple tidbits, drained	425 g
½ cup mayonnaise	110 g

- Combine grapes, pecans, cheese and pineapple. Fold in mayonnaise. Serve on lettuce leaves.

Pear Mousse

2 (15 ounce) cans sliced pears	2 (425 g)
1 (6 ounce) package lemon gelatin	170 g
1 (8 ounce) package cream cheese, softened	230 g
1 (8 ounce) carton whipped topping, thawed	230 g

- Drain pears and set aside liquid. Heat pear liquid and add enough water to equal ¾ cup (175 ml). Heat to boiling point. Add gelatin. Mix well and cool.
- Place pears and cream cheese in blender and process until smooth. Place into large bowl and fold in cooled but not congealed gelatin mixture and whipped topping. Mix until smooth.
- Pour into individual dessert dishes. Cover with piece of plastic wrap and refrigerate.

Watergate Salad

1 (20 ounce) can crushed pineapple with juice	570 g
2 (3 ounce) packages pistachio instant pudding mix	2 (85 g)
¾ cup chopped pecans	85 g
1 (12 ounce) carton whipped topping, thawed	340 g

- Mix pineapple with instant pudding mix until it thickens slightly. Add pecans. Mix well and fold in whipped topping.
- Pour into crystal bowl and refrigerate.

Mandarin Fluff

2 (11 ounce) cans mandarin oranges, well drained	2 (310 g)
1 cup miniature marshmallows	45 g
1 (8 ounce) carton whipped topping, thawed	230 g
½ cup chopped pecans	55 g

- Place oranges in bowl and stir in marshmallows (making sure marshmallows are not stuck together). Fold in whipped topping and pecans and refrigerate. Serve in individual sherbet glasses.

Crunchy Fruit Salad

2 red apples with peels, chopped	
⅓ cup sunflower seeds	45 g
½ cup green grapes	75 g
⅓ cup vanilla yogurt	75 g

- In bowl, combine apples, sunflower seeds, grapes and yogurt. Stir to coat salad. Refrigerate before serving.

Grapefruit-Avocado Salad

2 (15 ounce) cans grapefruit sections, drained	2 (425 g)
2 ripe avocados, peeled, sliced	
½ cup chopped slivered almonds	85 g
Prepared poppy seed salad dressing	

- Combine grapefruit, avocados and almonds.
- Toss with poppy seed dressing. Serve on bed of lettuce.

Ginger Dressing for Fruit Salad

1 cup vanilla yogurt	225 g
2 tablespoons honey	45 g
1 teaspoon sugar	5 ml
2 tablespoons finely minced, crystallized ginger	30 ml

• Combine all ingredients and mix well. Cover and refrigerate.

Classic Apple-Cranberry Salad

¼ cup mayonnaise	55 g
2 tablespoons peanut butter	35 g
1 teaspoon lemon juice	5 ml
1 teaspoon sugar	5 ml
2 Gala apples, with peel, chopped	
2 celery ribs, chopped	
⅓ cup cherry-flavored Craisins® (dried cranberries)	40 g
1 cup shredded lettuce	60 g
¼ cup chopped pecans	30 g

• In salad bowl, whisk together mayonnaise, peanut butter, lemon juice and sugar. Stir in apples, celery and Craisins® tossing to coat well. Cover and refrigerate.

• Arrange lettuce on 3 to 4 individual salad plates and top with chilled apple mixture and sprinkle evenly with pecans.

Spiced Cranberries

2 (16 ounce) cans whole cranberry sauce, chilled	2 (455 g)
⅓ cup orange marmalade, chilled	105 g
1 cup golden raisins	150 g
2 teaspoons pumpkin pie spice	10 ml

• Combine all ingredients in bowl and mix well. Refrigerate for 30 minutes.

Chilled Cranberry Salad

1 (14 ounce) can sweetened condensed milk	395 g
⅓ cup lemon juice	75 ml
1 (20 ounce) can crushed pineapple, drained	570 g
1 (16 ounce) can whole cranberry sauce	455 g
3 cups miniature marshmallows	135 g
1 (8 ounce) carton whipped topping, thawed	230 g

- In large bowl, combine sweetened condensed milk and lemon juice and mix well. Add pineapple, cranberry sauce and marshmallows and stir until they blend well. Fold in whipped topping and spoon into 9 x 13-inch (23 x 33 cm) baking dish. Place in freezer until hard, but not frozen through.

Cranberry Waldorf Salad

3 red delicious apples, unpeeled and cubed	
⅔ cup coarsely chopped pecans	75 g
¾ cup sweetened dried cranberries (Craisins)	90 g
⅓ cup shredded cheddar cheese	40 g

Dressing:

⅓ cup mayonnaise	55 g
2 tablespoons sugar	25 g

- In salad bowl, combine cubed apples, pecans and cranberries. In small bowl, combine mayonnaise and sugar. Toss with salad mixture. Refrigerate. When ready to serve, sprinkle cheese over top of salad.

Fruited Chicken Salad

1 (10 ounce) package spring salad mix	280 g
1 (6 ounce) package frozen, ready-to-serve chicken	
strips, thawed	170 g
½ cup fresh strawberries, sliced	85 g
½ cup fresh raspberries	60 g
½ fresh peach, sliced	
1 (8 ounce) bottle raspberry salad dressing	235 ml

- In salad bowl, combine salad mix, chicken strips, berries and peach. Toss with salad dressing.

Sunday Night Chicken Sandwiches

1 (10 ounce) package frozen breaded chicken breast patties	280 g
1 (8 ounce) carton guacamole dip	230 g
4 whole wheat hamburger buns, split	
⅓ cup thick-and-chunky salsa	90 g
½ (9 ounce) package shredded lettuce	½ (255 g)

- In skillet with very little oil, cook breaded chicken breast patties as directed on package.
- Spread thin layer of guacamole dip on bottom of each bun and top each with chicken patty; spread salsa on top of patty. Place 3 to 4 tablespoons (45 to 60 ml) shredded lettuce over salsa.
- Spread another thin layer of guacamole on top bun.

Chicken-Bacon Sandwiches

1 (12 ounce) can chicken breast meat, drained	340 g
⅓ cup mayonnaise	75 g
1 tablespoon dijon-style mustard	15 ml
1 celery rib, finely chopped	
¼ cup cooked, crumbled bacon	30 g
Sandwich bread	
Shredded lettuce	

- In medium bowl, combine chicken chunks, mayonnaise, mustard, celery, bacon, and salt and pepper to taste.
- Spread chicken mixture on 1 slice of whole wheat or white bread; top with shredded lettuce and another slice of bread.

Chicken-Bacon Salad Sandwiches

1 (12 ounce) can chicken breast meat, drained, crumbled	340 g
½ cup mayonnaise	110 g
1 tablespoon dijon-style mustard	15 ml
1 celery rib, finely chopped	
¼ cup ready-to-serve real bacon bits	30 g
4 medium size croissants	
Shredded lettuce	

- In medium bowl, combine crumbled chicken, mayonnaise, mustard, celery, bacon, salt and pepper to taste.
- Slice croissants in half horizontally and place salad mixture on bottom half of croissants. Sprinkle shredded lettuce on top and place top half on sandwich.

Wrap-That-Turkey Burger

1 pound ground turkey	455 g
⅓ cup shredded 4-cheese blend	40 g
¼ cup finely grated onion, drained	40 g
1 teaspoon Creole spicy seasoning	5 ml

Wrap:

4 fajita-size flour tortillas, warmed	
2 cups shredded lettuce	70 g
⅔ cup guacamole	155 g

- Combine ground turkey, shredded cheese, grated onion and spicy seasoning in bowl. Shape into 4 patties (make patties a little longer than round) and refrigerate about 30 minutes before cooking. Grill patties about 5 inches (13 cm) from heat for about 8 minutes or until thermometer reads 165° (75° C).
- Place tortillas on flat surface and arrange one-fourth lettuce on each tortilla. Place 1 patty on each tortilla and spread with guacamole. Fold tortilla in half to cover filling.

Wrap Up the Turkey

4 (8-inch) whole wheat tortillas	4 (20 cm)
Sun dried tomato GourMayo®	
1 pound thinly sliced deli roasted turkey	455 g
½ cup finely chopped lettuce	30 g
2 tablespoons chopped fresh cilantro	30 ml

- Place tortillas on flat surface and spread thin layer of GourMayo®. Layer each tortilla with 4 slices of turkey. Sprinkle with lots of lettuce and cilantro. Roll tightly and serve whole or cut on diagonal to serve smaller slices.

Apple Club Sandwich

Dressing:

⅓ cup mayonnaise	75 g
¼ teaspoon dried tarragon	1 ml
¼ teaspoon dillweed	1 ml
1 teaspoon mustard	5 ml
1 teaspoon lemon juice	5 ml

Sandwich:

4 slices of rye bread
4 thin slices deli turkey
4 thin slices deli ham
4 thin slices Monterey Jack cheese
Thin slices of tart apple
Lettuce leaves

- In small bowl, combine dressing ingredients and spread on 4 slices rye bread. On 2 slices of bread, layer turkey, ham and cheese; repeat layers and top with apple slices, lettuce leaf and remaining slices of bread.

Chicken Sandwich Olé

1 (10 ounce) package frozen breaded chicken breast patties	280 g
½ cup black bean dip	130 g
⅓ cup thick and chunky hot salsa	90 g

- Preheat oven to 325° (165° C). Heat chicken breast patties in oven as directed on package, adding 4 hoagie buns (or hamburger buns) the last 3 minutes of cooking time.
- Spread bottom of each hoagie bun liberally with bean dip and salsa. Top each with chicken patty and shredded lettuce and tomatoes. Serve immediately.

Reubens on a Bun

1 (1 pound) package smoked frankfurters	455 g
8 hot dog buns	
1 (8 ounce) can sauerkraut, drained	230 g
Caraway seeds	
Thousand island dressing	

- Pierce each frankfurter and place into split buns. Arrange 2 tablespoons (30 ml) sauerkraut over each frank. Sprinkle with caraway seed.
- Place in 9 x 13-inch (23 x 33 cm) shallow pan and drizzle with dressing. Heat until hot dogs are thoroughly hot.

Reuben Sandwiches

12 slices dark rye bread	
6 slices Swiss cheese	
12 thin deli slices corned beef	
4 cups deli coleslaw, drained	735 g

- On 6 slices of rye bread, layer cheese, 2 slices corned beef and lots of coleslaw. Top with remaining slices of bread.

Southwest Burgers

2 pounds lean ground beef	910 g
1 packet taco seasoning mix	
1 cup salsa, divided	265 g
1 (8 count) package kaiser buns	
8 slices hot pepper Jack cheese	

- Combine beef, taco seasoning and ¼ cup (65 g) salsa in large mixing bowl. Shape mixture into 8 patties.
- If you are grilling, cook patties about 12 minutes, turning once. To broil in oven, place patties on broiler pan 4 to 5 inches (10 cm) from heat and broil until they cook thoroughly. Turn once during cooking.
- When patties are almost done, place buns cut side down on grill and heat 1 or 2 minutes. Place 8 patties on bottom half of buns, top with cheese and cook an additional minute or until cheese melts. Top with heaping tablespoon salsa and top half of bun.

Ranch Cheeseburgers

1 (1 ounce) envelope dry ranch-style salad dressing mix	30 g
1 pound lean ground beef	455 g
1 cup shredded cheddar cheese	115 g
4 large hamburger buns, toasted	

- Combine dressing mix with beef and cheese. Shape into 4 patties. Cook on charcoal grill.

Jack's Firecrackers

1¼ pounds lean ground beef	570 g
2 ounce chunk Monterey Jack cheese with jalapeno peppers	60 g

- Preheat grill or broiler to high. Evenly divide ground beef into 8 large flat patties. Cut cheese into 4 cubes.
- Place one piece of cheese on top of each of 4 patties. Top each with remaining patties and press edges lightly to seal. Season with salt and pepper.
- Place burgers in broiler pan and broil or grill 8 to 10 minutes on each side. Serve on hamburger buns with lettuce and tomatoes.

Pizza Burger

1 pound lean ground beef   455 g
½ cup pizza sauce   125 g
4 slices mozzarella cheese

- Combine beef, ½ teaspoon (2 ml) salt and half pizza sauce.
- Mold into 4 patties and pan-fry over medium heat for 5 to 6 minutes on each side. Just before burgers are done, top each with 1 spoonful pizza sauce and 1 slice cheese. Serve on hamburger bun.

No Ordinary Sandwich

3 tablespoons crumbled blue cheese   35 g
¼ cup mayonnaise   55 g
2 hamburger buns
6 thin slices deli roast beef

- Combine crumbled blue cheese and mayonnaise and spread on cut side of both buns. Place 3 roast beef slices on each bottom bun and top with shredded lettuce and sliced tomatoes.

Hot Roast Beef Sandwich

1 (16 ounce) loaf French bread   455 g
¼ cup creamy dijon-style mustard   60 g
¾ pound sliced deli roast beef   340 g
8 slices American cheese

- Preheat oven to 325° (165° C). Split French bread and spread mustard on bottom slice. Layer slices of beef over mustard and cheese slices over beef with cheese on top.
- Cut loaf in quarters and place on baking sheet. Heat for about 5 minutes or until cheese just partially melts.

Cream Cheese Sandwich Spread

2 (8 ounce) packages cream cheese, softened	2 (230 g)
1 (2 ounce) jar dried beef, finely chopped	60 g
1 bunch green onions with tops, chopped	
¾ cup mayonnaise	170 g

- Combine all ingredients and 1 teaspoon (5 ml) salt until mixture spreads smoothly. Trim crust of whole wheat bread and spread cream cheese mixture on bread.
- Top with another slice of bread and slice into 3 strips or 4 quarters.

Meatball Heros

Any bread like club rolls, hot dog buns or French rolls will work.

1 (16 ounce) container marinara sauce	455 g
1 (16 ounce) package frozen bell peppers, thawed	455 g
½ onion, minced	
1 (12 ounce) package cooked Italian meatballs	340 g

- Combine marinara sauce, bell peppers and onion and cook in large saucepan on medium heat for 5 minutes.
- Add meatballs, cover and gently boil for about 5 minutes or until meatballs are hot. Spoon into split club rolls and serve hot.

Philly Meatball Sandwiches

1 tablespoon olive oil	15 ml
1 (16 ounce) package frozen chopped onions and bell peppers	455 g
½ (18 ounce) package frozen, cooked meatballs	½ (510 g)
6 toasted hoagie rolls	
1 (8 ounce) package shredded cheddar cheese	230 g

- In skillet with oil on medium heat, cook and stir onions and bell peppers for 5 minutes. Add meatballs, cover and cook, stirring occasionally, about 12 minutes or until meatballs are thoroughly hot.
- Spoon mixture into toasted rolls and sprinkle cheese over meatballs. Serve hot.

Burgers Italian Style

1½ pounds lean ground beef	680 g
½ cup spaghetti sauce, plus extra to spoon on burgers	125 g
¼ cup prepared Italian breadcrumbs	30 g
1 egg	
10 slices provolone cheese	
10 thick slices Italian bread	

- In bowl, combine ground beef, spaghetti sauce, breadcrumbs and egg, mix well. Shape into 5 patties. Broil patties on rack with tops about 3 inches (8 cm) from heat. Broil about 6 minutes on each side.

- On a baking sheet, lightly toast each bread slice. Place 1 slice cheese on 5 slices, top with patty and a second slice of cheese. Place another slice of bread on top and place baking sheet in oven. Leave in oven about 5 minutes or until cheese is slightly melted. Serve with additional spaghetti sauce.

Easy Dog Wraps

8 wieners	
8 slices cheese	
1 (8 ounce) package refrigerated crescent rolls	230 g
Mustard	

- Split wieners lengthwise and fill with folded cheese slice.
- Wrap in crescent dough roll and bake at 375° (190° C) for about 12 minutes. Serve with mustard.

Barking Dogs

10 wieners
5 slices cheese
10 corn tortillas

- Slice wieners lengthwise and halfway through. Cut each cheese slice in half and place inside each wiener. Wrap tortillas around wiener and secure with toothpick. Heat several inches of oil in frying pan. Fry dogs in oil until tortilla is crisp. Serve hot.

Cheese Doggies

Bacon slices
Sliced frankfurters
Cheddar cheese slices
Hot dog buns

- Use 1 bacon slice for each frankfurter. Place bacon on paper towel or paper plate, cover with paper towel and microwave for 45 seconds or until almost crisp.
- Cut lengthwise pocket in frankfurter and stuff with 1 strip cheese. Wrap bacon around doggie and secure with toothpick.
- Place in split hot dog bun and microwave for about 30 seconds or until hot dog is warm.

Cucumber Sauce for a Different Burger

1 seedless cucumber, peeled, coarsely grated, drained	
½ cup plain yogurt	115 g
¼ cup finely grated onion, drained	40 g
2 teaspoons dillweed	10 ml

- In bowl, combine cucumber, yogurt, grated onion, 2 teaspoons (10 ml) salt and dillweed. Use cucumber sauce for grilled hamburgers instead mayonnaise or mustard.

Couples Night Sandwich

1 (9 inch) round loaf focaccia bread	23 cm
6 deli ham slices	
6 slices Swiss cheese	
½ cup chopped, roasted red bell peppers, drained	130 g
1 (6 ounce) package baby spinach	170 g
Dressing:	
⅓ cup romano basil vinaigrette dressing	75 ml
2 tablespoons mayonnaise	30 g

Continued on following page

Continued from previous page

- Preheat oven to 325° (165° C). Place bread on cutting board and slice horizontally. Place layer of ham and cheese on top with red bell peppers and heavy layer of spinach.
- In small bowl, combine vinaigrette dressing and mayonnaise and drizzle mixture over spinach layer. Place top of loaf over spinach layer and wrap in foil. Bake 15 minutes. Cut focaccia into 4 or 6 wedges and serve immediately.

Apple-Ham Open-Face Sandwiches

4 kaiser bakery rolls (or buns)
Mayonnaise and mustard
16 slices American cheese
8 thin slices deli, boiled ham
1 red delicious apple, finely chopped

- Spread a little mayonnaise and mustard on top and bottom of 4 kaiser rolls and place on baking sheet. Top each with 1 slice of cheese, then slice of ham and about 2 tablespoons (15 g) chopped apple. Top with remaining slices of cheese.
- Broil 4 to 5 inches (10 cm) from broiler heat just until top slice of cheese melts. Serve immediately.

"Honey Do" Open-Face Sandwich

⅓ cup honey-mustard dressing   75 ml
4 kaiser rolls, split
8 thin slices deli honey ham
8 slices Swiss cheese

- Preheat oven to 400° (205° C). Spread honey-mustard on each split roll. Top each with ham and cheese slices.
- Place on baking sheet and bake 4 to 5 minutes or until cheese melts.

Ham Sandwiches

Kaiser rolls
16 slices American cheese
8 thin slices deli, boiled ham

- Spread a little mayonnaise and mustard on top and bottom of 4 kaiser rolls and place on baking sheet. Top each with 1 slice of cheese and slice ham. Top with remaining slices of cheese.
- Broil 4 to 5 inches (10 cm) from heat just until top slice of cheese melts. Serve immediately.

Grilled Open-Face Sandwich

2 cups cooked, ground ham (leftover or deli ham)	280 g
½ cup drained pickle relish	125 g
2 eggs, hard-boiled, chopped	
⅓ cup GourMayo®, a dijon flavored mayonnaise	75 g

- In bowl, combine ground ham, pickle relish, eggs and GourMayo®. Toast 5 slices of favorite bread and spread butter on untoasted side. Spread ham mixture on untoasted side of bread and broil until mixture browns slightly. Serve piping hot.

Guacamole Ham Salad Wrap

¾ cup guacamole	175 g
4 (8 inch) spinach tortillas	4 (20 cm)
¾ cup salsa	200 g
1 cup shredded 4-cheese blend	115 g
¾ pound deli ham, cut in thin strips	340 g
Shredded lettuce	

- Spread guacamole over half of each tortilla and layer salsa, cheese, ham strips and lettuce to within 2 inches (5 cm) of edges. Roll tightly.

Wrap It Up NOW!

4 burrito-size flour tortillas	
⅓ cup sweet-honey Catalina dressing	75 ml
4 thin slices deli ham	
4 slices Swiss cheese	
1½ cups deli coleslaw	275 g

- Spread tortillas with dressing and add 1 slice ham and 1 slice cheese on each tortilla. Spoon one-fourth coleslaw on top.
- Roll and wrap each in wax paper. Place in microwave and heat just until cheese begins to melt. Cut wraps in half to serve.

Party Sandwiches

1 cup bacon, cooked, crumbled	110 g
½ cup ripe olives, coarsely chopped	65 g
½ cup chopped pecans	55 g
1¼ cups mayonnaise	280 g

- Mix all ingredients. Spread on thin sliced white bread.
- Cut sandwiches into 3 strips.

Italian Sausage Sandwiches

1 pound sweet Italian sausage, cooked, casing removed	455 g
1 red bell pepper, chopped	
1 onion, chopped	
1⅔ cups Italian-style spaghetti sauce	420 g

- In skillet over medium heat, cook sausage, bell pepper and onion until sausage browns and is no longer pink.
- Stir in spaghetti sauce and heat until boiling. Simmer for 5 minutes; stir constantly. Pour mixture over split hoagie rolls.

B L T Wraps

Flour tortillas, spread with mayonnaise
Sliced turkey (2 per wrap)
Cooked bacon (2 per wrap)
Shredded lettuce
Chopped tomatoes

- Top each tortilla with 2 slices turkey, 2 slices bacon and shredded lettuce and tomatoes. Fold edges over to enclose filling. Serve immediately or wrap in wax paper and refrigerate.

Wow 'em Tenderloin Sandwich

Soft light cream cheese, softened
Orange marmalade
Thin slices (leftover) cooked pork tenderloin
Sliced red onion
Lettuce

- Spread thin layer of cream cheese on 2 slices of your favorite bread; on bottom slice, spread orange marmalade. Top with thin slices of pork tenderloin, red onion slice and lettuce leaf. Place second piece of bread on top.

Hot Cornbread Sandwich

2 (8 ounce) packages corn muffin mix	2 (230 g)
2 eggs, beaten	
⅔ cup milk	150 ml
12 slices American cheese	
6 slices deli ham slices	

- Preheat oven to 400° (205° C).
- In bowl, combine muffin mix, eggs and milk, mixing well. Pour half of mixture into 7 x 11-inch (18 x 28 cm) greased baking dish. Carefully place 6 slices of cheese, then ham slices over cheese and remaining cheese slices on top of ham. Spoon remaining cornbread batter over top of cheese.
- Bake for 25 minutes or until cornbread is golden brown. Cut into squares and serve hot.

A Family Sandwich

1 (16 ounce) loaf French bread, cut in half horizontally	455 g
Creamy dijon GourMayo® (from 11 ounce bottle)	310 g
8 sliced Swiss cheese	
8 slices deli-sliced honey ham	
8 sandwich-sliced dill pickles	

- Preheat oven to 375° (190° C). Spread dijon GourMayo® over cut sides of bread. Arrange half cheese and half ham on bottom slice and top with pickle slices. Layer remaining cheese and ham on top of pickles. Cover with top of bread and press down on sandwich; cut into quarters.
- Place on cookie sheet and bake for 5 minutes and serve immediately.

A Special Grilled Cheese Sandwich

Softened butter
1 loaf 7-grain bread

Filling for 1 sandwich:

2 tablespoons GourMayo® with chipotle	30 g
2 slices sharp cheddar cheese	
2 tablespoons real crumbled bacon	15 g
¼ of an avocado, thinly sliced	

- For each sandwich, spread softened butter on 2 thick slices of 7-grain bread and place one slice, butter side down in heavy skillet. Spread with 1 tablespoon (15 ml) of GourMayo® and one slice of cheese.
- Sprinkle with crumbled bacon and avocado slices. Top with second slice of cheese and remaining slice of bread spread with other tablespoon of GourMayo®.
- Heat skillet on medium-high and cook about 2 minutes or until light brown and cheese begins to melt.
- Turn sandwich over and cook another 2 minutes or until cheese is completely melted.

Barbecue Burger on a Muffin

1½ pounds ground pork	680 g
1 teaspoon minced garlic	5 ml
¼ teaspoon cayenne	1 ml
6 English muffins	
2 teaspoons dijon-style mustard	10 ml
½ cup barbecue sauce	130 g
1 cup refrigerated creamy coleslaw	185 g

- In bowl, combine ground pork, garlic, 1 teaspoon (5 ml) salt and cayenne and shape into 6 patties about ¾-inch (1.8 cm) thick.
- Using back of spoon, press an indentation in center for even grilling. Grill patties about 5 minutes on each side or until thermometer reaches 165° (75° C).
- Lightly toast each side of English muffins and spread with mustard and a little barbecue sauce. Place patties on bottoms of muffins and top with coleslaw and top of muffin. Serve extra barbecue sauce on the side, if you like.

Open Face Jumbo

8 slices bacon	
1 (8 ounce) package cream cheese, softened	230 g
¼ cup (½ stick) butter, softened	60 g
2 teaspoons lemon juice	10 ml
1 teaspoon Worcestershire sauce	5 ml
4 English muffins	
8 turkey slices	
8 ham slices	
8 slices Swiss cheese	

- Fry bacon until crisp, drain and set aside. In medium sized bowl, beat together cream cheese, butter, lemon juice and Worcestershire sauce; mix well.
- Spread on muffins. Top with turkey, ham and cheese slices. Broil on bottom rack of oven for 10 to 12 minutes. Top with bacon.

Crab-Avocado Burgers

4 frozen crab cakes, thawed	
1 ripe avocado	
¼ cup mayonnaise	55g
1 tablespoon lemon juice	15 ml
1 (4 ounce) can diced green chilies, drained	115 g
4 hamburger buns	

- Microwave crab cakes as directed on package. Mash avocado (with fork) together with mayonnaise, lemon juice and ½ teaspoon (2 ml) salt. Stir in green chilies.
- Place crab cakes on buns and spread with avocado-mayonnaise mixture. Serve as is or top with lettuce and sliced tomatoes.

Salmon Burgers

1 (15 ounce) can salmon	425 g
1 egg, slightly beaten	
¼ cup lemon juice	60 ml
⅔ cup seasoned breadcrumbs	80 g
Hamburger buns	
Mayonnaise	
Shredded lettuce	
Sliced tomatoes	

- Drain salmon and set aside 2 tablespoons (30 ml) liquid.
- In bowl, combine salmon, set aside salmon liquid, egg, lemon juice, breadcrumbs and a little salt and pepper. Form into patties and with a little oil, fry on both sides until golden.
- Serve hot on buns with mayonnaise, lettuce and sliced tomatoes.

Crab Salad Croissants

1 (8 ounce) package imitation crabmeat, flaked	230 g
1 sweet red bell pepper, finely chopped	
3 green onions, minced	
2 tablespoons sunflower seeds	15 g
1 teaspoon seasoned salt	5 ml
½ - ⅔ cup mayonnaise	110 - 150 g
Shredded lettuce	
6 croissants, split	

- In bowl, combine crabmeat, bell pepper, onions, sunflower kernels, seasoned salt and a little black pepper. Add mayonnaise and toss to blend well; add more mayonnaise if needed.
- Line croissants with shredded lettuce and top with crab salad.

Seafood Tortilla Wraps

2 (9-inch) garden spinach tortillas	2 (23 cm)
Mayonnaise	
1 cup shredded American cheese	115 g
1 (9 ounce) package spring salad mix	255 g
1 cup diced, drained tomatoes	255 g
4 finely chopped green onions	
1 (4 ounce) package albacore steak with lemon and	
cracked pepper, crumbled	115 g

- Heat broiler, place tortillas on baking sheet and broil very briefly on each side. Remover from oven and spread mayonnaise on side of tortilla. Sprinkle cheese over tortillas and return to oven just until cheese melts.
- Combine salad mix, tomatoes and green onions and sprinkle on tortillas. Place as much crumbled albacore on tortilla as needed. Roll or fold over to eat.

Fish and Chips Sandwiches

1 (12 ounce) box frozen breaded fish fillets, thawed	340 g
1 (8 ounce) loaf Italian bread	230 g
1 cup deli coleslaw	185 g
1 cup potato chips	25 g

- Heat fish fillets according to package directions. Remove from oven and preheat broiler. Slice bread in half lengthwise and broil, cut side up.
- Layer coleslaw, fish fillets and potato chips and cover with bread tops. To serve, cut into 4 quarters and serve immediately.

Chicken Pizza

4 (8-inch) flour tortillas	4 (20 cm)
2 cups deli chicken breast, diced	280 g
1 (11 ounce) can Mexicorn®, drained	310 g
1 (15 ounce) can black beans, rinsed, drained	425 g
2 tablespoons lemon juice	30 ml
1½ cups shredded Monterey Jack cheese with jalapeno peppers	170 g

- Preheat oven to 350° (175° C). Place tortillas on greased baking sheet and bake 10 minutes or until edges are light brown. Remove from oven, stack and press down to flatten.
- In skillet with a little oil, combine diced chicken, corn and black beans. Heat, stirring constantly until mixture is thoroughly hot and stir in lemon juice.
- Place tortillas on baking sheet and spoon about ¾ cup (175 ml) chicken-corn mixture on each tortilla. Sprinkle cheese on top of each pizza and return to oven for 2 minutes or just until cheese melts.

Caesar Salad Pizza

1 (12-inch) Italian pizza crust	32 cm
2 cups shredded mozzarella cheese	230 g
1 (6 ounce) package cooked chicken breast strips	170 g
2 cups shredded lettuce	70 g
3 fresh green onions, sliced	
¾ cup shredded cheddar and colby cheese	85 g
½ (8 ounce) bottle Caesar dressing	½ (235 ml)

- Preheat oven to 400° (205° C). Top pizza crust with mozzarella cheese and bake 8 minutes or until cheese melts. In bowl, combine chicken strips, lettuce, onions and remaining cheese with dressing and toss. Top hot pizza with salad and cut into wedges.

Deep-Dish Pizza

2 (13 ounce) packages refrigerated pizza dough	2 (370 g)
1 cup chopped red onion	160 g
2 tablespoons olive oil	30 ml
1 (10 ounce) package frozen chopped spinach, thawed, drained	280 g
1 cup ricotta cheese	245 g
1 cup shredded mozzarella cheese, divided	115 g
3 roma tomatoes, sliced	

- Preheat oven to 400° (205° C).
- Unroll 1 package of pizza dough and gently pull into 12-inch (32 cm) circle. Place dough on greased baking sheet and bake for 5 minutes.
- Cook onion in oil and add well drained spinach with salt and pepper to taste. Cook 2 minutes and spread over bottom of partially baked crust.
- In small bowl combine ricotta cheese and ¼ cup (30 g) mozzarella cheese. Spoon mixture over spinach layer and top with tomato slices.
- Sprinkle remaining mozzarella cheese over top. Unroll remaining pizza dough and place on top. Pinch together edges of dough and bake 20 minutes or until top is golden. Cut in wedges to serve.

Green Chile Grilled Cheese

4 slices cheddar cheese	
4 slices bread	
1 (4 ounce) can diced green chilies, drained	115 g
3 tablespoons butter, softened	45 g

- Place 1 slice cheese on 2 slices bread. Sprinkle with green chilies. Top with 2 remaining slices cheese and remaining 2 slices bread.
- Butter outside of sandwiches. In large skillet over medium heat, brown sandwiches on both sides until golden brown and cheese melts.

Watercress Tea Sandwiches

1 small bunch watercress	
5 eggs, hard-boiled, peeled	
6 tablespoons mayonnaise	85 g
1 tablespoon dijon-style mustard	15 ml

- Trim half watercress stems. Save rest for garnish.
- In food processor, coarsely chop eggs and add mayonnaise, mustard and a little salt. Process until smooth. Fold in chopped watercress and refrigerate.
- Trim crusts and spread mixture on thinly sliced white bread. Cut into finger sandwiches.

Cream Cheese Tea Sandwiches

1 (8 ounce) package cream cheese, softened	230 g
½ pound bacon, fried, finely chopped	230 g
12 - 14 slices whole wheat bread	
1 (12 ounce) package bean sprouts	340 g
Mayonnaise or butter	

- Using mixer, beat cream cheese until smooth. Add finely chopped bacon or chop cream cheese and bacon together in food processor.
- On 6 to 8 slices bread, spread bacon-cream cheese mixture. Add layer of bean sprouts. On other 6 to 8 slices bread, spread either mayonnaise or butter and place on top of bean sprouts to make 6 or 8 sandwiches. With sharp knife remove crust and cut each sandwich in 3 pieces. Refrigerate.

Cream Cheese Sandwiches

2 (8 ounce) packages cream cheese, softened	2 (230 g)
1 (4 ounce) can black olives, chopped	115 g
¾ cup finely chopped pecans	85 g
Pumpernickel rye bread	

- Beat cream cheese until creamy. Fold in olives and pecans. Trim crusts off bread. Spread cream cheese on bread.
- Slice sandwich into 3 finger strips.

Confetti Sandwiches

1 tablespoon lemon juice	15 ml
1 (8 ounce) package cream cheese, softened	230 g
½ cup grated carrots	55 g
¼ cup grated cucumber	30 g
¼ cup grated red onion	40 g
¼ cup grated green bell pepper	35 g

- Combine lemon juice with cream cheese and add enough mayonnaise to make cheese into spreading consistency. Fold in grated vegetables and spread on bread for sandwiches. Refrigerate.

Luncheon Sandwiches

1 loaf thinly sliced, sandwich bread	
1 cup (2 sticks) butter, softened	230 g
1 (5 ounce) jar cheese spread, softened	140 g
½ teaspoon Worcestershire sauce	2 ml

- Trim crust off bread. With mixer, beat butter and cheese spread until smooth and creamy and add Worcestershire sauce. Spread mixture on 3 slices bread to make triple-decker sandwich. Place fourth slice bread on top. Cut into finger sandwiches.

Marshmallow Sandwiches

Bread	
1 (7 ounce) jar marshmallow cream	200 g
Crunchy peanut butter	
Vanilla wafers	

- On 1 slice bread, spread marshmallow cream. On second slice bread, spread peanut butter. Put marshmallow and peanut butter sides together. Use vanilla wafers to make sandwiches, too.

Grandkid's Special

Peanut butter
Grape or plum jelly
4 slices white bread, crusts trimmed
2 eggs, well beaten
Butter
Powdered sugar

- Spread peanut butter and jelly on 2 slices of bread. Top with remaining 2 slices of bread. Beat eggs with 2 tablespoons (30 ml) water in shallow bowl. Dip each sandwich in egg.

- Melt about 2 tablespoons (30 g) butter in skillet and cook each sandwich on both sides until light brown. Take out of skillet and sprinkle lightly with powdered sugar.

Avocado Butter Spread

2 large ripe avocados	
⅓ cup lime juice	75 ml
⅓ cup extra-virgin olive oil	75 ml
A pinch dried tarragon	
½ teaspoon sugar	2 ml

- Slice avocados and place in food processor or blender. Add remaining ingredients and salt to taste. Pulse until smooth and buttery.

Super-Duper Reuben Sandwiches

½ cup mayonnaise	110 g
1 tablespoon chili sauce	15 ml
12 slices rye bread	
12 slices corned beef	
6 slices Swiss cheese	
1 (16 ounce) can sauerkraut, well drained	455 g
Butter, softened	

- Mix mayonnaise and chili sauce in bowl and spread over 6 slices of rye bread. Add slice of corned beef and cheese and then second slice of corned beef and sauerkraut.

- Top with remaining bread slices and spread top slices with butter. Place sandwiches, butter-side down in skillet and spread top of bread with butter.

- Cook sandwiches over low heat for 10 minutes or until bottom is brown. Turn and cook until golden brown and cheese melts.

Snap-Your-Fingers

Side Dishes
Vegetables

Potatoes Italian Style

1 (22 ounce) package frozen mashed potatoes, thawed	625 g
1 pint half-and-half cream	500 ml
1 cup grated parmesan cheese, divided	100 g
⅔ cup basil pesto (from 8 ounce jar of pesto)	155 g/230 g

- Place mashed potatoes, cream and an ample amount of salt and pepper in microwavable bowl. Microwave on HIGH for about 10 minutes, stirring once and cooking until potatoes are hot. Stir in half cheese, mixing well.
- Spread half potato-cheese mixture into 7 x 11-inch (18 x 28 cm) greased baking dish and top, spreading out, with basil pesto.
- Spoon remaining potato mixture on top of pesto. Sprinkle remaining parmesan cheese over top and return to microwave for another 2 minutes.

Potato Souffle

2⅔ cups instant mashed potato flakes	160 g
2 eggs, beaten	
1 cup shredded cheddar cheese	115 g
1 (3 ounce) can french-fried onions	85 g

- Prepare mashed potatoes according to package directions. Stir in eggs, cheese and stir until they blend.
- Spoon mixture into lightly greased 2-quart (2 L) dish. Sprinkle with onions. Bake uncovered at 325° (165° C) for 25 minutes.

Philly Potatoes

4½ cups instant mashed potatoes, prepared, hot	945 g
2 tablespoons freeze-dried chives	30 ml
1 (8 ounce) package cream cheese, softened	230 g
1 egg, slightly beaten	

- Mix all ingredients and blend well. Place in greased 3-quart (3 L) casserole. Bake covered at 350° (175° C) for 20 minutes. Uncover and bake for 15 minutes more.

Creamy Ranch Potatoes

4 medium russet potatoes, peeled, quartered	
¼ cup (½ stick) butter	60 g
⅓ cup ranch salad dressing	75 ml
2 tablespoons, cooked, crumbled bacon	15 g

- In saucepan, boil potatoes in water about 15 minutes or until tender. Drain and beat potatoes with electric mixer until smooth.
- Add butter, ½ teaspoon (2 ml) salt and a little black pepper and beat until butter melts. Gradually add salad dressing and beat until smooth.
- Spoon into serving bowl and top with crumbled bacon.

Cheddar Potatoes

1 (10 ounce) can cheddar cheese soup	280 g
⅓ cup sour cream	80 g
2 fresh green onions, chopped	
3 cups instant seasoned mashed potatoes, prepared	630 g

- In saucepan, heat soup and add sour cream, onion and little pepper. Stir in potatoes until they blend well. Pour into buttered 2-quart (2 L) casserole. Cook at 350° (175° C) for 25 minutes.

Creamy Potato Bake

6 - 8 baked potatoes	
1 (8 ounce) carton sour cream	230 g
1 (8 ounce) package cream cheese, softened	230 g
1½ cups shredded cheddar cheese	170 g

- Cut potatoes in half lengthwise. Scoop flesh out of potatoes, reserving skins and place in mixing bowl.
- Add salt to taste, sour cream and cream cheese and whip until all mix well. Spoon mashed potatoes back into potato skins and place in hot oven until potatoes are hot. Sprinkle cheddar cheese on top of potatoes.

Dinner-Bell Mashed Potatoes

8 medium to large potatoes	
1 (8 ounce) carton sour cream	230 g
1 (8 ounce) package cream cheese, softened	230 g
Butter	

- Preheat oven to 325° (165° C). Peel, cut up and boil potatoes until tender and drain.
- Whip hot potatoes and add sour cream, cream cheese, 1 teaspoon (5 ml) salt and ½ teaspoon (2 ml) pepper. Continue whipping until cream cheese melts. Pour in sprayed 3-quart (3 L) baking dish. Dot generously with butter.
- Cover with foil and bake for about 20 minutes.
- Bake 10 minutes longer if reheating.

Broccoli-Topped Potatoes

4 hot baked potatoes, halved	
1 cup diced cooked ham	140 g
1 (10 ounce) can cream of broccoli soup	280 g
½ cup shredded cheddar cheese	55 g

- Place hot baked potatoes on microwave-safe plate. Carefully fluff up potatoes with fork. Top each potato with ham.
- Stir soup in can until smooth. Spoon soup over potatoes and top with cheese. Microwave on HIGH for 4 minutes.

Creamy Mashed Potatoes

2 pounds baking potatoes	910 g
1 (8 ounce) package cream cheese, softened	230 g
1 teaspoon sugar	5 ml
¼ cup (½ stick) butter, softened	60 g

- Preheat oven to 325° (165° C). Peel and quarter potatoes and place in saucepan and cover with water. Cook for about 25 minutes or until tender.
- Drain and place potatoes in mixing bowl. Add cream cheese, sugar, 1 teaspoon (5 ml) salt and butter and beat until fluffy. Place in a greased 7 x 11-inch (18 x 28 cm) baking dish. Bake 25 minutes or until thoroughly hot.

Loaded Baked Potatoes

6 medium to large potatoes
1 (1 pound) package hot sausage   455 g
1 (16 ounce) package cubed processed cheese   455 g
1 (10 ounce) can diced tomatoes and green chilies, drained   280 g

- Cook potatoes in microwave. Brown sausage and drain. Add cheese to sausage and heat until cheese melts. Add tomatoes and green chilies. Serve sausage-cheese mixture over baked potatoes.

Ham-Baked Potatoes

4 potatoes, baked
1 cup diced cooked ham   140 g
1(10 ounce) can cream of mushroom soup   280 g
1 cup shredded cheddar cheese   115 g

- Place hot potatoes in microwave-safe plate. Cut in half lengthwise. Fluff up potatoes with fork. Top each potato with one-fourth ham.
- In saucepan, heat soup with ¼ cup (60 ml) water and heat just until spreadable. Spoon soup over potatoes and top with cheese.
- Microwave on HIGH for 4 minutes or until hot.

Loaded Potatoes

6 large baking potatoes, washed
2 cups cubed ham   280 g
1 (8 ounce) package cubed processed cheese   230 g
1 (11 ounce) can Mexicorn®, drained   310 g

- Cook potatoes in microwave until done. Combine ham, cheese and corn and stir well. With knife, cut potatoes down center and fluff insides with fork.
- Spoon generous amounts of ham-cheese mixture on each potato and reheat in microwave 2 to 3 minutes, if necessary.

Baked Potato Toppers

1 cup grated cheddar cheese	115 g
½ cup sour cream	120 g
¼ cup (½ stick) butter, softened	60 g
¼ cup chopped green onions	25 g

- Mix all ingredients and serve on baked potato.

A Better Potato Latke

1 large egg	
2 tablespoons chopped chives	5 g
2 tablespoons grated onion	20 g
2 tablespoons flour	15 g
1 tablespoon lemon juice	15 ml
2 pounds medium size potatoes, peeled	910 g
½ cup canola oil	125 ml

- Combine egg, chives, onion, flour, lemon juice and 1 teaspoon (5 ml) salt in large bowl.
- In food processor with shredding disk, shred potatoes and place in colander in sink; squeeze out liquid. Stir into egg mixture.
- In large skillet, place oil and heat until very hot. Drop ¼ cup (60 ml) potato mixture into hot oil (about 6 at a time) and flatten each latke into rounds. Cook about 8 minutes on both sides or until light brown. Transfer to large baking sheet that has been lined with paper towels. Keep warm.
- Repeat this process, stirring mixture each time before frying (you may need to add more oil after each batch).

Grilled New Potatoes

1 pound new potatoes	455 g
3 tablespoons orange marmalade	60 g
1 teaspoon brown sugar	5 ml
2 tablespoons butter, melted	30 g

- Cook new potatoes covered in boiling water until tender-crisp.
- Drain and cut in half. Thread on skewers. Combine marmalade, brown sugar and butter and brush mixture over potatoes.
- Grill over medium hot coals until potatoes are brown, about 5 minutes each side. Baste frequently. Salt and pepper to taste.

Potato Pancakes

2 pounds white potatoes, peeled, grated	910 g
1 onion, finely minced	
3 eggs, beaten	
½ cup seasoned dry breadcrumbs	60 g

- In large bowl, combine potatoes, onions, eggs, a little salt and pepper and breadcrumbs and mix well.
- In skillet, drop by spoonfuls in hot oil and brown on both sides.

Rosemary New Potatoes

2 pounds small red (new) potatoes, halved	910 g
¼ cup olive oil	60 ml
1 teaspoon dried rosemary	5 ml

- Place potatoes in saucepan with about 1 inch (2.5 cm) of water and a little salt. Cover and cook on medium heat, turning occasionally until tender (about 15 minutes). Drain and toss with olive oil, rosemary, 1 teaspoon (2 ml) salt and an ample amount of pepper. Cover again to keep warm.

Baked New Potatoes

1 pound new potatoes with peels	455 g
1 large onion, coarsely chopped	
1 clove garlic, minced	
½ cup (1 stick) butter	115 g

- Parboil new potatoes. Drain and quarter.
- In large skillet, saute onion and garlic with butter until onions are translucent. Add potatoes and toss to coat. Place in large baking dish. Add 1 teaspoon (5 ml) salt. Bake at 350° (175° C), basting occasionally, for 25 to 30 minutes until potatoes are fork tender.

Cheesy Potatoes

10 - 12 new potatoes with peels	
1 (8 ounce) carton sour cream	230 g
¼ cup (½ stick) butter, melted	60 g
1 (16 ounce) package processed cheese, sliced	455 g

- Rinse and scrub potatoes. Cut into ¼-inch (.6 cm) slices, place in large saucepan and cover with water. Cook for 25 minutes until slightly tender and drain.
- Place half potatoes in 9 x 13-inch (23 x 33 cm) baking dish. Sprinkle with a little salt and pepper.
- Spread half sour cream and half melted butter over top of potatoes. Place half sliced cheese on top.
- Repeat layers. Bake at 400° (205° C) about 20 minutes or until bubbly.

Maple-Pecan Sweet Potatoes

½ cup chopped, toasted pecans	55 g
1 (29 ounce) can sweet potatoes, drained	805 g
¼ cup (½ stick) butter, melted	60 g
½ cup pure maple syrup	125 ml

- Preheat oven to 350° (175° C). Toast pecans in oven for about 10 minutes. In bowl, mash sweet potatoes with fork (leaving some small chunks) and add melted butter and maple syrup; mixing well. Transfer to greased 7 x 11-inch (18 x 28 cm) baking dish.
- Sprinkle pecans over sweet potato mixture and bake uncovered for 25 minutes.

Sweet Potatoes and Pecans

2 (15 ounce) cans sweet potatoes, drained, divided	2 (425 g)
1½ cups packed brown sugar	330 g
¼ cup (½ stick) butter, melted	60 g
1 cup chopped pecans	110 g

- Slice half of the sweet potatoes and place in buttered, 2-quart (2 L) baking dish. Mix brown sugar, butter and pecans and sprinkle half mixture over sweet potatoes. Repeat layer. Bake uncovered at 350° (175° C) for 30 minutes.

Sweet Potato Casserole

1 (28 ounce) can sweet potatoes	795 g
½ cup chopped pecans	55 g
1½ cups packed light brown sugar	330 g
½ cup (1 stick) butter	115 g

- Slice sweet potatoes into 2-quart (2 L) casserole dish. Sprinkle pecans over sweet potatoes. Make syrup of brown sugar and butter with just enough water to make it thin enough to pour. Bring to boil and pour syrup over sweet potatoes.
- Bake at 350° (175° C) for 30 minutes or until potatoes brown.

Skillet Candied Sweet Potatoes

⅓ cup (⅔ stick) butter	75 g
2 (15 ounce) cans sweet potatoes, drained	2 (425 g)
1½ cups packed brown sugar	330 g
1 teaspoon cinnamon	5 ml

- In large skillet, melt butter and stir in sweet potatoes, brown sugar, cinnamon and a little salt. Cook on high heat just until mixture is hot; reduce heat, cover and simmer for 20 minutes.

Whipped Sweet Potatoes

2 (15 ounce) can sweet potatoes	2 (425 g)
¼ cup (½ stick) butter, melted	60 g
¼ cup orange juice	60 ml
1 cup miniature marshmallows	45 g

- Combine sweet potatoes, butter, orange juice and ½ teaspoon (2 ml) salt in mixing bowl.
- Beat until fluffy. Fold in marshmallows.
- Spoon into buttered 2-quart (2 L) casserole.
- Bake uncovered at 350° (175° C) for 25 minutes.

Penne Pasta in Creamy Pesto

1 (16 ounce) package penne regate pasta	455 g
1 (8 ounce) package Neufchatel cheese, softened	230 g
2 tablespoons butter	30 g
1 (6 ounce) carton basil pesto	170 g

- Cook pasta according to package directions. Drain, leaving about ½ cup (125 ml) pasta water in pan. While pasta is still hot, cut cheese into chunks and stir cheese and butter into pasta, stirring until both have melted.
- Gently stir in basil pesto, adding a tablespoon or two of water if mixture is too stiff. Serve hot.

Creamy Pasta

1 (8 ounce) jar roasted red peppers, drained	230 g
1 (14 ounce) can chicken broth	395 g
1 (3 ounce) package cream cheese	85 g
8 ounces pasta, cooked	230 g

- Combine red peppers and broth in blender and mix well.
- Pour into saucepan and heat to boiling.
- Turn heat down and whisk in cream cheese. Serve over pasta.

Ranch Spaghetti

1 (12 ounce) package spaghetti	340 g
¼ cup (½ stick) butter, cut in 3 pieces	60 g
¾ cup sour cream	180 g
¾ cup ranch dressing	175 ml
½ cup grated parmesan cheese	50 g

- Cook spaghetti according to package directions; drain and return to saucepan. Stir in butter, sour cream and ranch dressing and toss. Spoon into serving bowl and sprinkle with grated parmesan cheese. Serve immediately.

Wonderful Alfredo Fettuccine

1 (16 ounce) package fettuccine	455 g
2 tablespoons butter	30 g
¾ cup grated fresh parmesan cheese	75g
1¼ cups heavy cream	310 ml

- Cook fettuccine according to package directions.
- In large saucepan over medium heat, melt butter and stir in parmesan cheese, heavy cream and black pepper to taste. Cook for 1 minute, stirring constantly. Reduce heat and pour in fettuccine, tossing gently to coat fettuccine.

Creamy Fettuccine

1 (8 ounce) package fettuccine	230 g
1 pound Italian sausage	455 g
1 (10 ounce) can cream of mushroom soup	280 g
1 (16 ounce) carton sour cream	455 g

- Cook fettuccine and drain. Cut sausage into 1-inch (2.5 cm) pieces, brown over medium heat and cook for about 8 minutes. Drain sausage.
- Mix all ingredients and place in 2-quart (2 L) greased baking dish. Bake at 325° (165° C) for 30 minutes.

Spinach Fettuccine

1 (6 ounce) can tomato paste	170 g
1 (5 ounce) can evaporated milk	145 ml
½ cup (1 stick) butter	115 g
1 (12 ounce) package spinach fettuccine	340 g

- In saucepan, combine tomato paste, milk and butter and cook until butter melts. Season with a little salt and pepper. Cook fettuccine according to package directions. Serve sauce over fettuccine.

Pesto Sauce for Linguine or Angel Hair Pasta

½ cup extra-virgin olive oil	125 ml
2 teaspoons prepared minced garlic	10 ml
⅓ cup finely minced Italian parsley	20 g
½ teaspoon cayenne pepper	2 ml

- Combine all ingredients in jar with lid; shake well to blend. This sauce, plus a little salt and pepper, will season 1 pound (455 g) of pasta.

Artichoke Fettuccine

1 (12 ounce) package fettuccine	340 g
1 (14 ounce) can water-packed artichoke hearts, drained, chopped	395 g
1 (10 ounce) box frozen green peas, thawed	280 g
1 (16 ounce) jar alfredo sauce	455 g
2 heaping tablespoons crumbled blue cheese	45 g

- Cook fettuccine according to package directions. Drain and place in serving bowl to keep warm.
- In large saucepan, heat artichoke hearts, peas and alfredo sauce and stir well. Spoon into bowl with fettuccine and toss. Sprinkle with blue cheese and serve hot.

Special Macaroni and Cheese

1 (8 ounce) package small macaroni shells	230 g
1 (15 ounce) can stewed tomatoes	425 g
1 (8 ounce) package cubed processed cheese	230 g
3 tablespoons butter, melted	45 g

- Cook shells according to package directions and drain.
- In large bowl, combine shells, tomatoes, cheese cubes and butter. Pour into 2-quart (2 L) buttered baking dish.
- Bake covered at 350° (175° C) for 30 minutes.

Spice up the Macaroni

1 cup spiral pasta	75 g
⅓ cup (⅔ stick) butter	75 g
1 (8 ounce) package shredded Mexican processed cheese	230 g
1 (10 ounce) can diced tomatoes and green chilies	280 g
½ yellow onion, very finely diced	
1 (8 ounce) carton sour cream	230 g

- Cook pasta according to package directions, drain and add butter, stirring until butter melts. Set aside covered, keeping warm.
- Preheat oven to 325° (165° C). In large saucepan, combine processed cheese, tomatoes and green chilies and diced onion. Stir in macaroni and heat on low heat for 5 minutes, stirring occasionally. Fold in sour cream and pour into 2-quart (2 L) baking dish. Cover and bake for 20 minutes.

Macaroni and Cheese

1 cup macaroni	105 g
1½ cups small curd cottage cheese	340 g
1½ cups shredded cheddar or American cheese	170 g
¼ cup grated parmesan cheese	25 g

- Cook macaroni according to package directions and drain. Combine cottage cheese and both cheeses.
- Combine macaroni with cheese mixture. Spoon into greased 2-quart (2 L) baking dish. Bake covered at 350° (175° C) for 30 minutes.

Mom's Mac and Cheese

1 (10 ounce) package your favorite shape of macaroni	280 g
¼ cup (½ stick) butter	60 g
5 tablespoons flour	40 g
2¾ cups milk, divided	675 ml
1 (8 ounce) package shredded cheddar cheese, divided	230 g

- In saucepan cook macaroni according to package directions. Drain but do not rinse, then transfer to large mixing bowl.

- In heavy saucepan, melt butter and add flour; whisk to form smooth mixture. Slowly stir in about ¾ cup (175 ml) milk, whisking to avoid lumps. On medium heat, add remaining milk, bring to a boil, reduce heat to a gentle simmer, whisking until sauce is thick and smooth. Stir in three-fourths of cheese until it melts.

- Pour half sauce over drained macaroni, mixing well. Add remaining sauce, stirring well. Transfer to serving bowl and garnish with remaining cheese.

Skillet Ravioli and Broccoli

1 (16 ounce) package refrigerated cheese ravioli	455 g
1 (16 ounce) package frozen broccoli florets, thawed	455 g
1 (16 ounce) carton marinara sauce	455 g
¾ cup shredded mozzarella cheese	85 g

- In large saucepan with boiling water, cook ravioli for 8 minutes or until tender. Drain ravioli and return to saucepan.

- Cook broccoli according to package directions and drain. Stirring gently, add broccoli and marinara sauce to ravioli in skillet. Cook on medium heat, stirring often, just until mixture is thoroughly hot. Sprinkle with cheese, cover and cook 1 minute until cheese melts.

Colorful Bacon-Rice

¾ pound bacon	340 g
2½ cups cooked rice	395 g
1 (15 ounce) can sliced carrots, drained	425 g
1 (10 ounce) package frozen green peas, thawed	280 g

- In large skillet, fry bacon until crisp. Drain bacon on paper towels, leaving about ½ cup (125 ml) bacon drippings in skillet. Crumble bacon and set aside.
- Add rice, carrots and peas to skillet and cook, stirring occasionally until mixture is thoroughly hot. Stir in bacon and serve hot.

Tasty Rice

¼ cup (½ stick) butter	60 g
1 cup instant white rice	95 g
1 (15 ounce) can beef broth	425 g
¼ cup parmesan cheese	25 g

- Melt butter in 3-quart (3 L) casserole dish. Add rice and pour beef broth over rice. Sprinkle with parmesan cheese.
- Cover and bake at 350° (175° C) for 20 minutes.

Spanish Rice

6 tablespoons (¾ stick) butter, melted	85 g
1 onion, chopped	
2 cups cooked rice	315 g
1 (10 ounce) can diced tomatoes and green chilies	280 g

- In large bowl, combine butter, onion, rice, tomatoes and green chilies and salt to taste. Spoon mixture into buttered 3-quart (3 L) baking dish. Cover and bake at 350° (175° C) for 30 minutes.

Mushroom Rice

1 (6 ounce) package chicken Rice-a-Roni®	170 g
1 (4 ounce) can sliced mushrooms, drained	115 g
⅓ cup slivered almonds	55 g
1 (8 ounce) carton sour cream	230 g

- Prepare rice according to package directions. Fold in mushrooms, almonds and sour cream. Place in 3-quart (3 L) greased casserole. Bake covered at 350° (175° C) for 25 minutes.

Baked Rice

2 cups instant rice	190 g
½ cup (1 stick) butter, melted	115 g
1 (10 ounce) can cream of celery soup	280 g
1 (10 ounce) can cream of onion soup	280 g

- Combine rice, butter, soups and 1½ cups (375 ml) water.
- Pour into buttered 3-quart (3 L) baking dish.
- Cover and bake at 350° (175° C) for 25 minutes.

Chile-Rice Bake

1 cup instant rice	95 g
1 pint sour cream	455 g
1 (7 ounce) can diced green chilies	200 g
1 (8 ounce) package shredded Monterey Jack cheese	230 g

- Cook rice according to package directions. Add remaining ingredients plus ½ teaspoon (2 ml) salt. Place mixture in buttered baking dish. Bake covered at 325° (165° C) for 15 to 20 minutes or until hot.

Dinner Rice

2 cups cooked instant white rice	330 g
1 onion, chopped	
¼ cup (½ stick) butter, melted	60 g
1 (8 ounce) package shredded Mexican processed cheese	230 g

- Combine all ingredients; mix well. Spoon mixture into buttered 2-quart (2 L) baking dish. Bake covered at 325° (165° C) for 30 minutes.

Brown Rice

1 cup instant rice	95 g
1 (10 ounce) can French onion soup	280 g
1 (14 ounce) can beef broth	395 g
3 tablespoons butter, melted	45 g

- Put rice in bottom baking dish. Pour soups and butter on top. Bake covered at 350° (175° C) for 20 minutes.

Easy Rice

1 onion, finely chopped	
2 tablespoons (¼ stick) butter	30 g
1 cup instant white rice	95 g
2 (14 ounce) cans chicken broth	2 (395 g)

- In skillet, saute onion in butter until transparent. In 2-quart (2 L) baking dish combine onion, rice and broth. Cover and bake at 350° (175° C) for 30 minutes.

Skillet Beans and Rice

6 slices bacon	
1 (15 ounce) can Mexican stewed tomatoes	425 g
1 cup instant rice	95 g
2 (15 ounce) cans chili beans	2 (425 g)

- In skillet fry bacon until crisp and drain, reserving 2 tablespoons (30 ml) drippings. Cut bacon in 1-inch (2.5 cm) pieces and set aside.
- Dry skillet with paper towels and stir in stewed tomatoes, rice, reserved drippings and ⅓ cup (75 ml) water. Bring to boiling, reduce heat and simmer 3 minutes or until rice is tender and most of liquid has evaporated.
- Add chili beans and cook until mixture is thoroughly hot. Serve right from skillet or spoon into serving bowl and top with bacon pieces.

Broccoli and Wild Rice

2 (10 ounce) packages frozen chopped broccoli	2 (280 g)
1 (6 ounce) box long grain and wild rice	170 g
1 (8 ounce) jar processed cheese spread	230 g
1 (10 ounce) can cream of chicken soup	280 g

- Cook broccoli and rice according to package directions.
- Combine all ingredients and pour into buttered 2-quart (2 L) baking dish. Bake at 350° (175° C) for 25 minutes.

Pecan-Mushroom Rice

1½ cups pecan halves	170 g
1½ cups instant rice	145 g
1 (14 ounce) can chicken broth	395 g
¼ cup (½ stick) butter	60 g
2 (8 ounce) can whole mushrooms, drained	2 (230 g)
2 teaspoons prepared, minced garlic	10 ml
3 cups baby spinach leaves, stems removed	90 g
½ cup grated parmesan cheese	50 g

- In large saucepan, cook and stir pecans over medium heat for 5 minutes. Remove from pan and cool slightly.
- Cook rice in chicken broth and butter according to package directions. Gently stir in mushrooms, garlic, spinach, cheese and pecans. Serve immediately.

Chili Rice and Beans

2 (8.8 ounce) packages (microwavable) whole grain brown rice	2 (255 g)
2 (15 ounce) cans hot chili beans with liquid	2 (425 g)
1 (4.3 ounce) package precooked bacon, divided	115 g
1 (8 ounce) package shredded processed cheese	230 g

- Preheat oven to 350° (175° C).
- Cook rice 90 seconds in microwave and place in bowl. Add chili beans and half bacon, mix well. Spoon into greased 7 x 11-inch (18 x 28 cm) baking dish, cover and bake 20 minutes.
- Remove from oven and sprinkle cheese and remaining bacon over top. Return to oven for 5 minutes.

Italian-Style Rice and Beans

1 (16 ounce) package frozen chopped onions and bell peppers	455 g
2 tablespoons olive oil	30 ml
1 (15 ounce) can Italian stewed tomatoes	425 g
1 (15 ounce) can great northern beans, drained	425 g
1 cup instant rice	95 g

- In large saucepan, saute onions and bell peppers in oil.
- Add stewed tomatoes, beans, ½ cup (125 ml) water and rice and stir well. Over medium-high heat, cover and cook about 3 minutes. Uncover and continue cooking another 3 minutes, stirring once, or until rice is tender.

Instant Beans and Rice

1 (8.8 ounce) package (microwavable) rice	255 g
1 (15 ounce) can pinto beans	425 g
½ cup hot thick and chunky salsa	130 g
1 teaspoon cumin	5 ml

- Microwave rice in package for 90 seconds; transfer to saucepan and add beans, salsa, cumin and salt to taste. Heat on medium heat until thoroughly hot.

Supper Frittata

Canola oil	
2 cups cooked rice	315 g
1 (10 ounce) box frozen green peas, thawed	280 g
1 cup cooked, cubed ham	140 g
8 large eggs, beaten	
1 cup shredded pepper jack cheese, divided	115 g
1 teaspoon dried thyme	5 ml

- Preheat broiler.
- In large heavy skillet with ovenproof handle, heat a little oil, rice, peas and ham 3 to 4 minutes or until mixture is thoroughly hot.
- In separate bowl, whisk eggs, three-fourths of cheese, thyme and salt to taste. Add to mixture in skillet and shake pan gently to distribute evenly. On medium heat, cover and cook, without stirring, until set on bottom and sides (eggs will still be runny in center).
- Sprinkle remaining cheese over top. Place in oven and broil about 5 minutes or until frittata is firm in center.

Fried Poblano Rings

3 poblano chile peppers	
1 cup flour	120 g
1 cup milk or buttermilk	250 ml
3 cups canola oil	750 ml

- Slice poblanos in rings about ¼-inch (.6 cm) wide and remove seeds.
- Mix flour, salt and pepper to taste in shallow bowl. Dip chile rings into milk and then in flour mixture. Carefully place in hot oil in deep-fryer or saucepan. (Oil should be almost to smoking stage when chiles start cooking.) Fry until golden brown. Lightly salt.

Baked Bananas

10 bananas	
¾ cup (1½ sticks) butter, melted	170 g
¾ cup brown sugar	165 g
1 teaspoon vanilla	5 ml

- Preheat oven to 350° (175° C). Peel bananas and arrange pinwheel fashion in large glass pie plate. In saucepan, combine butter and brown sugar and heat just enough to mix well. Stir in vanilla and pour over bananas. Bake for 20 minutes or until bubbly.

Cinnamon Baked Apples

6 Granny Smith apples	
¾ cup mixed nuts	125 g
1 cup packed light brown sugar	220 g
1 teaspoon cinnamon	5 ml

- Preheat oven to 350° (175° C). Core apples without cutting through to bottom. Using potato peeler, peel 1-inch (2.5 cm) strip around top of apple. Combine nuts, sugar and cinnamon and stuff cavities and place apples in greased 2-quart (2 L) baking dish. Drizzle apple with 2 tablespoons (30 ml) water and bake for about 25 minutes. Serve warm or at room temperature.

Wild West Corn

3 (15 ounce) cans whole kernel corn, drained	3 (425 g)
1 (10 ounce) can diced tomatoes and green chilies, drained	280 g
1 (8 ounce) package shredded Monterey Jack cheese	230 g
1 cup cheese cracker crumbs	60 g

- In large bowl, combine corn, tomatoes and green chilies, and cheese and mix well. Pour into buttered 2½-quart (2.5 L) baking dish.
- Sprinkle cracker crumbs over casserole. Bake uncovered at 350° (175° C) for 25 minutes.

Corn au Gratin

3 (15 ounce) cans Mexicorn®, drained	3 (425 g)
1 (4 ounce) can sliced mushrooms, drained	115 g
1 (10 ounce) can cream of mushroom soup	280 g
1 cup shredded cheddar cheese	115 g

- Mix all ingredients in saucepan and heat slowly until cheese melts. Serve hot.

Mushrooms and Corn

½ cup fresh mushrooms, sliced	35 g
3 chopped green onions with tops	
2 tablespoons butter	30 g
1 (16 ounce) package frozen whole kernel corn	455 g

- Place all ingredients in 2-quart (2 L) saucepan and cook on medium heat for 5 to 10 minutes. Add salt and pepper to taste.

Italian Corn

1 (16 ounce) package frozen whole kernel corn	455 g
2 slices bacon, cooked, diced	
1 onion, chopped	
1 (15 ounce) can Italian stewed tomatoes	425 g

- Place all ingredients in 2-quart (2 L) pan. Cook until most liquid in tomatoes cooks out. Add a little salt and pepper and serve hot.

Corn Pudding

1 (8 ounce) package corn muffin mix	230 g
1 (15 ounce) can cream-style corn	425 g
½ cup sour cream	120 g
3 eggs, slightly beaten	

- Combine all ingredients and pour into buttered 2-quart (2 L) baking dish.
- Bake uncovered at 350° (175° C) for about 30 minutes.

Stuffed Corn

1 (15 ounce) can cream-style corn	425 g
1 (15 ounce) can whole kernel corn, drained	425 g
½ cup (1 stick) butter, melted	115 g
1 (6 ounce) package chicken stuffing mix	170 g

- Combine all ingredients plus seasoning packet and ½ cup (125 ml) water and mix well. Spoon into buttered 9 x 13-inch (23 x 33 cm) baking pan. Bake at 350° (175° C) for 30 minutes.

Atomic Salsa-Corn

1 (8 ounce) jar hot salsa	230 g
1 (16 ounce) package frozen whole kernel corn, thawed	455 g
¼ teaspoon garlic powder	1 ml
½ cup shredded Monterey Jack cheese	55 g

- Combine hot salsa, corn, garlic powder and ¼ cup (60 ml) water in saucepan. Cook on low-medium heat, stirring occasionally, for 6 minutes. Pour into serving bowl and sprinkle with cheese.

Shoe-Peg Corn

1 (8 ounce) package cream cheese, softened	230 g
½ cup (1 stick) butter, softened	115 g
3 (15 ounce) cans shoe-peg corn	3 (425 g)
1 (4 ounce) can diced green chilies	115 g

- With mixer, beat cream cheese and butter. Add corn and green chilies; mix well. Spoon into 7 x 11-inch (18 x 28 cm) greased baking dish. Bake covered at 350° (175° C) for 25 minutes.

Hot Corn Bake

3 (15 ounce) cans whole kernel corn, drained	3 (425 g)
1 (10 ounce) can cream of celery soup	280 g
1 cup salsa	265 g
1 (8 ounce) package shredded Mexican-cheese blend, divided	230 g

- Combine corn, soup, salsa and half cheese and mix well. Pour into buttered 3-quart (3 L) baking dish and sprinkle remaining cheese on top. Bake at 350° (175° C) for 20 to 30 minutes.

Corn Maize

¼ cup (½ stick) butter, melted	60 g
1 (3 ounce) package cream cheese, softened	85 g
2 (15 ounce) cans whole kernel corn, drained	2 (425 g)
⅓ cup salsa	90 g

- Beat together butter and cream cheese. Add corn and salsa.
- Pour into 2-quart (2 L) buttered baking dish.
- Bake covered at 350° (175° C) for 25 minutes. Serve hot.

Quick Corn-on-the-Cob

1 fresh ear corn-on-the-cob
Salt
Butter

- Microwave 1 ear of corn in its husk for 2 minutes on HIGH (the silky threads come off more easily after corn is cooked) turning once halfway through cooking.
- Or remove husk and silks and wrap ear in wax paper and cook 2 minutes on HIGH, turning once halfway through.
- For multiple ears, double or triple time for two or three ears.

Herb Butter for Corn-on-the-Cob

½ cup (1 stick) butter, softened	115 g
1 teaspoon dried oregano	5 ml
1 teaspoon basil	5 ml
1 tablespoon dried parsley	15 ml
1 teaspoon lemon juice	5 ml

- In bowl, combine butter, oregano, basil, parsley, lemon juice and ½ teaspoon (2 ml) salt, mix well. Transfer to piece of wax paper and roll into a log and refrigerate until firm. When ready to serve, slice herbed butter and serve with the corn.

Calico Corn

1 (16 ounce) package frozen whole kernel corn	455 g
1 bell pepper, chopped	
⅓ cup chopped celery	35 g
1 (10 ounce) can cheddar cheese soup	280 g

- Cook corn in microwave according to package directions and drain well.
- Add bell pepper and celery. Stir in soup and mix well.
- Pour into buttered 2-quart (2 L) baking dish and bake covered at 350° (175° C) for 30 minutes.

Creamy Succotash

2 onions, chopped	
2 tablespoons (¼ stick) butter	30 g
1 (10 ounce) package frozen baby lima beans, thawed	280 g
1 (10 ounce) package frozen whole kernel corn, thawed	280 g
⅔ cup heavy cream	150 ml

- Place onions in skillet with butter and saute until onions are clear, but not brown. Add lima beans and cook 5 minutes, stirring occasionally. Add corn with ample amount of salt and pepper; cook about 2 minutes.
- Stir in heavy cream and cook but do not boil, stirring, until cream is simmering, about 3 minutes or until vegetables are tender.

Spicy Hominy

1 (15 ounce) can yellow hominy, drained	425 g
1 (8 ounce) carton sour cream	230 g
1 (4 ounce) can diced green chilies	115 g
1¼ cups grated cheddar cheese	140 g

- Combine all ingredients and add a little salt. Pour into 1-quart (1 L) baking dish and bake at 350° (175° C) for about 20 minutes.

Fresh Asparagus with Vinaigrette

6 cups diagonally cut asparagus, steamed, chilled	1.1 kg
1 tablespoon sesame seeds, toasted	15 ml
2 tablespoons minced shallots	20 g

Dressing:

1 tablespoon olive oil	15 ml
1 tablespoon rice vinegar	15 ml
1 teaspoon fresh peeled, grated ginger	5 ml
½ teaspoon soy sauce	2 ml
½ teaspoon dried rosemary	2 ml
1 tablespoon honey	15 ml

- Place steamed asparagus, sesame seeds and shallots in serving bowl. Combine all dressing ingredients and pour over asparagus mixture and toss.

Asparagus Caesar

3 (15 ounce) cans asparagus spears, drained	3 (425 g)
¼ cup (½ stick) butter, melted	60 g
3 tablespoons lemon juice	45 ml
½ cup grated parmesan cheese	50 g

- Place asparagus in 2-quart (2 L) baking dish. Drizzle on butter and lemon juice. Sprinkle cheese and bake at 400° (205° C) for 15 to 20 minutes.

Sesame Asparagus

6 fresh asparagus spears, trimmed
1 tablespoon butter   15 ml
1 teaspoon lemon juice   5 ml
1 teaspoon sesame seeds   5 ml

- Place asparagus in skillet. Sprinkle with salt if desired. Add ¼ cup (60 ml) water and bring to boil. Reduce heat. Cover and simmer about 4 minutes. Melt butter and add lemon juice and sesame seeds. Drain asparagus and drizzle with butter mixture.

Quick Microwave Asparagus

1 bunch fresh asparagus
2 tablespoons olive oil   30 ml

- Wash asparagus and dry with paper towels and place in microwave-safe bowl. Drizzle with olive oil and cover with paper towel. Microwave 2 minutes; asparagus should be tender-crisp; if not, continue microwaving until tenderness is reached. (Time will vary depending on your microwave.)
- Slide asparagus to a serving plate and season with salt and pepper.

Parmesan Asparagus

1 bunch fresh asparagus
1 tablespoon olive oil   15 ml
2 tablespoons lemon juice   30 ml
⅓ cup freshly grated parmesan cheese   35 g

- Trim asparagus of woody ends and discard. Place asparagus and oil in large skillet over medium-high heat and saute just until tender-crisp and still bright green in color. Remove from heat and add lemon juice and an ample amount of salt and pepper. Sprinkle with parmesan cheese and serve.

Oven Baked Asparagus

1 bunch fresh asparagus, trimmed
2 tablespoons extra-virgin olive oil   30 ml
2 tablespoons balsamic vinegar   30 ml
⅓ cup freshly grated parmesan cheese   35 g

● Preheat oven to 400° (205° C). Arrange asparagus in single layer in shallow
  baking dish and drizzle olive oil over asparagus. Bake uncovered about
  10 minutes. To serve, sprinkle with a little salt and pepper, vinegar and
  parmesan cheese.

Creamed Asparagus

2 bunches fresh asparagus
1 teaspoon dried basil   5 ml
2 (10 ounce) cans cream of asparagus soup   2 (280 g)
¾ cup Italian breadcrumbs   90 g

● Preheat oven to 325° (165° C). Cut off tough ends of stalks and place in greased
  baking dish. Sprinkle with basil and a little salt. Bake uncovered for
  10 minutes. Place cream of asparagus soup in skillet with ⅓ cup (75 ml) water
  (or milk); heat just enough to mix with water. Spread over baked asparagus
  and sprinkle with Italian breadcrumbs. Bake for 30 minutes.

Baked Asparagus
with Lemon Dressing

2 bunches fresh asparagus
2 tablespoons olive oil   30 ml
1 teaspoon seasoned salt   5 ml

Dressing:
¼ cup lemon juice   60 ml
2 tablespoons finely minced shallots   20 g
⅓ cup olive oil   75 ml
2 eggs, hard-boiled, finely minced

● Preheat oven to 375° (190° C). Place asparagus on rimmed baking sheet and
  drizzle with olive oil; then sprinkle with seasoned salt. Toss to spread oil
  evenly and bake for 15 minutes.

● To make dressing, mix together lemon juice, shallots, a little salt and slowly
  whisk in oil to blend well. Arrange asparagus on serving platter and drizzle
  with lemon juice-olive oil mixture and garnish with minced eggs.

Asparagus Bake

2 (15 ounce) cans cut asparagus spears   2 (425 g)
3 eggs, hard-boiled, chopped
½ cup chopped pecans   55 g
1 (10 ounce) can cream of asparagus soup   280 g

● Arrange asparagus spears in buttered 2-quart (2 L) baking dish. Top with eggs
   and pecans. Heat asparagus soup and add liquid from asparagus spears. Spoon
   over eggs and pecans. Bake covered at 350° (175° C) for 25 minutes.

Almond Asparagus

⅓ cup (⅔ stick) butter   75 g
1 - 1½ pounds fresh asparagus   455 - 680 g
⅔ cup slivered almonds   110 g
1 tablespoon lemon juice   15 ml

● Melt butter in skillet and add asparagus and almonds and saute for 3 to 4
   minutes. Cover and steam about 2 minutes or until tender-crisp. Sprinkle
   lemon and a little salt and pepper over asparagus. Serve hot.

Yummy Cauliflower

1 head cauliflower, cut into florets
1 teaspoon prepared minced garlic   5 ml
⅓ cup mayonnaise   75 g
Dash hot sauce

● Steam cauliflower and garlic in 1½ quarts (1.5 L) water until tender; drain well.
   Transfer to food processor and add mayonnaise, ½ teaspoon (2 ml) salt and
   dash of hot sauce. Process until tender and creamy. Garnish with pepper.

Savory Cauliflower

1 head cauliflower
1 (1 ounce) envelope hollandaise sauce mix   30 g
Fresh parsley to garnish
Lemon slices to garnish, optional

- Cut cauliflower into small florets. Cook in salted water until barely tender. Do not overcook. Mix sauce according to package directions. Drain cauliflower, top with sauce and sprinkle with parsley. Garnish with lemon slices if you like.

Best Cauliflower

1 (16 ounce) package frozen cauliflower   455 g
1 (8 ounce) carton sour cream   230 g
1½ cups shredded American or cheddar cheese   170 g
4 teaspoons sesame seeds, toasted   20 ml

- Cook cauliflower according to package directions. Drain and place half cauliflower in 2-quart (2 L) baking dish. Sprinkle a little salt and pepper on cauliflower. Spread half sour cream and half cheese, top with half sesame seeds and repeat layers. Bake at 350° (175° C) for about 15 to 20 minutes.

Souper Cauliflower

1 (16 ounce) package frozen cauliflower, cooked, drained   455 g
1 (10 ounce) can cream of celery soup   280 g
¼ cup milk   60 ml
1 cup shredded cheddar cheese   115 g

- Place cauliflower in 2-quart (2 L) greased baking dish. In saucepan, combine soup, milk and cheese; heat and mix well. Pour over cauliflower. Bake at 350° (175° C) for 15 minutes.

Creamy Cauliflower

1 head cauliflower, broken into large florets
1 red bell pepper, chopped
1 small zucchini, chopped
1 (10 ounce) can cream of celery soup   280 g
⅓ cup milk   75 ml

- Place cauliflower florets, red bell pepper and zucchini in saucepan with about ¾ cup (175 ml) water and a little salt. Cover and cook on high heat about 10 minutes or until cauliflower is tender. Drain. In smaller saucepan combine soup and milk and heat, stirring until well mixed. Spoon cauliflower, bell pepper and zucchini into serving bowl and pour soup mixture over vegetables.

Best Green Beans

2 pounds fresh green beans, trimmed   910 g
½ pound bacon   230 g
1 bunch fresh green onions, sliced white parts only
1 (4 ounce) can chopped pimentos, drained   115 g

- In large saucepan over high heat, cook beans in ⅓ cup (75 ml) water for 10 minutes or until tender-crisp. Drain

- Cook bacon in skillet until crisp and drain, but set aside about 2 tablespoons (30 ml) drippings. Crumble bacon and place in small bowl. Wipe skillet of drippings; then add set aside drippings. Saute onion over medium-high heat for 1 minute.

- Spoon green beans into skillet with onions. Add pimentos and crumbled bacon; heat mixture until thoroughly hot.

Green Beans and Almonds

2 (16 ounce) packages frozen french-cut green beans   2 (455 g)
2 tablespoons butter   30 g
2 (8 ounce) cans water chestnuts, chopped   2 (230 g)
½ cup slivered almonds, toasted   85 g

- Cook beans according to package directions.
- Drain, add butter and heat just until butter melts. Fold in water chestnuts. Place in serving dish and sprinkle almonds over top.

Crunchy Green Beans

3 (15 ounce) cans whole green beans	3 (425 g)
2 (10 ounce) cans cream of mushroom soup	2 (280 g)
2 (11 ounce) cans water chestnuts, chopped	2 (310 g)
2 (3 ounce) cans french-fried onions	2 (85 g)

● Combine green beans, mushroom soup, water chestnuts, ½ teaspoon (2 ml) salt and a little pepper. Pour mixture into 2-quart (2 L) baking dish. Bake covered at 350° (175° C) for 30 minutes. Remove casserole from oven and sprinkle onions over top; bake for 10 more minutes.

Green Beans

1 pound fresh green beans	455 g
2 tablespoons soy sauce	30 ml
2 tablespoons butter	30 g
¼ teaspoon ground nutmeg	1 ml
½ cup toasted sesame seeds	65 g

● Cook green beans until tender-crisp, about 10 minutes, in medium saucepan.
● Combine soy sauce, nutmeg and butter. Cook over medium heat for a few minutes. Add to green beans and toss lightly. Add sesame seeds and toss again.

Seasoned Green Beans

4 slices bacon, chopped	
1 medium onion, chopped	
2 (15 ounce) cans green beans, drained	2 (425 g)
1 teaspoon sugar	5 ml

● Saute bacon and onion in skillet; drain. Add green beans and sugar and heat thoroughly.

Green Beans with Blue Cheese

1½ pounds fresh green beans, trimmed	680 g
1½ cups chopped, cooked ham (can be leftover)	210 g
¾ cup crumbled blue cheese	130 g
½ cup chopped walnuts, toasted	85 g

- Cut beans to 2-inch (5 cm) pieces and place in steamer basket. Over boiling water, steam beans for 5 minutes. Drain.
- In skillet saute ham in a little oil and add blue cheese and green beans, heat just until cheese has melted. Spoon into serving bowl and sprinkle walnuts over top.

Green Beans and Mushrooms

½ cup (1 stick) butter, divided	60 g
1 small onion, chopped	
1 (8 ounce) carton fresh shiitake mushrooms, sliced	230 g
2 pounds fresh green beans, trimmed	910 g
¾ cup chicken broth	175 ml

- In saucepan, melt half butter and saute onion and mushrooms; transfer to small bowl.
- In same saucepan, melt remaining butter and toss with green beans. Pour chicken broth over beans, bring to a boil; reduce heat, cover and simmer until liquid evaporates and green beans are tender-crisp. Stir in mushroom mixture and season with salt.

Cheddar Fresh Green Beans

1 (6 ounce) can cheddar french-fried onions	170 g
3 pounds fresh green beans, ends trimmed	1.4 kg
¼ cup (½ stick) butter	60 g
2 teaspoons salt free seasoning blend	10 ml

- Preheat oven to 325° (165° C). Place cheddar onions in pan and heat for about 15 minutes.
- In large saucepan, cook green beans in lightly salted water for about 10 minutes or until tender-crisp. Drain well.
- Place butter in small saucepan and over low heat, cook and stir about 5 minutes, being careful not to let butter burn. Remove from heat and add seasoning blend. Pour over beans and toss gently. When ready to serve, toss half cheddar onions with green beans and place in serving bowl. Sprinkle remaining onions over green beans.

Italian Green Beans

1 (16 ounce) package frozen Italian green beans	455 g
3 green onions with tops, chopped	
2 tablespoons butter	30 g
1 teaspoon mixed Italian seasoning	5 ml

- Mix all ingredients in 2-quart (2 L) saucepan and cook according to package directions.

Corny Green Beans

1 (16 ounce) package frozen green beans, thawed, drained	455 g
1 (16 ounce) package frozen whole kernel corn, thawed, drained	455 g
1 (10 ounce) can cream of chicken soup	280 g
1 (8 ounce) carton sour cream	230 g
1 (8 ounce) package shredded 4-cheese blend	230 g
2 cups crushed round butter-flavored crackers	120 g
2 tablespoons butter, melted	30 g

- Preheat oven to 350° (175° C). In large bowl, combine green beans, corn, soup, sour cream, cheese and a little salt, mixing well. Spoon into a greased 9 x 13-inch (23 x 33 cm) baking dish. Combine cracker crumbs and melted butter and sprinkle over top of casserole. Bake uncovered for 30 minutes.

Tangy Carrot Coins

2 (15 ounce) cans sliced carrots	2 (425 g)
2 tablespoons (¼ stick) butter	30 g
2 tablespoons brown sugar	30 g
1 tablespoon dijon-style mustard	15 ml

- Place all ingredients in saucepan. Cook and stir over medium heat for about 2 minutes. Serve hot.

Brown-Sugar Carrots

2 (15 ounce) cans carrots	2 (425 g)
¼ cup (½ stick) butter	60 g
3 tablespoons brown sugar	45 g
½ teaspoon ground ginger	2 ml

- Drain carrots but set aside 2 tablespoons (30 ml) liquid. Combine liquid with butter, brown sugar and ginger. Heat thoroughly. Add carrots, stirring gently, and cook 3 minutes. Serve hot.

Creamy Carrots
with Toasted Almonds

2 (15 ounce) cans sliced carrots	2 (425 g)
1 (10 ounce) can cream of celery soup	280 g
½ cup milk	125 ml
⅓ cup chopped almonds, toasted	55 g

- In saucepan, combine carrots, soup and milk. Over medium heat stir to mix and heat thoroughly. Stir almonds before serving. Serve hot.

Glazed Carrots

1 (16 ounce) package frozen baby carrots	455 g
¼ cup apple cider	60 ml
¼ cup apple jelly	80 g
1½ teaspoons dijon-style mustard	7 ml

- In saucepan place carrots and apple cider and bring to boil. Reduce heat. Cover and simmer about 8 minutes or until carrots are tender. Remove cover and cook on medium heat until liquid evaporates. Stir in jelly and mustard. Cook until jelly melts and carrots glaze.

Caramelized Carrots

1 (16 ounce) package baby carrots	455 g
2 teaspoons soy sauce	10 ml
2 tablespoons brown sugar	30 g
1 tablespoon olive oil	15 ml

- Preheat oven to 425° (220° C). Place carrots in single layer in buttered 7 x 11-inch (18 x 28 cm) baking pan. Combine soy sauce, brown sugar, olive oil and a little salt. Spoon over carrots. Bake for 15 minutes, stirring once.

Simply Sweet Carrots

1 (16 ounce) package baby carrots	455 g
1 (14 ounce) can chicken broth	395 g
½ cup apricot preserves	160 g
1 tablespoon soy sauce	15 ml
1 tablespoon fresh grated ginger	15 ml

- Place carrots and broth in saucepan and bring to a boil; reduce heat to medium and cook for about 14 minutes or until carrots are tender-crisp and liquid is reduced to about ¼ cup (60 ml).
- Stir in apricot preserves, soy sauce and fresh grated ginger; cook another 10 minutes, stirring constantly until mixture thickens and carrots are glazed.

Carrots and Peas

1 (15 ounce) can sliced carrots, drained	425 g
1 (15 ounce) can green peas, drained	425 g
¼ cup (½ stick) butter	60 g
⅓ cup chopped cashews	45 g

- In saucepan, combine carrots, peas, butter and cashews.
- Heat until butter melts and mix well. Serve hot.

Kid-Pleasing Carrots

1 (16 ounce) package baby carrots	455 g
¾ cup orange juice	175 ml
2 tablespoons butter	30 g
2 tablespoon brown sugar	30 g
½ teaspoon ground cumin	2 ml

- Combine all ingredients in saucepan with ¼ cup (60 ml) water. Cook on medium-high about 10 minutes or until carrots are tender and liquid is cooked out.

Dilled Baby Carrots

1 (12 ounce) package fresh baby carrots	340 g
3 chicken bouillon cubes or 2 teaspoons bouillon granules	10 ml
6 tablespoons (¾ stick) butter	85 g
2 teaspoons dillweed	10 ml

- Boil carrots in water with dissolved bouillon cubes until tender (about 8 minutes). Drain.
- Place in skillet with melted butter. Cook on low heat for only a few minutes and make sure butter coats all carrots.
- Sprinkle dillweed over carrots and shake to make sure dill is on all carrots. Place in serving dish and serve immediately.

Cheddar-Broccoli Bake

1 (10 ounce) can cheddar cheese soup	280 g
½ cup milk	125 ml
1 (16 ounce) bag frozen broccoli florets, cooked	455 g
1 (3 ounce) can french-fried onions	85 g

- In 2-quart (2 L) baking dish, mix soup, milk and broccoli.
- Bake at 350° (175° C) for 20 minutes.
- Stir and sprinkle onions over broccoli mixture. Bake for 10 more minutes or until onions are golden.

Buttered Vegetables

½ cup (1 stick) butter	115 g
2 yellow squash, sliced	
1 (16 ounce) package broccoli florets	455 g
1 (10 ounce) package frozen corn	280 g

- Melt butter in large skillet and combine all vegetables. Saute vegetables for about 10 to 15 minutes or until tender-crisp.

Crunchy Broccoli

2 (10 ounce) packages frozen broccoli florets	2 (280 g)
1 (8 ounce) can sliced water chestnuts, drained, chopped	230 g
½ cup (1 stick) butter, melted	115 g
1 (1 ounce) packet dry onion soup mix	30 g

- Place broccoli in microwave-safe dish, cover and microwave for 5 minutes. Turn dish and cook another 4 minutes. Add water chestnuts. Combine melted butter and soup mix and blend well. Toss with cooked broccoli.

Broccoli-Stuffed Tomatoes

4 medium tomatoes	
1 (10 ounce) package frozen chopped broccoli	280 g
1 (6 ounce) roll garlic cheese, softened	170 g
½ teaspoon garlic salt	2 ml

- Cut tops off tomatoes and scoop out pulp. Cook broccoli according to package directions and drain well. Combine broccoli, cheese and garlic salt. Heat just until cheese melts. Stuff broccoli mixture into tomatoes and place on baking sheet.
- Bake at 375° (190° C) for about 10 minutes.

Broccoli with Jazzy Cheese Sauce

1 (24 ounce) package frozen broccoli florets, thawed	680 g
1 (10 ounce) can cream of celery soup	280 g
¾ cup milk	175 ml
¼ teaspoon garlic powder	1 ml
¼ teaspoon cayenne pepper	1 ml
1½ cups cubed processed cheese	210 g

Continued on following page

Continued from previous page

- Place broccoli in microwave-safe bowl and microwave on HIGH about 4 minutes or until tender. Keep warm.
- In saucepan, combine celery soup, milk, garlic powder and cayenne pepper. Heat, stirring until well blended. On low heat, stir in cheese until melted. Spoon over broccoli.

Broccoli Fritters

1 (16 ounce) package frozen chopped broccoli	455 g
2 eggs, lightly beaten	
1 small onion, chopped	
½ cup chopped pecans	55 g
½ cup self-rising flour	65 g

- Cook broccoli according to package directions and drain well. Combine broccoli, eggs, onion, pecans and flour, mixing well.
- Place about ¼ inch (.6 cm) of oil in skillet and heat. Drop broccoli mixture by tablespoonfuls into hot oil and cook, in batches 2 minutes on each side or until light brown. Remove to wire rack on baking pan and keep warm in 200° (93° C) oven until each batch is cooked.

Vegetable Medley

1 (16 ounce) package frozen broccoli, cauliflower and carrots	455 g
1 (16 ounce) package frozen corn	455 g
2 (10 ounce) cans fiesta nacho cheese soup	2 (280 g)
½ cup milk	125 ml

- Combine broccoli mixture and corn in 2-quart (2 L) greased baking dish.
- Combine soup and milk in saucepan and heat just enough to mix well. Pour over vegetables.
- Cover and bake at 350° (175° C) for about 20 minutes.

Creamy Vegetable Casserole

1 (16 ounce) package frozen broccoli, carrots and cauliflower	455 g
1 (10 ounce) can cream of mushroom soup	280 g
1 (8 ounce) carton garden-vegetable cream cheese	230 g
1 cup seasoned croutons	40 g

- Cook vegetables according to package directions, drain and place in large bowl. In saucepan, place soup and cream cheese and heat just enough to mix easily. Pour into vegetable mixture and mix well. Pour into 2-quart (2 L) baking dish.
- Sprinkle with croutons. Bake uncovered at 375° (190° C) for 25 minutes or until bubbly.

Veggies to Love

1 (16 ounce) package frozen broccoli, cauliflower and carrots	455 g
1 (10 ounce) can cream of celery soup	280 g
⅓ cup milk	75 ml
1 (3 ounce) can french-fried onions	85 g

- Cook vegetables according to package directions. Add soup and milk, mix well. Pour into buttered 2-quart (2 L) baking dish and sprinkle french-fried onions over top. Bake at 350° (175° C) for 30 minutes or until bubbly.

Roasted Vegetables

1½ pounds assorted fresh vegetables (squash, carrots, red bell peppers, zucchini, cauliflower and/or broccoli)	680 g
1 (11 ounce) can water chestnuts, drained	310 g
2 tablespoons (¼ stick) butter, melted	30 g
1 (1 ounce) packet savory herb with garlic soup mix	30 g

- Cut all vegetables in 2-inch (5 cm) pieces and place in greased 2-quart (2 L) baking dish with water chestnuts. Combine melted butter and soup mix, drizzle over vegetables and stir well. Cover and bake vegetables at 400° (205° C) for 20 to 25 minutes or until tender and stir once.

Creamy Cabbage Bake

1 head cabbage, shredded
1 (10 ounce) can cream of celery soup   280 g
⅔ cup milk   150 ml
1 (8 ounce) package shredded cheddar cheese   230 g

- Place cabbage in 2-quart (2 L) buttered baking dish. Pour celery soup diluted
  with milk over top of cabbage. Bake covered at 325° (165° C) for 30 minutes.
  Remove from oven, sprinkle with cheese and bake uncovered until it melts.

Quick Fix Cabbage Supper

1 pound Polish sausage, cut in ⅓-inch slices   455 g/8 mm
1 bell pepper, seeded, diced
1 red onion, diced
1 medium size cabbage, cut up
1 (15 ounce) can stewed tomatoes   425 g

- In large skillet, brown sausage slices and remove with slotted spoon; set
  aside. In same skillet with hot drippings, saute bell pepper and red onion for 3
  minutes. Stir in cabbage, cover and cook, stirring occasionally, for 10 minutes.
- Stir in stewed tomatoes and sliced sausage; bring to a boil; reduce heat and
  cook for about 10 minutes or until thoroughly hot.

Scalloped Cabbage

2 small cabbages, cut up
1 (10 ounce) can cream of celery soup   280 g
1 cup shredded cheddar cheese   115 g
⅓ cup crumbled saltine crackers   20 g

- Preheat oven to 350° (175° C). Cut whole cabbages into quarters to easily
  remove thick white core. Place cut up cabbage in saucepan with 2 cups (500
  ml) water and 1 teaspoon (2 ml) salt. Cook 8 minutes and drain. Transfer
  cabbage to 2-quart (2 L) buttered baking dish.
- In saucepan on medium heat, combine celery soup, ½ cup (125 ml) water
  and cheddar cheese; whisk, stirring constantly, until mixture is heated and
  cheese begins to melt. Pour mixture over cabbage and sprinkle with crumbled
  crackers. Bake uncovered 20 minutes.

Speedy Cabbage

1 head cabbage, shredded	
2 tablespoons (¼ stick) butter	30 g
3 tablespoons sour cream	45 g
½ teaspoon sugar	2 ml

- Saute cabbage in butter and about 2 tablespoons (30 ml) water until tender (about 3 to 4 minutes), stirring constantly.
- Stir in sour cream and about ½ teaspoon (2 ml) each of salt and pepper and a little sugar. Serve hot.

Spinach to Like

2 (10 ounce) packages frozen, chopped spinach	2 (280 g)
1 (8 ounce) carton sour cream	230 g
½ (1 ounce) packet dry onion soup mix	½ (30 g)
⅔ cup seasoned breadcrumbs	80 g

- Cook spinach according to package directions and drain well. Add sour cream and onion soup mix to spinach.
- Pour into 2-quart (2 L) baking dish. Sprinkle breadcrumbs on top. Bake at 350° (175° C) for 30 minutes.

Favorite Spinach

2 (10 ounce) packages frozen chopped spinach, thawed, well drained	2 (280 g)
1 (1 ounce) packet dry onion soup mix	30 g
1 (8 ounce) carton sour cream	230 g
⅔ cup shredded Monterey Jack cheese	75 g

- Combine spinach, onion soup mix and sour cream. Pour into buttered 2-quart (2 L) baking dish. Bake at 350° (175° C) for 20 minutes. Take out of oven, sprinkle cheese over top and place casserole back in oven for 5 minutes.

Super Spinach Bake

¼ cup (½ stick) butter	60 g
⅔ cup cracker crumbs	40 g
2 (10 ounce) packages frozen chopped spinach, thawed, drained	2 (280 g)
1 (8 ounce) package shredded cheddar cheese, divided	230 g
1 (8 ounce) carton sour cream	230 g
1 tablespoon dry onion soup mix	15 ml

- Preheat oven to 325° (165° C). Melt butter in skillet over medium heat and add cracker crumbs. Cook, stirring often, for 5 minutes or until crumbs are light brown; set aside.

- In medium bowl, combine spinach, half cheese, sour cream and soup mix. Spoon into sprayed 7 x 11-inch (18 x 28 cm) baking dish. Top with browned crumbs.

- Bake uncovered for 25 minutes. Remove from oven, sprinkle remaining cheese over top and return to oven for 5 minutes.

Herbed Spinach

2 (16 ounce) packages frozen chopped spinach	2 (455 g)
1 (8 ounce) package cream cheese, softened	230 g
¼ cup (½ stick) butter, melted	60 g
1 (6 ounce) package herbed-seasoned stuffing	170 g

- Cook spinach according to package directions. Drain and add cream cheese and half butter. Season with a little salt and pepper.

- Pour into buttered baking dish. Spread herb stuffing on top and drizzle with remaining butter. Bake at 350° (175° C) for 25 minutes.

Easy Spinach Bake

2 (8 ounce) packages cream cheese, softened   2 (230 g)
1 (10 ounce) can cream of chicken soup   280 g
2 (16 ounce) packages frozen chopped spinach, thawed,
   well drained   2 (455 g)
1 cup round crushed, buttery crackers   60 g

● In mixing bowl, beat cream cheese until smooth. Add soup and mix well. Stir
in spinach. Spoon into well greased 3-quart (3 L) baking dish. Sprinkle cracker
crumbs over top of casserole. Bake uncovered at 325° (165° C) for 35 minutes.

Wilted Spinach with Walnuts

2 (8 ounce) packages baby spinach   2 (230 g)
1 teaspoon minced garlic   5 ml
2 tablespoons olive oil   30 ml
Seasoned salt
¼ cup walnut halves, toasted   30 g

● In large skillet, saute spinach and garlic in hot oil on medium-high heat for 6
minutes or until spinach is wilted. Sprinkle a little seasoned salt over spinach
and mix. Toss with whole toasted walnuts. (To toast walnuts, place in a
300°/150° C oven for about 6 minutes.)

Creamy Spinach

1 (16 ounce) package frozen chopped spinach   455 g
1 (8 ounce) carton whipping cream   250 ml
3 tablespoons butter   45 g
½ cup grated parmesan cheese   50 g

● Cook spinach according to package directions. Place whipping cream in
heavy saucepan and cook on medium heat until cream is reduced by half. Stir
in spinach, stirring well to coat spinach. Add butter and cheese while heat is
still on medium and stir until mixture is thoroughly hot. Stir in a little salt and
pepper.

Spinach and Ravioli Supreme

1 (6 ounce) package baby spinach	170 g
½ cup extra-virgin olive oil	125 ml
⅔ cup pine nuts	85 g
2 (10 ounce) packages refrigerated cheese ravioli	2 (280 g)

- In food processor, combine spinach, oil, pine nuts and an ample amount of salt and pepper. Pulse until mixture is well blended. Place mixture in pint jar.
- In boiling water, cook cheese ravioli according to package directions and drain. Stir in ¾ cup (175 ml) spinach mixture and toss gently. Serve hot. Refrigerate remaining spinach mixture for another use; it can be kept for 1 week.

Creamed Spinach Bake

1 (16 ounce) package frozen chopped spinach	455 g
2 (3 ounce) packages cream cheese, softened	2 (85 g)
3 tablespoons butter	45 g
1 cup Italian-style seasoned breadcrumbs	120 g

- In saucepan, cook spinach with ¾ cup (175 ml) water for 6 minutes, drain thoroughly and pat dry with paper towels. Add cream cheese and butter and heat until they melt and mix well with spinach.
- Pour into greased 2-quart (2 L) baking dish. Sprinkle a little salt over spinach and cover with breadcrumbs.
- Bake uncovered at 350° (175° C) for 15 to 20 minutes.

Eggplant in Marinara Sauce

1 medium eggplant	
Olive oil	
1 (16 ounce) carton marinara sauce	455 g
1 (8 ounce) package shredded mozzarella cheese	230 g

- Cut eggplant into ½-inch (1.2 cm) slices and brush with olive oil. Place slices on greased baking pan and broil for 6 to 8 minutes.
- While eggplant is broiling, spoon marinara sauce in 9 x 13-inch (23 x 33 cm) baking dish. Top with half eggplant slices and half cheese; repeat layers. Bake at 325° (165°) for about 10 minutes or until hot and bubbly.

Cheesy Baked Eggplant

1 eggplant
½ cup mayonnaise   110 g
1 cup seasoned breadcrumbs   60 g
¼ cup grated parmesan cheese   25 g

- Peel eggplant and slice ½-inch (1.2 cm) thick. Spread both sides with mayonnaise and dip in mixture of crumbs and cheese. Coat both sides well. Place in single layer in shallow baking dish. Bake at 400° (205° C) for 20 minutes.

Baked Eggplant

1 medium eggplant
¼ cup (½ stick) butter, melted   60 g
1 (5 ounce) can evaporated milk   150 ml
1½ cups cracker crumbs   90 g

- Peel, slice and boil eggplant until tender enough to mash. Season with a little salt and pepper. Add all other ingredients.
- Pour into 2-quart (2 L) buttered baking dish. Bake at 350° (175° C) for 25 minutes.

Brussels Sprouts and Onions

1 (10 ounce) container brussels sprouts   280 g
1 (10 ounce) bag pearl onions   280 g
3 slices bacon
1 teaspoon chopped fresh thyme   5 ml

- In large saucepan, bring to a boil 1½ quarts (1.5 L) water and a little salt. Add brussels sprouts and onions and cook 2 minutes, drain. (Some of the onion outer layer may need to be removed).
- Cook bacon until crisp in skillet, drain on paper towels, returning bacon drippings to skillet.
- Add sprouts, onions, fresh thyme and salt to taste and stir to coat vegetables with drippings. Heat just until ingredients are warm and spoon into serving dish. Top with crumbled bacon.

Creamy Brussels Sprouts

4 cups fresh brussels sprouts	350 g
1 onion, chopped	
¼ cup (½ stick) butter	60 g
1 pint carton sour cream	455 g

- Take each brussels sprout and cut a crisscross gash on bottom of each so that the tougher ends cook as quickly as the tops. In saucepan, steam or boil sprouts until tender.
- Saute onion in skillet with butter; add sour cream and heat, stirring constantly. Gently mix in sprouts. Serve immediately.

Baked Squash

5 cups squash, cooked, drained	900 g
¾ cup grated Monterey Jack cheese	85 g
1 (10 ounce) can cream of chicken soup	280 g
1 (16 ounce) box herb dressing mix	455 g

- Place cooked squash in mixing bowl and season with salt to taste. Add cheese and soup; blend well. Mix dressing according to package directions. Place half dressing in 9 x 13-inch (23 x 33 cm) greased baking dish. Spoon squash mixture on top and sprinkle remaining dressing on top. Bake uncovered at 375° (190° C) for 30 minutes.

Creamy Squash

6 - 8 medium yellow squash, cut in small pieces	
1 (8 ounce) package cream cheese, cubed, softened	230 g
2 tablespoons (¼ stick) butter	30 ml
½ teaspoon sugar	2 ml

- Place squash in large saucepan. Cover with water and boil for 10 to 15 minutes or until tender. Drain liquid, and add cream cheese, butter, ¾ teaspoon (4 ml) each of salt and pepper, and sugar. Cook over low heat and stir until cream cheese melts. Serve hot.

Posh Squash

8 medium yellow squash, sliced
½ green bell pepper, seeded, chopped
1 small onion, chopped
1 (8 ounce) package cubed Mexican processed cheese   230 g

- Combine squash, bell pepper and onion in large saucepan and just barely cover with water. Cook 10 to 15 minutes until tender. Drain and add cheese. Stir until cheese melts and pour into buttered 2-quart (2 L) baking dish. Bake at 350° (175° C) for 15 minutes.

Seasoned Squash and Onion

8 yellow squash, sliced
2 onions, chopped
¼ cup (½ stick) butter   60 g
1 cup grated American cheese   115 g

- Cook squash and onion in small amount of water until tender and drain. Add butter and cheese and toss. Serve hot.

Stir-Fry Squash-Onions

¼ cup extra-virgin olive oil   60 ml
4 medium zucchini, sliced
3 medium yellow squash, sliced
1 red and 1 green bell pepper, julienned
2 yellow onions, sliced, cut into rings

- Heat skillet with oil on medium heat and stir-fry zucchini, squash, bell peppers and onions about 30 minutes, tossing several times to allow vegetables to brown lightly. Season with 1 teaspoon (5 ml) each of salt and pepper and serve immediately.

Sunny Yellow Squash

6 - 8 medium yellow squash, cut up
1 (8 ounce) package cream cheese, softened, cubed   230 g
2 tablespoons (¼ stick) butter   30 g
1 teaspoon sugar   5 ml

- In saucepan, add squash with a little water and boil until tender. Drain. Add
  cream cheese, butter, sugar and a little salt and pepper. Cook over low heat and
  stir until cream cheese melts.

Creamed Yellow Squash

6 medium size yellow squash
2 tablespoons butter   30 g
1 (8 ounce) package cream cheese   230 g
½ cup seasoned breadcrumbs, optional   60 g

- Cut squash into small chunks and place in saucepan. Just barely cover with
  water and bring to a boil. Reduce heat to medium, stirring several times and
  cook about 10 to 15 minutes or until some chunks become very soft. Drain.
  Spoon into serving dish and keep warm.
- While saucepan is still on medium heat, stir in butter, cream cheese and salt
  and pepper to taste; stir and heat until butter and cream cheese is creamy. Pour
  over squash and sprinkle seasoned breadcrumbs over top.

Seasoned Zucchini and Leeks

¼ cup (½ stick) butter   60 g
2 large leeks, finely chopped
6 small-medium zucchini, chopped
1 teaspoon garlic powder   5 ml

- Place butter in skillet and saute leeks about 2 minutes. Stir in zucchini, garlic
  powder and 1 teaspoon (5 ml) salt. Cover and cook on medium heat for 15
  minutes, stirring occasionally.

Fried Zucchini

3 large zucchini, grated
5 eggs
⅓ (12 ounce) box round buttery crackers, crushed   ⅓ (340 g)
½ cup grated parmesan cheese   50 g

- Combine zucchini, eggs and cracker crumbs; mix well. Add cheese and a little salt and pepper. Drop by spoonfuls into skillet with a little oil. Fry about 15 minutes; brown each side.

Zucchini and Creamy Penne

4 medium zucchini, sliced
1 (16 ounce) package penne pasta   455 g
1 (8 ounce) carton whipping cream   230 g
6 ounces crumbled goat cheese   170 g

- In saucepan, cook zucchini in a little salted water, drain and add 1 tablespoon (15 ml) olive oil. Cook penne according to package directions. Drain and add another tablespoon olive oil.
- While zucchini and pasta are still hot, combine and stir in whipping cream and goat cheese; toss. Serve hot.

Walnut Zucchini

6 - 8 zucchini, julienned
½ red bell pepper, julienned
¼ cup (½ stick) butter   60 g
1 cup chopped walnuts   130 g

- Saute zucchini and bell pepper in butter until tender. Shake pan and toss zucchini to cook evenly. Pour off any excess butter.
- Add chopped walnuts and a little salt and pepper. When walnuts blend and heat, serve immediately.

Creamy Zucchini

6 - 8 medium zucchini, sliced	
1 teaspoon beau monde seasoning	5 ml
1 (8 ounce) carton sour cream	230 g
¼ cup grated parmesan cheese	60 ml

- Saute zucchini in 2 tablespoons (30 g) butter. Cook on low for 5 minutes. Stir in seasoning, sour cream and cheese. Heat but do not boil.

Speedy Zucchini and Fettuccine

1 (9 ounce) package refrigerated fettuccine	255 g
⅓ cup extra-virgin olive oil, divided	75 ml
1 tablespoon minced garlic	15 ml
4 small zucchini, grated	
1 tablespoon lemon juice	15 ml
½ cup pine nuts, toasted	65 g
⅓ cup grated parmesan cheese	35 g

- Cook fettuccine according to package directions, drain and place in serving bowl. Heat large skillet over high heat and add 2 tablespoons (30 ml) oil, garlic and zucchini. Saute for 1 minute.
- Add zucchini mixture to pasta. Add lemon juice, pine nuts and salt and pepper to taste. Stir in remaining olive oil and toss to combine. To serve, sprinkle parmesan cheese over top of dish.

Zucchini Patties

1½ cups grated zucchini	190 g
1 egg, beaten	
2 tablespoons flour	15 g
⅓ cup finely minced onion	55 g
3 tablespoons olive oil	45 ml

- Mix all ingredients except oil and add ½ teaspoon (2 ml) salt. Heat oil in skillet. Drop zucchini mixture by tablespoons into skillet at medium to high heat. Turn and brown both sides. Remove and drain on paper towels.

Zucchini and Fettuccine Toss

2 pounds small zucchini, cubed	910 g
¼ cup (½ stick) butter	60 g
2 (9 ounce) packages fresh fettuccine	2 (255 g)
⅓ cup grated parmesan cheese	50 g

- In skillet, saute zucchini in butter about 5 minutes, stirring several times. Cook fettuccine according to package directions; drain well and combine with cooked zucchini. Sprinkle dish with parmesan cheese. Serve hot.

TIP: If you want to make this a main dish, stir in 2 cups (280 g) cubed leftover cooked ham.

Swiss Cheesy Peas

3 (15 ounce) cans green peas and onions, drained	3 (425 g)
1 (8 ounce) carton sour cream	230 g
1 (8 ounce) package grated Swiss cheese	230 g
2 cups crushed corn flakes	70 g

- In large bowl, combine peas, onions, sour cream, Swiss cheese and salt to taste. Spoon into buttered 3-quart (3 L) baking dish. Sprinkle corn flakes over top. Bake uncovered at 350° (175° C) for 35 minutes.

Sesame Peas

1 (10 ounce) package frozen green peas	280 g
2 tablespoons sesame seeds	15 g
1 teaspoon sugar	5 ml
¼ cup (½ stick) butter	60 g

- Cook peas according to package directions and drain.
- In saucepan, heat remaining ingredients. Pour over peas. Serve hot.

Parmesan Peas

2 (10 ounce) packages frozen green peas	2 (280 g)
3 tablespoons butter, melted	45 g
1 tablespoon lemon juice	15 ml
⅓ cup grated parmesan cheese	35 g

- Microwave peas in 2 tablespoons (30 ml) water for 3 minutes. Rotate bowl and cook for another 3 minutes. Stir in butter, lemon juice and parmesan.

Minted Peas

1 teaspoon dried mint leaves	5 ml
Pinch of sugar	
1 (10 ounce) package frozen tiny peas, thawed	280 g

- In saucepan, combine ½ cup (125 ml) water, mint, sugar, salt and pepper to taste and bring to boil. Add peas and cook for 2 minutes. Drain slightly and add lump of butter.

Creamed Peas and Potatoes

2 pounds small new potatoes, quartered	910 g
1 (10 ounce) can cream of mushroom soup	280 g
⅓ cup milk	75 ml
1 (10 ounce) package frozen peas with pearl onions	280 g

- Cook new potatoes in boiling water for 25 minutes; drain. Add soup, milk, peas and ½ teaspoon (2 ml) pepper; stir occasionally.

Cheesy Peas Please

1 (10 ounce) can cream of mushroom soup	280 g
1 (6 ounce) roll garlic cheese	170 g
2 (15 ounce) cans green peas, drained	2 (425 g)
⅛ teaspoon cayenne	.5 ml

- In saucepan, heat soup and cheese until cheese melts. Add peas and cayenne and heat.

Italian White Beans

1 onion, coarsely chopped	
1 bell pepper, seeded, chopped	
2 teaspoons minced garlic	10 ml
2 tablespoons olive oil	30 ml
2 (15 ounce) cans great northern beans, drained	2 (425 g)
1 teaspoon sugar	5 ml
1 teaspoon white wine vinegar	5 ml
1 roll commercially prepared polenta	
½ cup grated parmesan cheese	50 g

- In large saucepan, saute onion, bell pepper and garlic in olive oil. Stir in beans, sugar, vinegar and salt and pepper to taste. Cook and stir over medium heat until mixture is hot. Serve over sliced, heated polenta sprinkled with parmesan cheese.

Southwest Bean Bake

1 (15 ounce) can kidney beans, rinsed, drained	425 g
1 (15 ounce) can navy beans, rinsed, drained	425 g
1 (15 ounce) can Mexican stewed tomatoes	425 g
¾ cup salsa	175 g
¼ cup packed light brown sugar	55 g

- Heat oven to 400° (205° C). Combine all ingredients and pour into 3 quart (3 L) greased baking dish. Bake for 20 minutes.

Chili-Baked Beans

2 (15 ounce) cans pork and beans, drained	2 (425 g)
1 (15 ounce) can chili with beans	425 g
¼ cup molasses	60 ml
1 teaspoon chili powder	5 ml

- In 2-quart (2 L) baking dish, combine pork and beans, chili, molasses and chili powder. Heat until bubbly.

Classic Baked Bean Stand-By

3 (18 ounce) cans baked beans   3 (510 g)
½ cup chili sauce   135 g
⅓ cup packed brown sugar   75 g
4 slices bacon, cooked, crumbled

- In buttered 3-quart (3 L) baking dish, combine baked beans, chili sauce and brown sugar. Bake at 325° (165° C) for 30 minutes. When ready to serve, sprinkle bacon on top.

Lima Beans

1 (16 ounce) package frozen baby lima beans   455 g
1 cup chopped celery   100 g
3 tablespoons butter   45 g
2 teaspoons lemon juice   10 ml

- Place all ingredients in 2-quart (2 L) saucepan and add ⅓ cup (75 ml) water. Cook until vegetables are tender-crisp.

Barbecued Baby Limas

1 (10 ounce) package frozen baby lima beans   280 g
⅓ cup chili sauce   90 g
¼ teaspoon chili powder   1 ml
2 tablespoons brown sugar   30 g

- Cook lima beans according to package directions, drain and add chili sauce, chili powder and brown sugar, mixing gently.
- Simmer ingredients together for about 10 minutes to blend flavors.

Fried Green Tomatoes

1 pound green tomatoes	455 g
1 cup flour	120 g
1 - 2 tablespoons light brown sugar	15 - 30 g
Canola oil	

- Cut ends off tomatoes, slice ⅓-inch (8 mm) thick and lay on paper towels to drain. Mix flour, brown sugar, ½ teaspoon (2 ml) each of salt and pepper in shallow bowl.
- Dredge tomatoes in flour thoroughly. Heat oil and carefully place each slice in skillet. When 1 side of tomato is crispy and golden turn to brown other side. Drain on paper towels and serve immediately.

Baked Tomatoes with Basil

3 large tomatoes	
1½ cups seasoned breadcrumbs	180 g
¼ cup (½ stick) butter	60 g
Dried basil	

- Cut tomatoes in half or slice tomatoes in ½ to 1-inch (1.2 to 2.5 cm) thick slices and place on baking sheet. Sprinkle slices generously with breadcrumbs and top with butter and basil. Bake at 350° (175° C) for 10 to 15 minutes or until light brown on top.

Stewed-Tomato Casserole

2 (15 ounce) cans Mexican-style stewed tomatoes	2 (425 g)
2 onions, sliced	
1¼ cups cracker crumbs	75 g
1 cup shredded cheddar cheese	115 g

- In 2-quart (2 L) baking dish layer tomatoes, onions, cracker crumbs and cheese and repeat layers. Sprinkle with a little salt and pepper. Bake at 350° (175° C) for 35 minutes.

Stewed Okra and Tomatoes

2 tablespoons olive oil	30 ml
1 small onion, chopped	
4 - 5 cups okra pods, trimmed	400 - 500 g
1 (15 ounce) can stewed tomatoes	425 g

- In skillet on medium heat, place oil and chopped onion and saute for 5 minutes. Add okra, stewed tomatoes and bring to a boil. Reduce heat, cover and simmer for 15 minutes.

Fried Okra

Small, fresh garden okra
Milk or buttermilk
Cornmeal
Canola oil

- Thoroughly wash and drain okra. Cut off top and ends and slice. Toss okra with a little milk or buttermilk (just enough to make cornmeal stick). Sprinkle cornmeal and a little salt and pepper over okra and toss. Heat 2 or 3 tablespoons (30 to 45 ml) oil in skillet. Fry okra, turning several times, until okra is golden brown and crisp.

Black-Eyed Peas and Okra

3 (15 ounce) cans black-eyed peas, drained	3 (425 g)
¾ cup shredded ham	105 g
1 onion, chopped	
1 pound small fresh whole okra pods	455 g

- In large saucepan, combine peas, ham and onion and bring to a boil.
- Place okra on top of pea-onion mixture and do not stir.
- Bring to boil again, lower heat, cover and simmer about 5 to 10 minutes or until okra is tender. Serve hot.

Southern Hoppin' John

1 pound bulk sausage	455 g
1 (16 ounce) package frozen chopped onion and bell peppers	455 g
1 (14 ounce) can chicken broth	395 g
1¼ cups instant rice	120 g
2 (15 ounce) cans black-eyed peas	2 (425 g)

- In large pot, brown and cook sausage, onions and bell peppers over medium-high heat. Drain and add chicken broth, rice and salt and pepper to taste. Bring to a boil, reduce heat and simmer for 15 minutes, stirring occasionally.
- Drain and rinse peas and add to pot. Simmer for an additional 10 minutes or until liquid is absorbed.

Hoppin' John

4 slices bacon	
1 onion, chopped	
1 cup instant rice	95 g
1 (15 ounce) can black-eyed peas with liquid	425 g

- Fry bacon and drain. Saute onion in bacon grease.
- In large saucepan, combine onion, bacon grease, a little salt, rice and 1½ cups (375 ml) water. Bring to boil. Cover, lower heat and simmer for 10 minutes. Add bacon and black-eyed peas and simmer 5 more minutes. Remove from heat and allow to stand for 5 minutes until liquid absorbs.

Caramelized Onions

2 tablespoons butter	30 g
2 tablespoons bacon drippings	30 ml
3 yellow onions, sliced	

- Melt butter with bacon drippings in large skillet over medium-high heat. Add onions with a little salt and ¼ teaspoon (1 ml) pepper and saute about 20 minutes or until light golden brown.

Cheesy Baked Onions

4 yellow onions, peeled, sliced
½ cup (1 stick) butter   115 g
25 round, buttery crackers, crushed
⅓ cup grated parmesan cheese   35 g

- Saute onions in butter until transparent. Spread half onions in buttered
  2-quart (2 L) buttered casserole dish. Top with half crackers and half cheese.
  Repeat layers.
- Bake uncovered at 325° (165° C) for 30 minutes.

Cheesy Onion Casserole

5 sweet onions, sliced
½ cup (1 stick) butter   115 g
1 cup shredded cheddar cheese   115 g
22 saltine crackers, crushed

- Saute onions in butter until soft. In buttered 2-quart (2 L) baking dish layer
  half onions, half cheese, half crackers and repeat layers. Bake at 325° (165° C)
  for 30 minutes.

Onion Tart

Frozen 8-inch piecrust (from 15 ounce package of 2)   20 cm/425 g
2 medium-size onions, sliced
¼ cup (½ stick) butter   60 g
5 eggs, well beaten

- Preheat oven to 375° (190° C). Line pie pan with crust and refrigerate while
  making filling.
- In skillet, saute onion in butter; cook only until onions are transparent but still
  firm. Sprinkle with an ample amount of salt and pepper and spoon onions into
  piecrust. Pour beaten eggs over onions. Cook for 5 minutes and then reduce
  heat to 250° (120° C) and bake for another 25 minutes or until custard is set and
  light brown on top.

Creamed Onions and Peas

1 (10 ounce) can cream of celery soup	280 g
½ cup milk	125 ml
3 (15 ounce) jars tiny white onions, drained	3 (425 g)
1 (10 ounce) package frozen peas	280 g
½ cup slivered almonds	85 g
3 tablespoons grated parmesan cheese	20 g

- Preheat oven to 350° (175° C). In large saucepan, combine soup and milk, heat and stir until bubbly. Gently stir in onions, peas and almonds, mixing well.
- Spoon into greased 2-quart (2 L) baking dish. Sprinkle with parmesan cheese.
- Cover and bake for 30 minutes.

Onion Rings

1 yellow onion, sliced	
2⅓ cups biscuit mix, divided	280 g
1 cup beer	250 ml
2 eggs, slightly beaten	

- Separate onion rings and toss with ⅓ cup (40 g) biscuit mix. Stir together remaining biscuit mix, beer, eggs and a little salt.
- Heat oil to 375° (190° C) in deep fryer or large saucepan. Dip onion rings, a few at a time into batter, letting excess drip back into bowl. Fry for about 2 minutes and, turning with fork, fry until golden brown and drain on paper towels.

Celery with Water Chestnuts

1 bunch celery, chopped diagonally	
1 (8 ounce) can water chestnuts, drained, chopped	230 g
¼ cup slivered almonds, toasted	40 g
¼ cup (½ stick) butter, melted	60 g

- Boil celery in salted water just until tender-crisp and drain. Saute water chestnuts and almonds in melted butter. Toss celery with water chestnut-almond mixture. Serve hot.

Herb-Seasoned Vegetables

1 (14 ounce) can seasoned chicken broth with Italian herbs	395 g
½ teaspoon garlic powder	2 ml
1 (16 ounce) package frozen vegetables	455 g
½ cup grated parmesan cheese	50 g

- Heat broth, garlic and vegetables to boil. Cover and cook over low heat for 5 minutes or until tender-crisp and drain. Place in serving dish and sprinkle cheese over vegetables.

Cheesy Macaroni Stuffed Peppers

4 large green bell peppers	
1 (22 ounce) carton refrigerated macaroni and cheese	625 g
1 cup shredded cheddar cheese	115 g

- Preheat oven to 350° (175° C). Cut peppers in half lengthwise and remove seeds and veins. Steam, covered in simmering water for 8 minutes; drain well. Heat macaroni and cheese in microwave as instructed on package and generously fill each pepper half with macaroni and cheese and place in greased baking dish.
- Bake for about 10 minutes or just until macaroni and cheese is bubbly. Remove from oven and sprinkle 1 tablespoon (15 ml) cheddar cheese over each pepper and return to oven for 5 minutes. Sprinkle a little paprika over top of each pepper before serving.

Hot Mustard Sauce for Vegetables

1 (10 ounce) can cream of celery soup	280 g
½ cup milk	125 ml
2 tablespoons prepared mustard	30 g
Pinch of sugar	

- In saucepan, combine soup, milk, mustard and pinch of salt and sugar. Heat until well blended. Serve over cooked vegetables.

Black Bean Salsa

1 (15 ounce) can black beans with jalapeno, rinsed, drained	425 g
1 (8 ounce) can whole kernel corn, drained	230 g
⅓ cup chopped red onion	55 g
⅓ cup lime juice	75 ml
1 teaspoon minced garlic and fajita seasoning	5 ml

- Place half of beans in shallow bowl and mash slightly. Combine mashed beans, whole beans and all remaining ingredients and refrigerate for 30 minutes before serving.

Rush-Hour
Main Dishes

Chicken
Beef
Pork
Seafood

Adobe Chicken

2 cups cooked brown rice	390 g
1 (10 ounce) can diced tomatoes and green chilies, drained	280 g
3 cups chopped cooked chicken	420 g
1 (8 ounce) package shredded Monterey Jack cheese, divided	230 g

- Combine rice, tomatoes and green chilies, chicken and half cheese.
- Spoon into buttered, 7 x 11-inch (18 x 28 cm) baking dish. Cook covered at 325° (165° C) for 30 minutes.
- Uncover, sprinkle remaining cheese over casserole and return to oven for 5 minutes.

Alfredo Chicken

5 - 6 boneless, skinless chicken breast halves	
1 (16 ounce) package frozen broccoli florets, thawed	455 g
1 red bell pepper, seeded, chopped	
1 (16 ounce) jar alfredo sauce	455 g

- Preheat oven to 325° (165° C). Brown and cook chicken breasts in large skillet with a little oil until juices run clear. Transfer to greased 9 x 13-inch (23 x 33 cm) baking dish.
- Microwave broccoli according to package directions and drain. (If broccoli stems are extra long, trim and discard.) Spoon broccoli and bell pepper over chicken.
- In small saucepan, heat alfredo sauce with ¼ cup (60 ml) water. Pour over chicken and vegetables. Cover and cook for 15 to 20 minutes.

Almond Crusted Chicken

1 egg	
¼ cup seasoned breadcrumbs	30 g
1 cup sliced almonds	190 g
4 boneless, skinless chicken breast halves	
1 (5 ounce) package grated parmesan cheese	140 g

Continued on following page

Continued from previous page

Sauce:

1 teaspoon minced garlic	5 ml
⅓ cup finely chopped onion	55 g
2 tablespoons oil	30 ml
1 cup white wine	250 ml
¼ cup teriyaki sauce	60 ml

- Preheat oven to 350° (175° C).
- Place egg and 1 teaspoon (5 ml) water in shallow bowl and beat. In another shallow bowl, combine breadcrumbs and almonds. Dip each chicken breast in egg, then in almond mixture and place in greased 9 x 13-inch (23 x 33 cm) baking pan. Bake uncovered for 20 minutes. Sprinkle parmesan cheese over each breast and bake for another 15 minutes or until almonds and cheese are golden brown.
- While chicken is cooking, saute garlic and onion in oil in small saucepan. Add wine and teriyaki; bring to a boil, reduce heat and simmer about 10 minutes or until mixture is reduced by half.
- To serve, divide sauce among four plates and place chicken breast on top.

Wild Rice and Chicken

1 (6 ounce) package long grain-wild rice mix	170 g
4 boneless, skinless chicken breast halves	
½ cup (1 stick) butter, divided	115 g
1 large red bell pepper, chopped	

- Prepare rice according to package directions. In large skillet, cook chicken in 2 tablespoons (30 g) butter and make sure each chicken breast browns on both sides. Remove chicken and keep warm. Add remaining butter to pan drippings and saute red pepper until tender. Add to rice. Serve with cooked chicken breasts.

Wine and Chicken

6 - 8 boneless, skinless chicken breast halves	
1 (10 ounce) can cream of mushroom soup	280 g
1 (10 ounce) can cream of onion soup	280 g
1 cup white wine	250 ml

- In skillet, brown chicken in little bit of oil. Place in 9 x 13-inch (23 x 33 cm) baking dish. Combine soups and wine and pour over chicken. Bake covered at 375° (190° C) for 25 minutes. Uncover and bake another 20 minutes.

Chicken and Orzo Supper

1 (5.6 once) box chicken-flavored orzo	155 g
1 (7 ounce) package cooked chicken strips	200 g
1 (10 ounce) package frozen corn	280 g
1 (10 ounce) package frozen cut green beans	280 g
¼ cup extra-virgin olive oil	60 ml
1 teaspoon minced garlic	5 ml

- Cook orzo according to package directions. Add remaining ingredients, ¼ cup (60 ml) water and a little salt and pepper, mixing well. Cook on low heat, stirring several times, until mixture is hot (about 10 to 15 minutes).

Alfredo Chicken Spaghetti

1 (8 ounce) package thin spaghetti, broken in thirds	230 g
2 teaspoons minced garlic	10 ml
1 (16 ounce) jar alfredo sauce	455 g
About ¼ cup milk	60 ml
1 (10 ounce) box broccoli florets, thawed	280 g
2 cups cooked, diced chicken	280 g

- Cook spaghetti according to package directions and drain. Place back in saucepan and stir in garlic, alfredo sauce and milk, mixing well. Add drained broccoli florets and cook on medium heat, stirring several times, for about 5 minutes or until broccoli is tender, adding more milk if mixture gets too dry.
- Stir in diced chicken and spoon into serving bowl.

Asparagus-Cheese Chicken

1 tablespoon butter	15 ml
4 boneless, skinless chicken breast halves	
1 (10 ounce) can broccoli-cheese soup	280 g
1 (10 ounce) package frozen asparagus cuts	280 g
⅓ cup milk	75 ml

- Heat butter in skillet and cook chicken 10 minutes or until brown on both sides. Remove chicken and set aside.
- In same skillet, combine soup, asparagus and milk. Heat to boil, return chicken to skillet and reduce heat to low.
- Cover and simmer for 25 minutes until chicken is no longer pink and asparagus is tender.

Bacon-Wrapped Chicken

6 boneless, skinless chicken breast halves	
1 (8 ounce) carton cream cheese with onion and chives	230 g
Butter	
6 bacon strips	

- Flatten chicken to ½-inch (1.2 cm) thickness. Spread 3 tablespoons (45 g) cream cheese over each. Dot with butter and a little salt; roll. Wrap each with bacon strip. Place seam-side down in greased 9 x 13-inch (23 x 33 cm) baking dish.
- Bake uncovered at 375° (190° C) for 35 to 40 minutes or until juices run clear. To brown, broil 6 inches (15 cm) from heat for about 3 minutes or until bacon is crisp.

Cheesy Crusted Chicken

¾ cup mayonnaise (not light)	170 g
½ cup grated parmesan cheese	50 g
5 - 6 boneless, skinless chicken breast halves	
1 cup Italian seasoned dry breadcrumbs	120 g

- Preheat oven to 400° (205° C). Combine mayonnaise and cheese. Place chicken breasts on sheet of wax paper and spread mayonnaise-cheese mixture over chicken. Sprinkle heavily with breadcrumbs and turn breasts over and sprinkle heavily with breadcrumbs.
- Place chicken on large greased baking pan making sure pieces do not touch. Bake 20 minutes (25 minutes if chicken pieces are fairly large). Chicken pieces can be sliced and placed on serving platter.

Glazed Chicken

4 skinless, boneless chicken breast halves
1 (20 ounce) can pineapple chunks   570 g
½ cup refrigerated dijon-style honey-mustard   125 g
1 green bell pepper, thinly sliced
1 red bell pepper, thinly sliced
Couscous, cooked

- Cut chicken breasts into strips, add a little salt and pepper and brown in large
  skillet with a little oil. Add liquid from pineapple, cover and simmer for
  15 minutes.

- Add honey-mustard, bell peppers and pineapple chunks to chicken. Bring
  to a boil, reduce heat, cover and simmer for another 15 minutes. Serve over
  couscous.

Chicken and Shrimp Curry

2 (10 ounce) cans cream of chicken soup   2 (280 g)
⅓ cup milk   75 ml
1½ teaspoons curry powder   7 ml
1 (12 ounce) can boned chicken   340 g
1 (6 ounce) can shrimp, drained, veined   170 g
Rice, cooked

- In saucepan, heat soup, milk and curry powder; stir in chicken pieces and
  shrimp. Serve over rice.

Chicken for Lunch

4 thick cooked deli chicken breast slices
1 (3 ounce) package cream cheese, softened   85 g
3 tablespoons salsa   45 g
2 tablespoons mayonnaise   30 g

- Place chicken slices on a bed of shredded lettuce on individual salad plates.

- Use mixer to blend cream cheese, salsa and mayonnaise. Place heaping
  tablespoon (15 ml) on top of chicken slices. Serve cold.

Baked Chicken and Mushrooms

2 (10 ounce) cans cream of mushrooms soup	2 (280 g)
1 soup can milk	
2 teaspoons curry powder	10 ml
1 (4 ounce) can sliced mushrooms	115 g
2½ cups cooked rice (use instant)	415g
1 (8 ounce) can green peas, drained	230 g
3 cups cooked, cubed chicken	420 g
2 cups slightly crushed potato chips	110 g

- Preheat oven to 350° (175° C). In large bowl, combine soup, milk, curry powder, mushrooms, rice, peas, chicken and salt and pepper to taste; mix well.
- Spoon into greased 9 x 13-inch (23 x 33 cm) baking pan. Cover and bake for 20 minutes. Remove from oven and sprinkle with crushed potato chips and return to oven for another 15 minutes.

Cheesy Swiss Chicken

4 boneless, skinless chicken breast halves	
⅓ cup refrigerated honey-mustard dressing	75 ml
1 (8 slices) package fully cooked bacon	
4 slices Swiss cheese	

- In large skillet with a little oil, cook chicken breasts on medium-high heat for 5 minutes. Remove chicken to cutting board and liberally spread each breast with honey-mustard dressing.
- Top with 2 slices bacon for each breast and cover with 1 slice of Swiss cheese. Carefully lift each chicken breast back into skillet and place 1 tablespoon (15 ml) water in skillet. Cover and cook on low-medium heat for 10 minutes.

Zesty Orange Chicken

½ cup white wine	125 ml
½ cup frozen orange juice concentrate, thawed	125 ml
½ cup orange marmalade	160 g
½ teaspoon ground ginger	2 ml
½ teaspoon ground cinnamon	2 ml
1 large fryer chicken, quartered	
2 (11 ounce) cans mandarin oranges, drained	2 (310 g)
½ cup green grapes, halved	75 g
1½ cups instant brown rice, cooked	320 g

- Preheat oven to 350° (175° C). Combine wine, orange juice concentrate, marmalade, ginger and cinnamon in greased 9 x 13-inch (23 x 33 cm) baking dish.
- Add chicken quarters, turning to coat chicken. Bake uncovered, basting occasionally, for 30 minutes. Add oranges and grapes to dish and bake for additional 5 minutes. Serve over brown rice.

Curried Chicken Casserole

1 (10 ounce) box chicken flavor rice and macaroni	280 g
2 (5 ounce) cans chunk white chicken	2 (140 g)
1 teaspoon curry powder	5 ml
⅓ cup raisins, optional	55 g

- In skillet, prepare rice and macaroni according to package directions. Once rice cooks, add curry powder, chicken with liquid, and raisins and mix well. Cover and remove from heat. Let stand for 10 minutes and serve.

Creamy Tarragon Chicken

1½ cups flour, divided	180 g
6 boneless, skinless chicken breast halves	
2 tablespoons olive oil	30 ml
1 (10 ounce) can chicken broth	280 g
1 cup milk	250 ml
2 teaspoons dried tarragon	10 ml
1 (4 ounce) can sliced mushrooms, drained	115 g
2 (8 ounce) packages (microwavable) roasted chicken rice	2 (230 g)

- Mix flour and a little salt and pepper on wax paper and coat chicken, saving extra flour. Heat oil in large skillet over medium-high heat and cook chicken breasts, turning once, about 10 minutes or until light brown. Transfer to plate.

- In the same skillet, stir in 2 tablespoons (15 g) flour-salt mixture. Whisk in chicken broth, milk and tarragon, heat, stirring constantly, until bubbly. Add mushrooms and return chicken to skillet. Cover and simmer for 10 to 15 minutes or until sauce has thickened.

- Microwave rice according to package directions and place on serving platter. Spoon chicken and sauce over rice.

Chicken Curry

2 (10 ounce) cans cream of mushroom soup	2 (280 g)
2 teaspoons curry powder	10 ml
⅓ cup chopped almonds	55 g
4 boneless, skinless chicken breast halves, cooked, cubed	
Hot, cooked rice	

- In large saucepan combine soup, 1 soup can water, curry powder, almonds and cubed chicken. Cook on medium heat, stirring often for 15 to 20 minutes. Serve over rice.

Cashew Chicken and Veggies

1 pound boneless, skinless chicken breasts	455 g
2 tablespoons cornstarch	30 ml
1 tablespoon soy sauce	15 ml
1 teaspoon grated fresh ginger	5 ml
1(16 ounce) package frozen broccoli florets, thawed	455 g
1 (10 ounce) package frozen green peas, thawed	280 g
1 (1.2 ounce) packet savory herb with garlic soup mix	30 g
⅔ cup cashews	90 g
1 (6 ounce) package chicken and herb-flavored rice, cooked	170 g

- Cut chicken crosswise into ¼-inch (.6 cm) wide strips. In medium bowl, combine cornstarch, soy sauce and ginger, mixing well. Add chicken strips, stirring to coat well. Set aside. In large skillet with a little oil, stir-fry broccoli and peas for 3 minutes, remove vegetables to warm plate.

- In same skillet with a little oil, stir-fry chicken until all pieces change color. Stir in ½ cup (125 ml) water and soup mix. Cook on medium heat about 5 minutes until chicken is well coated with soup mix. Return cooked vegetables and add cashews to skillet and cook until thoroughly hot. Serve chicken and vegetables over hot flavored rice.

Chicken-Broccoli Skillet

3 cups cubed, cooked chicken	420 g
1 (16 ounce) package frozen broccoli florets	455 g
1 (8 ounce) package cubed processed cheese	230 g
⅔ cup mayonnaise	150 g
Hot, cooked rice	

- In skillet, combine chicken, broccoli, cheese and ¼ cup (60 ml) water. Cover and cook over medium heat until broccoli is tender-crisp and cheese melts. Stir in mayonnaise and heat through, but do not boil. Serve over rice.

Chicken a la Orange

1 (11 ounce) can mandarin oranges, drained	310 g
1 (6 ounce) can frozen orange juice concentrate, thawed	175 ml
1 tablespoon lemon juice and cornstarch	15 ml
4 boneless, skinless chicken breast halves	
1 tablespoon Mrs. Dash® garlic and herb seasoning	15 ml
2 tablespoons butter	30 g

Continued on following page

Continued from previous page

- In saucepan, combine oranges, orange juice concentrate, lemon juice, ⅔ cup (150 ml) water and cornstarch. Cook on medium heat, stirring constantly until mixture thickens. Set aside.
- Sprinkle chicken breasts with Mrs. Dash® seasoning and place in skillet with butter. Cook about 7 minutes on each side until brown. Lower heat and spoon orange juice mixture over chicken, cover and simmer about 20 minutes, adding a little water if sauce gets too thick.

Chicken Quesadillas

3 boneless, skinless chicken breast halves, cubed	
1 (10 ounce) can cheddar cheese soup	280 g
⅔ cup chunky salsa	175 g
10 flour tortillas	

- Cook chicken in skillet, stirring often until juices evaporate. Add soup and salsa; heat thoroughly. Spread about ⅓ cup (75 ml) soup mixture on half tortilla within ½ inch (1.2 cm) of edge. Moisten edge with water, fold over and seal. Place tortillas on 2 baking sheets. Bake at 400° (205° C) for 5 to 6 minutes.

Chicken and Brown Rice Supper

3 cups instant brown rice	565 g
¼ cup (½ stick) butter	60 g
3 cups cooked, cubed chicken breasts	420 g
½ cup golden raisins	75 g
½ cup chopped red bell pepper	75 g

Dressing:

2 tablespoons lemon juice	30 ml
1 tablespoon dijon-style mustard	15 ml
3 tablespoons honey	65 g
¼ cup toasted, slivered almonds	40 g

- Preheat oven to 350° (175° C). Cook brown rice according to package directions, adding butter and salt and pepper to taste.
- While rice is still hot, stir in cubed chicken, raisins and chopped bell pepper. Transfer to greased 7 x 11-inch (18 x 28 cm) baking dish. In jar with lid, combine all dressing ingredients and shake until well blended. Drizzle over rice-chicken mixture and sprinkle with almonds. Bake uncovered for 15 minutes.

Chile Pepper Chicken

5 boneless, skinless chicken breast halves
1 (1 ounce) package hot and spicy recipe Shake 'N Bake®
    coating mixture   30 g
1 (4 ounce) can diced green chilies   115 g
Chunky salsa

- Dredge chicken in coating mixture and place in greased 9 x 13-inch
  (23 x 33 cm) baking dish. Bake at 375° (190° C) for 25 minutes. Remove from
  oven, spread green chilies over chicken breasts and bake for 5 minutes. Serve
  with salsa over each chicken breast.

Chicken and Green Chile Casserole

1 green bell pepper, seeded, chopped
3 ribs celery, chopped
¾ cup chopped green onions   70 g
½ cup (1 stick) butter   115 g
1 (7 ounce) can diced green chilies   200 g
1½ cups instant rice   145 g
1 (8 ounce) carton sour cream   230 g
3 cooked chicken breasts, sliced
1 (14 ounce) can chicken broth   395 g

- Preheat oven to 325° (165° C). Combine bell pepper, celery and green onions in
  skillet with butter and saute 5 minutes.
- Transfer to mixing bowl. Stir in green chilies, rice, sour cream, chicken,
  chicken broth, ¼ cup (60 ml) water and salt and pepper to taste. Pour into
  greased 9 x 13-inch (23 x 33 cm) baking dish. Cover and bake 20 minutes;
  uncover and cook another 10 minutes.

Parmesan Chicken

1 (1 ounce) package dry Italian salad dressing mix	30 g
½ cup grated parmesan cheese	50 g
¼ cup flour	30 g
¾ teaspoon garlic powder	4 ml
5 boneless, skinless chicken breast halves	

- Preheat oven to 375° (190° C). In shallow bowl, combine salad dressing mix, cheese, flour and garlic. Moisten chicken with a little water and coat with cheese mixture. Place in sprayed 9 x 13-inch (23 x 33 cm) baking pan. Bake for 25 minutes or until chicken is light brown and cooked thoroughly.

Chicken Cacciatore

1 (2½ pound) frying chicken	1.1 kg
2 onions, sliced	
1 (15 ounce) can stewed tomatoes	425 g
1 (8 ounce) can tomato sauce	230 g
1 teaspoon dried oregano	5 ml
1 teaspoon celery seed	5 ml
Cooked noodles or spaghetti	

- Quarter chicken and sprinkle with plenty of salt and black pepper. Place in large skillet on medium-high heat, with a little oil. Add sliced onions and cook until chicken is tender, about 15 minutes.

- Add stewed tomatoes, tomato sauce, oregano and celery seed. Bring mixture to a boil; reduce heat and simmer uncovered for about 20 minutes.

- Serve over noodles or spaghetti.

Chicken-Mushroom Bake

1 (4 ounce) can sliced mushrooms	115 g
1 (10 ounce) can cream of chicken soup	280 g
1 (8 ounce) carton sour cream	230 g
½ cup cooking sherry	125 ml
1 (1 ounce) packet dry onion soup mix	30 g
2 cups cooked, cubed chicken	280 g
Rice, cooked	

● Preheat oven to 350° (175° C). In large bowl, combine mushrooms, soup, sour cream, sherry, onion soup mix and chicken. Spoon into greased 3-quart (3 L) baking dish and bake 30 minutes. Serve over rice.

Chicken Parmesan and Spaghetti

1 (14 ounce) package frozen, cooked, breaded chicken cutlets, thawed	395 g
1 (28 ounce) jar spaghetti sauce	794 g
2 (5 ounce) packages grated parmesan cheese, divided	2 (140 g)
1 (8 ounce) package thin spaghetti, cooked	230 g

● Preheat oven to 400° (205° C). Place cutlets in buttered 9 x 13-inch (23 x 33 cm) baking dish and top each with about ¼ cup (65 g) spaghetti sauce and 1 heaping tablespoon (15 ml) parmesan. Bake for 15 minutes.

● Place cooked spaghetti on serving platter and top with cutlets. Sprinkle remaining cheese over cutlets. Heat remaining spaghetti sauce and serve with chicken and spaghetti.

Chicken Couscous

1 (5.6 ounce) package toasted pine nut couscous, cooked	155 g
1 rotisserie chicken, skinned, boned, cubed	
1 (15 ounce) can baby green peas, drained	425 g
⅓ cup golden raisins	50 g
1 (2.8 ounce) can french-fried onions	85 g

● Preheat broiler.

Continued on following page

Continued from previous page

- Combine couscous, chicken, peas and raisins in microwaveable dish. Heat on MEDIUM about 2 minutes, stirring once, until mixture is warmed.
- Spoon into greased 7 x 11-inch (18 x 28 cm) baking dish; sprinkle with french-fried onions. Place under broiler and broil for about 3 minutes or just until onions are slightly brown.

Chicken Squares

2 (12 ounce) cans chicken breast chunks	2 (340 g)
1 (8 ounce) carton cream cheese, softened	230 g
¼ cup finely chopped onion	40 g
2 tablespoons sesame seeds	15 g
1 (8 count) package refrigerated crescent rolls	

- Preheat oven to 350° (175° C). Drain chicken and pour liquid in mixing bowl. Combine chicken liquid with cream cheese and beat until creamy. Add chicken, onion, sesame seeds and salt and pepper to taste.
- Open package of crescent rolls, but do not divide into triangles. Keep 2 triangles together to form 4 squares. Pinch seam in middle of each square together and pat into larger square.
- Spoon about ½ cup (125 ml) chicken mixture into center of each square. Fold corners up into center and lay like flower petals so roll seals. Repeat for all squares. Place each roll on sprayed baking sheet and bake about 15 minutes or until golden brown.

Glazed Chicken over Rice

4 boneless, skinless chicken breast halves, cubed	
1 (20 ounce) can pineapple chunks	570 g
½ cup honey-mustard grill-and-glaze sauce	125 ml
1 red bell pepper, seeded, chopped	
2 cups instant white rice, cooked	330 g

- Place a little oil in skillet and brown chicken. Reduce heat to medium and cook for 15 minutes. Add pineapple, honey-mustard sauce and bell pepper and bring to a boil.
- Reduce heat to low and simmer 15 minutes or until sauce thickens slightly. Serve over rice.

Chicken-Broccoli Casserole

2 (3 ounce) packages ramen chicken-flavor noodles	2 (85 g)
1 (10 ounce) can cream of chicken soup	280 g
⅔ cup milk	150 ml
1 cup shredded mozzarella cheese	115 g
2 cups cooked, cubed chicken breasts	280 g
1 (10 ounce) package frozen broccoli florets, thawed	280 g
¼ cup roasted sunflower seeds	30 g

- In large saucepan, prepare noodles according to package directions, adding seasoning packets. Drain most of liquid.
- Stir in soup, milk and cheese and mix well. Add chicken and broccoli and heat thoroughly, while stirring occasionally. Transfer to serving dish and sprinkle sunflower seeds over top of casserole. Serve immediately.

Chicken and Noodles

1 (3 ounce) package chicken-flavored ramen noodles	85 g
1 (16 ounce) package frozen broccoli, cauliflower and carrots	455 g
⅔ cup sweet-and sour-sauce	150 ml
3 boneless, skinless chicken breast halves, cooked, cut into thin strips	

- Set aside seasoning packet from noodles. In saucepan, cook noodles and vegetables in 2 cups (500 ml) boiling water for 3 minutes, stirring occasionally, and drain.
- Combine noodle-vegetable mixture with seasoning packet, sweet-and-sour sauce and a little salt and pepper. (You may want to add 1 tablespoon/15 ml soy sauce.) Add chicken and heat thoroughly.

Honey-Glazed Chicken

4 skinless, boneless chicken breast halves	
1 (20 ounce) can pineapple chunks	570 g
½ cup refrigerated dijon-style honey-mustard	125 ml
1 green bell pepper, thinly sliced	
1 red bell pepper, thinly sliced	
Couscous, cooked	

- Cut chicken breasts into strips, add a little salt and pepper and brown in large skillet with a little oil. Add liquid from pineapple, cover and simmer for 15 minutes.

- Add honey-mustard, pepper slices and pineapple chunks to chicken. Bring to a boil, reduce heat, cover and simmer for 15 minutes. Serve over couscous.

Chicken and Sausage Casserole

1 pound pork sausage	455 g
1 (16 ounce) package fresh mushrooms, sliced	455 g
2 red bell peppers, seeded, chopped	
3 cups cooked, cubed chicken	420 g
1 (6 ounce) box long-grain and wild rice mix, cooked	170 g
1 (10 ounce) can cream of chicken soup	280 g
1 (10 ounce) can chicken broth	280 g
2 cups buttery cracker crumbs	120 g

- Preheat oven to 350° (175° C). In large skillet, brown and cook sausage, drain. Add mushrooms and bell peppers and saute for 5 minutes. Stir in chicken and mix well.

- In large saucepan, combine chicken soup, chicken broth and cooked rice. Stir in sausage-chicken mixture and gently mix to blend well. Spoon into greased 9 x 13-inch (23 x 33 cm) baking dish. Sprinkle buttery crumbs over top and bake 30 minutes.

Chicken and Sauerkraut

6 large, boneless, skinless chicken breast halves
1 (16 ounce) can sliced potatoes, drained   455 g
1 (16 ounce) can sauerkraut, drained   455 g
¼ cup pine nuts or ½ teaspoon caraway seeds   30 g/2 ml

- In sprayed large skillet, season chicken with pepper to taste and cook over medium heat until chicken browns on both sides, about 15 minutes.
- Add potatoes to skillet. Spoon sauerkraut over potatoes, cover and cook over low heat about 35 minutes until chicken is done.
- Toast pine nuts in dry skillet on medium heat, stirring constantly, until golden brown. Sprinkle chicken and sauerkraut with toasted pine nuts or caraway seeds and serve.

Honey-Roasted Chicken

3 tablespoons soy sauce   45 ml
3 tablespoons honey   65 g
2½ cups crushed wheat cereal   150 g
½ cup very finely minced walnuts   45 g
5 - 6 boneless, skinless chicken breast halves

- Preheat oven to 400° (104° C). In shallow bowl, combine soy sauce and honey and set aside. In another shallow bowl, combine crushed cereal and walnuts.
- Dip both sides of each chicken breast in soy sauce-honey mixture and dredge in cereal-walnut mixture. Place each piece on sprayed foil-lined baking sheet. Bake for 25 minutes (about 35 minutes if breasts are very large).

Chicken Taco Pie

1½ pounds boneless, skinless chicken breast halves   680 g
1 (1.5 ounce) packet taco seasoning mix   45 g
1 green bell pepper, finely chopped
1 red bell pepper, finely chopped
1½ cups shredded Mexican 3-cheese blend   170 g
1 (8 ounce) package corn muffin mix   230 g
1 egg
⅓ cup milk   75 ml

- Preheat oven to 400° (205° C). Cut chicken into 1-inch (2.5 cm) chunks and cook on medium-high heat in large skillet with a little oil. Cook about 10 minutes, drain.

Continued on following page

Continued from previous page

- Stir in taco seasoning, bell peppers and ¾ cup (175 ml) water. Reduce heat and simmer, stirring several times for another 10 minutes. Spoon into buttered 9-inch (23 cm) deep-dish pie pan and sprinkle with cheese.
- Prepare corn muffin mix with egg and milk, mixing well. Spoon over top of pie and bake for 20 minutes or until top is golden brown. Let set about 5 minutes before serving.

Honey-Mustard Chicken

⅓ cup dijon-style mustard	85 g
½ cup honey	170 g
2 tablespoons dried dillweed	30 ml
1 (2½ pound) chicken, quartered	1.1 kg

- Combine mustard, honey and dillweed. Arrange chicken quarters in 9 x 13-inch (23 x 33 cm) baking dish. Pour mustard mixture over chicken. Turn chicken over and make sure mustard mixture covers chicken.
- Bake covered at 375° (190° C) for 30 minutes. Uncover and bake for another 10 minutes.

Chicken Stir-Fry

1 pound chicken tenders, cut in half lengthwise	455 g
2 tablespoons cornstarch	15 g
1 (16 ounce) package frozen broccoli, cauliflower and carrots, thawed	455 g
1 (10 ounce) package sugar snap peas	280 g
1 (15 ounce) can pineapple chunks, reserve liquid	425 g
⅔ cup stir-fry sauce	150 ml

- Place chicken tenders, cornstarch and salt and pepper to taste, in large resealable plastic bag; seal and shake to coat chicken. In large skillet with a little oil on medium-high heat, stir-fry chicken for about 10 minutes or until thoroughly cooked. Transfer to plate.
- In same skillet with a little oil, add vegetables and stir-fry for about 3 minutes. Add pineapple and cook until vegetables are tender-crisp. Add stir-fry sauce and pineapple liquid and simmer for about 10 minutes. Add chicken to vegetable mixture and toss to mix.

Honey-Mustard Grilled Chicken

½ teaspoon lemon pepper	2 ml
¾ cup mayonnaise	170 g
2 tablespoons country dijon-style mustard	60 g
¼ cup honey	85 g
4 - 5 boneless, skinless chicken breast halves	

- In bowl, combine lemon pepper, mayonnaise, mustard and honey, mixing well. Brush about half mayonnaise mixture over each piece of chicken and sprinkle with lemon pepper and grill over hot coals until done. Serve with remaining mayonnaise-mustard mixture.

Grilled Chicken with Broccoli Slaw

1 (3 pound) chicken, quartered	1.4 kg
3 tablespoons olive oil	45 ml
⅔ cup barbecue sauce	175 g
¼ cup mayonnaise	55 g
3 tablespoons cider vinegar	45 ml
2 tablespoons sugar	25 g
1 (12 ounce) package broccoli slaw	340 g
1 cup shredded carrots	110 g

- Brush chicken quarters with oil and sprinkle with salt and pepper. Grill 30 to 35 minutes, turning once or twice or until juices run clear when thigh part is pierced and a meat thermometer inserted registers 170° (75° C). Brush with barbecue sauce and grill just until sauce is brown, but not charred.

- Combine mayonnaise, vinegar and sugar, mixing well. Spoon over broccoli slaw and carrots and toss. Refrigerate.

Spicy Chicken and Rice

3 cups cooked, sliced chicken	420 g
2 cups cooked brown rice	390 g
1 (10 ounce) can fiesta nacho cheese soup	280 g
1 (10 ounce) can diced tomatoes and green chilies	280 g

Continued on following page

Continued from previous page

- Combine chicken, rice, cheese soup, and tomatoes and green chilies and mix well. Spoon mixture into buttered 3-quart (3 L) baking dish.
- Cook covered at 350° (175° C) for 35 minutes.

Grilled Chicken with Raspberry-Barbecue Sauce

1 (12 ounce) jar seedless raspberry preserves	340 g
½ cup barbecue sauce	130 g
2 tablespoons raspberry vinegar	30 ml
2 tablespoons dijon-style mustard	30 g
1 (2½ pound) chicken, quartered	1.1 kg

- In bowl, combine preserves, barbecue sauce, vinegar and mustard and have ready when chicken quarters are nearly done.
- Season chicken quarters liberally with seasoned salt and pepper. Grill chicken, covered with grill lid, over medium-high heat for about 8 minutes on each side. Baste sauce over quarters last 2 minutes of cooking. Serve with remaining sauce.

Sunday Chicken

5 - 6 boneless, skinless chicken breast halves	
½ cup sour cream	120 g
¼ cup soy sauce	60 ml
1 (10 ounce) can French onion soup	280 g

- Place chicken in greased 9 x 13-inch (23 x 33 cm) baking dish.
- In saucepan, combine sour cream, soy sauce and soup and heat just enough to mix well. Pour over chicken breasts.
- Bake covered at 375° (190° C) for 35 minutes.

Glazed Drumsticks

1 (20 ounce) package frozen chicken drumsticks	570 g
½ cup hoisin sauce	130 g
2 tablespoons light soy sauce	30 ml
1 teaspoon minced garlic	5 ml

- Preheat broiler. Place drumsticks in a single layer, in greased 9 x 13-inch (23 x 33 cm) baking dish and broil for 10 minutes. Turn drumsticks and broil another 10 minutes. Reduce heat to 325° (165° C).
- In bowl, combine hoisin sauce, soy sauce and garlic, mixing well. Brush chicken drumsticks lightly with sauce and bake for 25 minutes. During baking time, remove from oven and brush with remaining sauce and continue cooking until glaze bubbles and browns.

Tempting Chicken

3 boneless, skinless chicken breast halves	
3 boneless, skinless chicken thighs	
1 (16 ounce) jar tomato-alfredo sauce	455 g
1 (10 ounce) can tomato-bisque soup	280 g

- Preheat oven to 350° (175° C). In large skillet, brown chicken pieces in little oil and place in sprayed 9 x 13-inch (23 x 33 cm) baking pan.
- Combine tomato-alfredo sauce, tomato-bisque soup and ½ cup (125 ml) water and pour over chicken. Cover and simmer for about 20 minutes; uncover chicken and cook another 15 minutes.

Tasty Skillet Chicken

5 large boneless, skinless chicken breast halves, cut in strips	
1 green bell pepper, julienned	
1 red bell pepper, julienned	
2 small yellow squash, seeded, julienned	
1 (16 ounce) bottle thick-and-chunky salsa	455 g

- With a little oil in large skillet, saute chicken for about 5 minutes. Add peppers and squash and cook for another 5 minutes or until peppers are tender-crisp. Stir in salsa and bring to a boil; lower heat and simmer for 10 minutes. Serve over rice.

Sunshine Chicken

1 chicken, quartered
Flour
1 cup barbecue sauce   265 g
½ cup orange juice   125 ml

● Place chicken in bowl of flour and coat well. In skillet with a little oil, brown
  chicken and place in sprayed, shallow 9 x 13-inch (23 x 33 cm) baking pan.
  Combine barbecue sauce and orange juice. Pour over chicken. Bake covered at
  350° (175° C) for 30 minutes. Remove from oven, spoon sauce over chicken and
  bake uncovered for another 15 minutes.

Sweet-Spicy Chicken Thighs

3 tablespoons chili powder   25 g
3 tablespoons honey   65 g
2 tablespoons lemon juice   30 ml
10 - 12 chicken thighs

● Preheat oven to 425° (220° C). Line 10 x 15-inch (25 x 38 cm) shallow baking
  pan with heavy foil and set metal rack on top. Combine chili powder, honey,
  lemon juice and lots of salt and pepper. Brush mixture over chicken thighs,
  place on rack and turn thighs to coat. Bake, turning once, for about 35 minutes.

So-Good Chicken

4 - 5 boneless, skinless chicken breasts
1 (10 ounce) can golden mushroom soup   280 g
1 cup white cooking wine   250 ml
1 (8 ounce) carton sour cream   230 g

● Wash, dry chicken breasts with paper towels and sprinkle a little salt and
  pepper over each. Place chicken in sprayed 9 x 13-inch (23 x 33 cm) baking
  dish. Preheat over to 375° (190° C). In bowl, combine mushroom soup, wine
  and sour cream and mix well. Spoon over chicken breasts. Cook covered for
  30 minutes. Uncover, and cook for another 10 minutes.

Sweet-and-Sour Chicken

2 - 3 pounds chicken pieces	910 g - 1.4 kg
Canola oil	
1 (1 ounce) packet dry onion soup mix	30 g
1 (6 ounce) can frozen orange juice concentrate, thawed	175 ml

- In skillet, brown chicken pieces on both sides in a little oil. Place in 9 x 13-inch
  (23 x 33 cm) baking dish. In small bowl, combine onion soup mix, orange juice and
  ⅔ cup (150 ml) water and stir well. Pour over chicken. Bake uncovered at 375°
  (190° C) for 30 minutes.

Requested Favorite Chicken

6 boneless, skinless chicken breast halves	
Canola oil	
1 (16 ounce) jar thick-and-chunky hot salsa	455 g
1 cup packed light brown sugar	220 g
1 tablespoon dijon-style mustard	15 ml
Cooked brown rice	

- Preheat oven to 350° (175° C). In large skillet with a little oil, brown chicken
  breasts and place in greased 9 x 13-inch (23 x 33 cm) baking dish. Combine
  salsa, brown sugar, mustard and ½ teaspoon (2 ml) salt and pour over chicken.
  Cover and bake for 35 minutes. Serve over brown rice.

Italian Crumb Chicken

5 - 6 boneless, skinless chicken breast halves	
¾ cup mayonnaise	170 g
⅓ cup grated parmesan cheese	35 g
½ cup Italian seasoned breadcrumbs	60 g

- Preheat oven to 400° (205° C). Place all chicken breasts on foil-lined baking
  pan. Combine mayonnaise, 2 teaspoons (10 ml) pepper and parmesan
  cheese in bowl; mix well. Spread mixture over chicken breasts and sprinkle
  breadcrumbs on both sides. Place in oven uncovered and bake 20 to 25
  minutes.

Quick Chicken Supper

1 (16 ounce) package frozen broccoli florets, thawed	455 g
1 (10 ounce) can cream of chicken soup	280 g
⅔ cup mayonnaise	150 g
1 cup shredded cheddar cheese	115 g
3 cups cooked, cubed chicken	420 g
2 cups crushed cheese crackers	120 g

- Preheat oven to 375° (190° C). In large bowl, combine broccoli, soup, mayonnaise, cheese and chicken, mixing well. Pour into greased 3-quart (3 L) baking dish; cover and bake 20 minutes. Sprinkle crackers over casserole and bake uncovered for 10 minutes.

Saucy Chicken

5 - 6 boneless, skinless chicken breast halves	
2 cups thick, chunky salsa	530 g
⅓ cup packed light brown sugar	75 g
1½ tablespoons dijon-style mustard	22 ml
Hot, cooked rice	

- Place chicken breasts in greased 9 x 13-inch (23 x 33 cm) baking dish. Combine salsa, sugar and mustard and pour over chicken. Cover and bake at 350° (175° C) for 45 minutes. Serve over rice.

Italian Chicken and Rice

3 boneless, chicken breast halves, cut into strips	
1 (14 ounce) can chicken broth seasoned with Italian herbs	395 g
¾ cup instant rice	70 g
¼ cup grated parmesan cheese	25 g

- Cook chicken in non-stick skillet until brown and stir often. Remove chicken. To skillet add broth and rice. Heat to boiling point. Cover and simmer over low heat for 15 minutes. (Check to see if it needs more water.) Stir in cheese. Return chicken to pan. Cover and cook for 5 minutes or until done.

Skillet Chicken and Peas

4 - 5 boneless, skinless chicken breast halves	
2 (10 ounce) can cream of chicken soup	2 (280 g)
2 cups instant rice	190 g
1 (10 ounce) package frozen green peas	280 g

- Heat a little oil in very large skillet. Add chicken and cook until it browns. Transfer chicken to plate and keep warm. To skillet, add soup, 1¾ cups (425 ml) water and ½ teaspoon (2 ml) pepper and paprika. Heat to a boil, stir in rice and peas, reduce heat. Place chicken on top and cook on low heat for 15 minutes.

Skillet Chicken and Stuffing

1 (6 ounce) box stuffing mix for chicken	170 g
1 (16 ounce) package frozen whole kernel corn	455 g
¼ cup (½ stick) butter	60 g
4 boneless, skinless chicken breast halves, cooked	

- In large skillet, combine contents of seasoning packet in stuffing mix, corn, 1⅔ cups (400 ml) water and butter. Bring to a boil Reduce heat, cover and simmer for 5 minutes. Stir in stuffing mix just until moist. Cut chicken into thin slices. Mix with stuffing-corn mixture. Cook on low heat until thoroughly hot.

Chicken-Green Bean Bake

2 cups instant rice	190 g
1 (16 ounce) package shredded processed cheese	455 g
1 (16 ounce) package frozen cut green beans, thawed	455 g
3 cups cooked, cubed chicken	420 g
2 cups coarsely crushed potato chips	110 g

- Preheat oven to 325° (165° C). Cook rice in large saucepan according to package directions and stir in cheese and an extra ¼ cup (60 ml) water. Stir and mix until cheese melts.
- Cook green beans according to package directions; drain. Stir in rice-cheese mixture and add cubed chicken; mix well. Spoon into sprayed 9 x 13-inch (23 x 33 cm) baking dish. Top with potato chips and bake 20 minutes until chips are light brown.

Creamy Chicken and Veggies

6 small boneless, skinless chicken breast halves
1 (16 ounce) bottle creamy Italian dressing   500 ml
1 (16 ounce) package frozen broccoli, cauliflower and
    carrots, thawed   455 g

- Sprinkle chicken with pepper and salt to taste. Place a little oil in large, heavy non-stick skillet over medium-high heat. Add chicken breasts and cook 4 minutes on each side. Pour about ¾ dressing over chicken; cover and simmer for about 8 minutes. Add vegetables, cover and cook for another 10 minutes or until vegetables are tender.

Chop Suey Veggies and Chicken

3 cups cooked, cubed chicken   420 g
2 (10 ounce) cans cream of chicken soup   2 (280 g)
2 (15 ounce) cans chop suey vegetables, drained   2 (425 g)
1 (8 ounce) can sliced water chestnuts, drained   230 g
1 (16 ounce) package frozen onions and bell peppers   455 g
½ teaspoon hot sauce   2 ml
½ teaspoon curry powder   2 ml
2 cups chow mein noodles   110 g

- Preheat oven to 350° (175° C). In large bowl, combine all ingredients, except chow mein noodles. Spoon into greased 9 x 13-inch (23 x 33 cm) baking dish. Sprinkle chow mein noodles over top and bake uncovered for 30 minutes.

Confetti Squash and Chicken

1 pound yellow squash, sliced	455 g
1 pound zucchini, sliced	455 g
2 cups cooked, cubed chicken	280 g
1 (10 ounce) can cream of chicken soup	280 g
1 (8 ounce) carton sour cream	230 g
1 (4 ounce) can chopped pimento, drained	115 g
½ cup (1 stick) butter, melted	15 g
1 (6 ounce) box herb stuffing mix	170 g

- Preheat oven to 350° (175° C). In large saucepan, cook squash and zucchini in salted water about 10 minutes. Drain and stir in chicken, soup, sour cream and pimentos, mixing well.
- Combine melted butter and stuffing mix and add to vegetable-chicken mixture and mix well. Spoon into greased 9 x 13-inch (23 x 33 cm) baking dish. Cover and bake 30 minutes.

Creamy Chicken and Broccoli

5 large chicken breast halves	
2 (10 ounce) cans cream of chicken soup	2 (280 g)
½ cup milk	125 ml
1 (16 ounce) package frozen broccoli florets, thawed	455 g
Cooked instant brown rice	

- In very large skillet (with lid) sprinkle chicken with salt and pepper and brown breasts in a little oil. On medium-high heat, stir into skillet both cans of soup and milk. Stir to mix and as you are stirring, spoon soup mixture over top of chicken breasts. When mixture is well mixed and hot, reduce heat to low, cover and simmer for 20 minutes.
- Place broccoli florets around chicken and into creamy sauce. Return heat to high until broccoli is heated; again reduce heat and simmer about 10 minutes or until broccoli is tender-crisp.
- Serve chicken and sauce over brown rice.

Creamy Chicken and Pasta

1 (10 ounce) package penne pasta	280 g
1 tablespoon olive oil	15 ml
2 (12 ounce) cans white chicken meat, drained	2 (340 g)
2 tablespoons pesto	30 g
¾ cup whipping cream	175 ml

- In large saucepan, cook penne pasta according to package directions. Drain and place back in saucepan. Gently stir in oil, chicken, prepared pesto, whipping cream and salt and pepper to taste. Place saucepan over low heat and simmer, stirring often, (but do not let mixture boil) until cream is absorbed into pasta. Spoon into serving bowl and serve immediately.

Easy Chicken and Dumplings

3 cups cooked, chopped chicken	420 g
2 (10 ounce) cans cream of chicken soup	2 (280 g)
1 tablespoon chicken bouillon granules	15 ml
1 (8 ounce) can refrigerated buttermilk biscuits	230 g

- Combine chopped chicken, soup, chicken bouillon granules and 4½ cups (1.1 L) water in large kettle or Dutch oven. Boil mixture and stir to mix well.

- Separate biscuits and cut in quarters, making 4 pieces out of each biscuit. Drop biscuit pieces, 1 at a time, into boiling chicken mixture, stir gently. When all biscuits are dropped, reduce heat to low and simmer, stirring occasionally, for about 15 minutes.

Crunchy Chip Chicken

1½ cups crushed sour cream potato chips	85 g
1 tablespoon dried parsley	15 ml
1 egg, beaten	
1 tablespoon Worcestershire sauce	15 ml
4 large boneless, skinless chicken breast halves	
¼ cup canola oil	60 ml

- In shallow bowl, combine potato chips and parsley. In another shallow bowl, combine beaten egg, Worcestershire sauce and 1 tablespoon (15 ml) water. Dip chicken pieces in egg mixture, then dredge chicken in potato chip mixture. Heat oil in heavy skillet and fry chicken pieces in skillet for about 10 minutes; turn each piece over and cook for another 10 minutes until golden brown or until juice of chicken is no longer pink.

Moist-Crunchy Baked Chicken

¼ pound (1 stick) butter, melted	115 g
2 tablespoons mayonnaise	30 g
2 tablespoons marinade for chicken	30 ml
1 (6 ounce) can french-fried onions, crushed	170 g
6 boneless, skinless chicken breasts halves	

- Preheat oven to 375° (190° C). In shallow bowl, combine melted butter, mayonnaise and marinade for chicken. Place crushed onions in another shallow bowl.
- Dry chicken breasts with paper towels and dip first into butter mixture and dredge each chicken breast in crushed onions. Place in large baking pan, arranging so pieces do not touch.
- Bake 25 minutes or until chicken juices run clear.

Lemony Chicken and Noodles

½ (16 ounce) package wide egg noodles	½ (455 g)
1 (10 ounce) package frozen sugar snap peas, thawed	280 g
1 (10 ounce) can chicken broth	280 g
1 teaspoon fresh grated lemon peel	5 ml
2 cups cubed skinless rotisserie chicken meat	280 g
½ cup whipping cream	125 ml

- In large saucepan with boiling water, cook noodles according to package directions, but add snap peas to noodles 1 minute before noodles are done. Drain and return to saucepan. Add chicken broth, lemon peel, chicken pieces and ½ teaspoon (2 ml) each of salt and pepper; heat, stirring constantly until thoroughly hot. Over low heat, gently stir in heavy cream. Serve hot.

Roasted Chicken

1 (14 ounce) can chicken broth	395 g
1 (8 ounce) can whole kernel corn, drained	230 g
2 cups cooked, cubed chicken breast	280 g
1 (5 ounce) box couscous	140 g
1 cup roasted red bell peppers	260 g
¼ cup toasted pine nuts	30 g

- In saucepan over medium-high heat, combine chicken broth, corn, chicken, couscous and bell peppers. Cover and simmer 10 minutes. Sprinkle pine nuts over top.

Parmesan Crusted Chicken

1 egg white, beaten	
1½ cups breadcrumbs	180 g
1 teaspoon dried parsley	5 ml
½ cup grated parmesan cheese	50 g
4 small boneless, skinless chicken breast halves	
Olive oil	
¼ cup minced shallots	40 g
½ cup dry white wine	125 ml
½ cup heavy cream	125 ml
½ cup chicken broth	125 ml
¼ cup (½ stick) butter, cut in chunks	60 g
¾ teaspoon dried sage	4 ml

- Preheat oven to 425° (220° C).
- Combine beaten egg white and 1 tablespoon (15 ml) water. In shallow bowl, combine breadcrumbs, parsley, cheese and salt and pepper to taste.
- Dip each piece of chicken in egg white; then dredge in crumb mixture. Place in heavy skillet with a little oil and saute chicken until golden. Transfer to greased baking dish and bake uncovered for 15 minutes.
- Saute shallots in a little oil in saucepan. Add wine, cream and chicken broth; simmer until reduced by half. Stir in butter and sage. Serve over chicken.

Sassy Red Pepper Chicken

4 boneless, skinless chicken breast halves	
1½ cups seasoned breadcrumbs	180 g
1 teaspoon garlic powder	5 ml
1 large egg, beaten	
½ cup canola oil, divided	125 ml

Red Pepper Sauce:

¾ cup drained, diced roasted red peppers	195 g
½ cup vinegar	125 ml
½ cup ketchup	135 g
⅔ cup sugar	135 g
1 teaspoon paprika	5 ml

- Place chicken breasts between 2 sheets plastic wrap and, using a meat mallet, flatten chicken to ¼-inch (.6 cm) thickness; set aside. In shallow bowl, combine breadcrumbs and garlic powder and place beaten egg with 2 tablespoons (30 ml) water in second shallow bowl. Dip chicken in egg mixture and then dredge chicken in breadcrumbs.

- Pour ¼ cup (60 ml) oil in large skillet and cook 2 chicken breasts for 5 minutes on each side. Remove from skillet to keep warm. Repeat procedure with remaining oil and chicken.

- Place all pepper sauce ingredients in saucepan, bring to a boil, reduce heat and cook for 25 minutes, stirring often. Spoon sauce over chicken to serve.

Rolled Chicken Florentine

6 boneless, skinless chicken breast halves	
6 thin slices deli ham	
6 thin slices Swiss cheese	
1 (10 ounce) package frozen chopped spinach, thawed, drained	280 g
2 (10 ounce) cans cream of chicken soup	2 (280 g)
4 green onions, finely chopped	
1 (10 ounce) box chicken flavored Rice-a-Roni®	280 g

- With flat side of meat mallet, pound chicken to ¼-inch (.6 cm) thickness. Place ham slice, cheese slice and one-fourth well drained spinach on each chicken piece and roll chicken from short end, jelly-roll style. Secure with

Continued on following page

Continued from previous page

wooden toothpicks. Place chicken in buttered 9 x 13-inch (23 x 33 cm) glass baking dish. Cover with plastic wrap and microwave on HIGH for 4 minutes.

- Preheat oven to 325° (165° C). In bowl, stir together chicken soup, onions, ⅔ cup (150 ml) water and black pepper to taste, stirring to blend well. Pour over chicken rolls, cover and bake for 25 minutes or until chicken is fork-tender.

- Cook rice according to package directions and place on serving platter and spoon chicken and sauce over rice.

Skillet Chicken and More

4 boneless, skinless chicken breast halves	
Canola oil	
2 (10 ounce) cans cream of chicken soup	2 (280 g)
2 cups instant rice	190 g
1 (16 ounce) package broccoli florets	455 g

- Brown chicken breasts on both sides in very large skillet with a little oil and simmer 10 minutes. Remove chicken and keep warm. Add soup and 2 cups (500 ml) water. Heat to boiling.

- Stir in instant rice and broccoli florets. Use a little salt, pepper and paprika (if you have it) on chicken and place on top of rice. Cover dish and cook on low 15 minutes or until liquid evaporates.

Stir-Fry Cashew Chicken

1 pound chicken tenders, cut into strips	455 g
1 (16 ounce) package frozen broccoli, cauliflower and carrots	455 g
1 (8 ounce) jar stir-fry sauce	230 g
⅓ cup cashew halves	70 g
1 (12 ounce) package chow mein noodles	340 g

- In 12-inch (32 cm) wok, place a little oil and stir-fry chicken strips over high heat for about 4 minutes. Add vegetables and stir-fry for another 4 minutes or until vegetables are tender.

- Stir in stir-fry sauce and cashews. Cook just until mixture is hot. Serve over chow mein noodles.

Luncheon Chicken Pie

1 (12 ounce) package shredded cheddar cheese, divided	340 g
1 (10 ounce) package frozen peas and carrots, thawed	280 g
1 red bell pepper, seeded, chopped	
2 cups cooked, finely diced chicken breasts	280 g
3 large eggs, beaten	
¾ cup biscuit mix	90 g
1½ cups half-and-half cream	375 ml

- In large bowl, combine 2 cups (230 g) cheese, peas and carrots, bell pepper and chicken. Spread into buttered 10-inch (25 cm) deep-dish pie plate. In mixing bowl, combine eggs and baking mix, whisk until smooth. Stir in cream and salt to taste. Spoon mixture over cheese-vegetable mixture, but do not stir.
- Cover and bake 30 minutes or until center of pie is firm. Sprinkle remaining cheese over top and bake for 5 more minutes.

Stir-Fry Chicken and Veggies

1¼ cups instant rice	120 g
¼ cup (½ stick) butter	60 g
1½ pounds chicken tenderloin strips	680 g
1 (16 ounce) package frozen broccoli, cauliflower and carrots	455 g
2 red bell peppers, julienned	
½ cup stir-fry sauce	125 ml
Rice, cooked	

- Cook rice according to package directions and keep warm. In large non-stick skillet, melt butter and stir-fry chicken strips for about 5 minutes, or until light brown.
- Stir in vegetables and cook 8 minutes longer. Pour in stir-fry sauce, mixing well; cover and cook 2 minutes or until thoroughly hot. Serve over rice.

Pimento Cheese-Stuffed Chicken

4 large skinless, boneless chicken breast halves	
½ cup milk	125 ml
1 large egg, beaten	
2 cups seasoned breadcrumbs	240 g
1 (16 ounce) carton pimento cheese	455 g

- Preheat oven to 350° (175° C). Dry chicken breasts with paper towels and sprinkle well with salt and pepper.

Continued on following page

Continued from previous page

- Combine milk and beaten egg in shallow bowl, mixing well and place breadcrumbs in second shallow bowl. Dip chicken in milk mixture and dredge in breadcrumbs.
- In large skillet over medium-high heat, pour in a little oil to ⅛ inch (.4 cm) depth and cook chicken about 10 to 12 minutes on each side. Transfer to baking sheet. Hold chicken with tongs and cut slit in 1 side of each chicken breast to form a pocket. Spoon about ¼ cup (35 g) pimento cheese into each pocket and bake for another 5 minutes or until cheese melts.

Swiss-Cheesy Chicken

4 boneless, skinless chicken breast halves
½ cup refrigerated honey-mustard dressing   125 ml
1 package (8 slices) fully cooked bacon
4 slices Swiss cheese

- In large skillet with a little oil, cook chicken breasts on medium-high heat for 5 minutes. Remove chicken to cutting board and liberally spread each breast with honey-mustard dressing.
- Top with 2 slices of bacon for each breast and cover with a slice of Swiss cheese. Carefully lift each chicken breast back into skillet and place 1 tablespoon (15 ml) water in skillet. Cover and cook on low-medium heat for 10 minutes.

Ranch Chicken to Go

1 (8 ounce) package pasta	230 g
½ cup (1 stick) butter, melted	115 g
1 (10 ounce) can cream of chicken soup	280 g
1 (1 ounce) packet ranch-style salad dressing mix	30 g
2 (15 ounce) cans peas and carrots, drained	2 (425 g)
3 cups cooked, cubed chicken	420 g
1 (2.8 ounce) can french-fried onions	85 g

- Preheat oven to 350° (175° C).
- Cook pasta according to package directions.
- In a saucepan, combine butter, soup, dry dressing mix, peas and carrots. Heat on medium, stirring occasionally, until all ingredients are well mixed and thoroughly hot.
- Toss with cooked pasta and chicken and spoon into greased 3-quart (3 L) baking dish. Cover and bake 15 minutes. Sprinkle on onion rings and bake 15 more minutes.

Sweet 'n Spicy Chicken

1 pound boneless, skinless chicken breast halves	455 g
1 (1 ounce) packet taco seasoning	30 g
1 (16 ounce) jar chunky salsa	455 g
1½ cups peach preserves	480 g
Rice, cooked	

- Cut chicken into ½-inch (1.2 cm) cubes and place in large, plastic bag. Add taco seasoning and toss to coat. In skillet, brown chicken in a little oil.
- Combine salsa and preserves, stir into skillet and bring mixture to a boil. Reduce heat, cover and simmer until juices run clear, about 15 minutes. Serve over rice.

Skillet Roasted Chicken

1 (2½ - 3 pound) chicken, quartered	1.1 - 1.4 kg
Canola oil	
2 teaspoons sage	10 ml
2 teaspoons prepared minced garlic	10 ml
2 (10 ounce) cans cream of chicken soup	2 (280 g)
Rice, cooked and buttered	

- Dry chicken quarters with paper towels. Sprinkle with sage and salt and pepper to taste. Place in large skillet with a little oil. Cook on both sides over medium-high heat for about 15 minutes. Combine garlic, chicken soup and ½ cup (125 ml) water in saucepan. Heat just enough to blend ingredients.
- Pour over chicken, cover and cook on low heat for 10 minutes or until chicken heats thoroughly. Serve over rice.

Special Chicken Couscous

1¼ cups chicken broth	310 ml
1 (5.6 ounce) package pine nut couscous mix	155 g
1 rotisserie chicken, skinned, boned, cut up	
1 (4 ounce) can diced pimentos	115 g
½ cup crumbled feta cheese	70 g
1 (10 ounce) package frozen green peas, drained, optional	280 g
1 tablespoon dried basil	15 ml
1 tablespoon lemon juice	15 ml

- Heat broth and seasoning packet from couscous in microwave on HIGH for 4 minutes or until broth begins to boil. Place couscous in large bowl and stir in broth, cover and let stand for 5 minutes. Fluff couscous with fork and add chicken, pimento, cheese, peas, basil and lemon juice. Toss and serve warm.

Spicy Orange Chicken

1 pound boneless skinless chicken tenders	455 g
3 tablespoons olive oil, divided	45 ml
2 tablespoons soy sauce	30 ml
1 (16 ounce) package frozen stir-fry vegetables, thawed	455 g
1 (6 ounce) package chow mein noodles	170 g
⅔ cup orange marmalade	160 ml
2 teaspoons lime juice	10 ml
½ teaspoon dried ginger	2 ml
½ teaspoon cayenne	2 ml

- In large skillet over medium-high heat, lightly brown chicken tenders in 2 tablespoons (30 ml) oil. Add soy sauce and stir-fry vegetables and cook about 8 minutes or until vegetables are tender-crisp.

- In saucepan, combine marmalade, remaining oil, lime juice, ginger and cayenne and mix well. Heat and pour over stir-fry and toss. Serve over chow mein noodles.

Cheesy Chicken and Potatoes

1 (20 ounce) package frozen hash browns with	
peppers and onions, thawed	570 g
1 tablespoon minced garlic	15 ml
2-2½ cups bite-size chunks rotisserie chicken	280 - 350 g
1 bunch green onions, sliced	
1 cup shredded cheddar cheese	115 g

- Add a little oil to large skillet over medium-high heat, cook potatoes for 7 minutes and turn frequently.

- Add garlic, chicken, green onions and ⅓ cup (75 ml) water and cook for 5 to 6 minutes. Remove from heat and stir in cheese. Serve immediately right from skillet.

Stir-Fry Chicken Spaghetti

1 pound boneless, skinless chicken breast halves	455 g
Canola oil	
1½ cups sliced mushrooms	110 g
1½ cups bell pepper strips	140 g
1 cup sweet-and-sour stir-fry sauce	250 ml
1 (16 ounce) package spaghetti, cooked, drained	455 g
¼ cup (½ stick) butter	60 g

- Salt and pepper chicken and cut into thin slices. In large skillet with a little oil, brown chicken slices and cook for 5 minutes on low-medium heat. Transfer to plate and reserve.
- In same skillet adding a little more oil, stir-fry mushrooms and bell pepper strips for 5 minutes. Add chicken strips and sweet-and-sour sauce, stirring until ingredients are thoroughly hot.
- While spaghetti is still hot and drained, add butter, stirring until butter is melted. Place in large bowl and toss with chicken mixture.

Sunny Chicken Supper

4 boneless, skinless chicken breast halves	
1½ teaspoons curry powder	7 ml
1½ cups orange juice	375 ml
2 tablespoons brown sugar	30 g
1 cup rice	185 g
1 teaspoon mustard	5 ml

- Rub chicken breasts with curry powder and a little salt and pepper. In large skillet, combine remaining ingredients and mix well. Top with chicken breasts and bring to a boil. Reduce heat, cover and simmer for 30 minutes.
- Remove from heat and let stand, covered until all liquid has absorbed, about 10 minutes.

Supreme Chicken

1 (16 ounce) package frozen onions and bell peppers	455 g
Olive oil	
3 cup cooked, diced chicken	420 g
1 (6 ounce) package long-grain and wild rice, cooked	170 g
1 (10 ounce) can cream of chicken soup	280 g
1 (4 ounce) can diced pimentos	115 g
1 (15 ounce) can French-style green beans, drained	425 g
½ cup slivered almonds	85 g
1 cup mayonnaise	225 g
3 cups lightly crushed potato chips	170 g

- Preheat oven to 350° (175° C). In skillet with a little oil, saute onions and bell peppers. In large bowl, combine onions and bell peppers, chicken, rice, chicken soup, pimentos, green beans, almonds, mayonnaise, and salt and pepper to taste. Mix until well blended.
- Butter a deep 9 x 13-inch (23 x 33 cm) baking dish and spoon mixture into dish. Sprinkle crushed potato chips over casserole and bake for 35 minutes or until chips are light brown.

Spaghetti Toss

1 (10 ounce) package thin spaghetti	280 g
1 (10 ounce) package frozen sugar snap peas	280 g
2 tablespoons butter	30 g
3 cups rotisserie cooked chicken strips	420 g
1 (11 ounce) can mandarin oranges, drained	310 g
⅔ cup stir-fry sauce	150 ml

- Cook spaghetti according to package directions; stir in peas and cook an additional minute. Drain and stir in butter until butter melts. Spoon into bowl. Add chicken strips, oranges and stir-fry sauce; toss to coat.

Summertime-Limeade Chicken

6 large boneless, skinless chicken breast halves	
1 (6 ounce) can frozen limeade concentrate, thawed	175 ml
3 tablespoons brown sugar	40 g
½ cup chili sauce	135 g
Rice, cooked, buttered	

- Sprinkle chicken breasts with a little salt and pepper and place in lightly greased skillet. Cook on high heat and brown on both sides for about 10 minutes. Remove from skillet, set aside and keep warm.
- Add limeade concentrate, brown sugar and chili sauce to skillet. Boil, stirring constantly, for 10 minutes.
- Return chicken to skillet and spoon sauce over chicken. Reduce heat, cover and simmer for 15 minutes. Serve over rice.

Southwest Pizza

1 (12 inch) pre-baked pizza crust	32 cm
¾ cup guacamole	180 g
1 (10 ounce) package cooked southwest-style chicken breast, sliced	280 g
½ cup roasted red peppers, drained, sliced	130 g
1 (4 ounce) can sliced ripe olives	115 g
1 (8 ounce) package shredded Mexican 4-cheese blend	230 g

- Preheat oven to 350° (175° C).
- Place pizza crust on greased cookie sheet and spread guacamole over crust. Top with chicken, red peppers and olives, spreading evenly. Top with cheese.
- Bake for 15 minutes or just until cheese bubbles and is slightly brown. Cut pizza into wedges to serve.

Ginger-Orange Glazed Cornish Hens

1 cup fresh orange juice	250 ml
2 tablespoons peeled, minced fresh ginger	30 ml
1 tablespoon soy sauce	15 ml
3 tablespoons honey	65 g
2 (about 1½ pounds) cornish hens, halved	2 (680 g)
½ teaspoon ground ginger	2 ml

Continued on following page

Continued from previous page

- Preheat oven to 450° (230° C). In saucepan, combine orange juice, minced ginger, soy sauce and honey and cook on high heat, stirring constantly, for 3 minutes or until thick and glossy.
- Place hens in greased baking pan and sprinkle with ground ginger, ½ teaspoon (2 ml) each of salt and pepper. Spoon glaze mixture over hens and bake 25 minutes, brushing glaze over hens several times during cooking.

Jambalaya

1 (8 ounce) package jambalaya mix	230 g
1 (6 ounce) package frozen chicken breast strips, thawed	170 g
1 (11 ounce) can Mexicorn®	310 g
1 (2 ounce) can chopped black olives	60 g

- Combine jambalaya mix and 2¼ cups (560 ml) water in soup or large saucepan. Heat to boiling, reduce heat and cook slowly for 5 minutes.
- Add chopped chicken, corn and black olives. Heat to boiling, reduce heat and simmer for about 20 minutes.

Tortellini and Chicken Supper

1 (9 ounce) package refrigerated cheese tortellini	255 g
1 (10 ounce) package frozen green peas, thawed	280 g
1 (8 ounce) carton cream cheese with chives and onion	230 g
½ teaspoon Creole seasoning	2 ml
½ cup sour cream	120 g
1 (9 ounce) package frozen cooked chicken breasts	255 g

- Cook cheese tortellini in saucepan according to package directions. Place peas in colander and pour hot pasta water over green peas. Return tortellini and peas to saucepan.
- Combine cream cheese, Creole seasoning and sour cream in smaller saucepan and heat on low, stirring well until cream cheese melts. Spoon mixture over tortellini and peas and toss, keeping heat on low. Heat cooked chicken in microwave according to package directions. Spoon tortellini and peas in serving bowl and place chicken on top.

Family Night Spaghetti

6 frozen breaded, cooked chicken breasts	
1 (8 ounce) package spaghetti, cooked	230 g
1 (18 ounce) jar spaghetti sauce	510 g
1 (26 ounce) package shredded mozzarella cheese, divided	735 g

- Bake chicken breasts according to package directions; keep warm.
- Cook spaghetti as instructed on package; drain and arrange on platter.
- Place spaghetti sauce in saucepan with 1 cup (115 g) mozzarella cheese and heat slightly, not boiling. Spoon about half sauce over spaghetti and arrange chicken breasts over top. Spoon remaining spaghetti sauce over chicken and sprinkle remaining cheese over top.

Turkey and Rice Supper

¾ pound cooked, sliced deli turkey	340 g
2 cups cooked instant brown rice	425 g
1 (10 ounce) can cream of chicken soup	280 g
1 (10 ounce) can diced tomatoes and green chilies	280 g
1½ cups crushed tortilla chips	130 g

- Preheat oven to 350° (175° C).
- Place turkey slices in bottom of sprayed 7 x 11-inch (18 x 28 cm) baking dish. In bowl, combine rice, chicken soup and tomatoes and green chilies and mix well. Spoon over turkey slices.
- Sprinkle crushed tortilla chips over top of casserole and bake, uncovered, for 30 minutes.

Baked Turkey and Dressing

1 (6 ounce) package turkey stuffing	170 g
3 cups diced, cooked turkey	420 g
2 tablespoons dried parsley flakes	30 ml
1 (10 ounce) can cream of chicken soup	280 g
1 (8 ounce) carton sour cream	230 g
¼ cup (½ stick) butter, melted	60 g
1 teaspoon ground cumin	5 ml
1½ cups shredded mozzarella cheese	170 g

Continued on following page

Continued from previous page

- Preheat oven to 350° (175° C).
- In large mixing bowl, combine all ingredients except mozzarella cheese. Mix well and spoon into greased 9 x 13-inch (23 x 33 cm) baking dish. Cover and bake 30 minutes.
- Sprinkle with cheese and bake uncovered just until cheese begins to melt.

Turkey Casserole

1 (7 ounce) package herb-seasoned stuffing	200 g
1 cup whole cranberry sauce	280 g
1 (12 ounce) can turkey	340 g
1 (10 ounce) can turkey gravy	280 g

- Prepare stuffing according to package directions. Combine prepared stuffing and cranberry sauce in medium bowl and set aside.
- In buttered, 2-quart (2 L) baking dish place turkey. Pour gravy over turkey and spoon stuffing mixture over casserole. Bake uncovered at 375° (190° C) for 20 minutes or until hot.

Chilly Night's Turkey Bake

1 (6 ounce) package stuffing mix for chicken, divided	170 g
1½ pounds cooked turkey, cut into 1-inch strips	360 ml/2.5 cm
1 (10 ounce) can cream of chicken soup	280 g
½ cup sour cream	120 g
1 (16 ounce) package frozen mixed vegetables, thawed, drained	455 g

- Preheat oven to 350° (175° C).
- Sprinkle ½ cup (25 g) dry stuffing mix evenly over bottom of sprayed 9 x 13-inch (23 x 33 cm) baking dish and set aside.
- In bowl, combine remaining stuffing and 1 cup (250 ml) water and stir just until moist and set aside.
- Place turkey strips (deli turkey can be used) over dry stuffing mix in baking dish.
- In bowl, mix soup, sour cream and vegetables, spoon over turkey strips and top with moistened stuffing. Bake uncovered for 25 minutes.

Turkey and the Works

1 (6 ounce) stuffing mix for turkey	170 g
½ (16 ounce) can whole cranberry sauce	½ (455 g)
Canola oil	
1 pound turkey tenderloin, cut in thin slices	455 g
1 (12 ounce) jar turkey gravy	340 g

- Preheat oven to 325° (165° C). Prepare stuffing mix according to package directions; (besides water, you will need ½ stick butter). Measure 1 cup (280 g) of cranberry sauce and stir into prepared stuffing mix.
- In skillet with a little oil, brown turkey slices and let them simmer, covered for about 10 minutes or until liquid has evaporated.
- Place turkey slices in 7 x 11-inch (18 x 28 cm) buttered baking dish. Cover with turkey gravy and then spoon prepared stuffing mix over turkey and gravy. Cover and bake for 25 minutes.

Turkey and Noodles

1 (8 ounce) package noodles	230 g
2½ cups diced, cooked turkey	350 g
1 (1 ounce) package prepared chicken gravy	30 g
2 cups round, buttery cracker crumbs	120 g

- Boil noodles according to package directions and drain.
- Arrange alternate layers of noodles, turkey and gravy in greased 2-quart (2 L) baking dish. Cover with crumbs.
- Bake uncovered at 350° (175° C) for 35 minutes.

Turkey Tenders

1 pound turkey tenders	455 g
1 (6 ounce) package roasted-garlic long grain, wild rice	170 g

Glaze:

⅔ cup honey	225 g
2 teaspoons grated, peeled fresh ginger	10 ml
1 tablespoon marinade for chicken	15 ml
1 tablespoon soy sauce and lemon juice	15 ml

- Place a little oil in heavy skillet and cook turkey tenders about 5 minutes on each side or until brown.
- Combine all glaze ingredients, mix well and pour into skillet. Bring mixture to a boil, reduce heat and simmer for 15 minutes; spoon glaze over turkey every 5 minutes. Prepare rice according to package directions and serve turkey over rice.

Turkey-Asparagus Alfredo

1 bunch fresh asparagus
1 red bell pepper, julienned
1 (16 ounce) jar alfredo sauce   455 g
½ pound deli smoked turkey, cut into strips   230 g

- In large skillet bring ½ cup (125 ml) water to a boil. Cut off woody ends of asparagus and cut into thirds. Add asparagus and bell peppers to skillet and cook on medium-high heat for 4 minutes or until tender-crisp, drain.
- With skillet on medium-high heat, stir in alfredo sauce and turkey strips. Bring to a boil, reduce heat and simmer until mixture is thoroughly hot.

Turkey-Broccoli Bake

1 (16 ounce) package frozen broccoli spears, thawed   455 g
2 cups cooked, diced turkey   280 g
1 (10 ounce) can cream of chicken soup   280 g
½ cup mayonnaise   110 g
2 tablespoons lemon juice   30 ml
⅓ cup grated parmesan cheese   35 g

- Preheat oven to 350° (175° C). Arrange broccoli spears in bottom of sprayed 9 x 13-inch (23 x 33 cm) baking dish and sprinkle with diced turkey.
- In saucepan, combine chicken soup, mayonnaise, lemon juice, cheese and ¼ cup (60 ml) water. Heat just enough to mix well. Spoon over broccoli and turkey. Cover and bake for 20 minutes, uncover and continue baking for another 10 minutes.

Turkey-Rice Olé

1 pound ground turkey	455 g
1 (5.5 ounce) package Mexican rice mix	155 g
1 (15 ounce) can black beans, rinsed, drained	425 g
1 cup thick and chunky salsa	265 g
1 (10 ounce) package small original corn chips	280 g
1 cup shredded pepper Jack cheese	115 g

- Brown turkey in large skillet and break up large pieces with fork. Add rice mix and 2 cups (500 ml) water, bring to a boil, reduce heat and simmer about 8 minutes or until rice is tender.
- Stir in beans and salsa; cook just until mixture is thoroughly hot. Place corn chips in individual salad or serving bowl and spoon turkey mixture over corn. Sprinkle cheese over each serving.

Pizza Pies

½ pound bulk turkey sausage	230 g
⅔ cup pizza sauce	170 g
1 (10 ounce) package refrigerated pizza dough	280 g
½ cup shredded mozzarella cheese	55 g

- Preheat oven to 400° (205° C).
- Brown sausage in skillet and stir to break up pieces of meat. Drain fat, add pizza sauce and heat until bubbly.
- Unroll pizza dough, place on flat surface and pat into an 8 x 12-inch (20 x 32 cm) rectangle. Cut into 6 squares.
- Divide sausage mixture evenly among squares and sprinkle with cheese. Lift one corner of each square and fold over filling to make triangle. Press edges together with tines of fork to seal. Bake 12 minutes or until light brown. Serve immediately.

Dipping Sauce for Chicken Nuggets

1 (18 ounce) package frozen, cooked chicken nuggets	510 g
1 cup barbecue sauce	265 g
½ teaspoon mustard	2 ml
¾ cup apricot preserves	240 g

- Place number of chicken nuggets you need in a 325° (165° C) oven and heat for 20 minutes.
- Place barbecue sauce, mustard and preserves in microwave-safe bowl and microwave on HIGH for 30 seconds, stirring occasionally or until hot.

Chicken Dipping

1½ cups cornbread stuffing mix	75 g
¼ cup canola oil	60 ml
4 boneless, skinless chicken breast halves	

- Place stuffing mix in plastic bag and crush with rolling pin.
- Add oil to center of 9 x 13-inch (23 x 33 cm) baking pan and spread around entire pan.
- Cut chicken breasts into 3 or 4 pieces, dip in stuffing mix and place in baking pan. Arrange chicken, making sure pieces are not touching. Bake at 350° (175° C) uncovered for 25 minutes. Remove from oven, turn pieces and bake another 15 minutes.

Dipping Sauce:

¼ cup honey	85 g
3 tablespoons spicy brown mustard	45 g

- To serve, dip chicken in dipping sauce and enjoy.

Smothered Beef Patties

1½ pounds lean ground beef	680 g
½ cup chili sauce	135 g
½ cup buttery cracker crumbs	30 g
1 (14 ounce) can beef broth	395 g

- Combine beef, chili sauce and cracker crumbs and form into 5 or 6 patties. In skillet, brown patties and pour beef broth over patties.
- Bring to a boil. Reduce heat and cover and simmer for 35 minutes.

Bueno Taco Casserole

2 pounds lean ground beef	910 g
1½ cups taco sauce	375 ml
2 (15 ounce) cans Spanish rice	2 (425 g)
1 (8 ounce) package shredded Mexican 4-cheese blend, divided	230 g

- In skillet, brown ground beef and drain. Add taco sauce, Spanish rice and half cheese. Spoon into buttered 3-quart (3 L) baking dish. Cover and bake at 350° (175° C) for 35 minutes. Uncover and sprinkle remaining cheese on top and return to oven for 5 minutes.

Yummy Creamy Pasta Shells

1¼ pounds lean ground beef	570 g
1 onion, chopped	
1 (10 ounce) can cream of celery soup	280 g
1 package shells and cheese sauce	

- In skillet, brown beef and onion and stir until beef crumbles.
- Add a little pepper and garlic salt if desired. Add soup and mix.
- Prepare shells and cheese according to package directions. Stir into beef mixture. Simmer for 20 minutes.

Cheesy Beefy Gnocchi

1 pound lean ground beef	455 g
1 (10 ounce) can cheddar cheese soup	280 g
1 (10 ounce) can tomato-bisque soup	280 g
2 cups gnocchi or shell pasta	150 g

- In skillet, cook beef until brown and drain. Add soups, 1½ cups (375 ml) water and pasta. Bring mixture to a boil. Cover and cook over medium heat for 10 to 12 minutes, stirring often.

Tex-Mex Supper

1 pound lean ground beef	455 g
1 large onion, chopped	
1 (15 ounce) can pinto beans, drained	425 g
2 teaspoons cumin	10 ml
½ head lettuce, torn	
2 large tomatoes, chopped, drained	
2 avocado, peeled, diced	
1 (8 ounce) package shredded cheddar cheese	230 g
1 (10 ounce) package small chips	280 g
1 (8 ounce) bottle Catalina salad dressing	230 g

- Saute beef and onion in skillet. Drain grease and add beans, cumin, salt and pepper to taste and ½ cup (125 ml) water and simmer until water cooks out.
- In large serving bowl, combine lettuce, tomatoes and avocado and toss. When ready to serve, toss salad with warm beef mixture, cheese, chips and dressing. Serve immediately.

Quick Skillet Supper

1½ pounds lean ground beef	680 g
⅔ cup stir-fry sauce	150 ml
1 (16 ounce) package frozen stir-fry vegetables	455 g
2 (3 ounce) packages Oriental-flavor ramen noodles	2 (85 g)

- Brown and crumble ground beef in large skillet. Add 2½ cups (625 ml) water, stir-fry sauce to taste, vegetables and seasoning packets with ramen noodles. Cook and stir on low-medium heat for about 5 minutes.
- Break noodles, add to beef-vegetable mixture and cook about 6 minutes. Stir to separate noodles as they soften.

Taco Pie Pan Bake

1 pound lean ground beef	455 g
1 (11 ounce) can Mexicorn®, drained	310 g
1 (8 ounce) can tomato sauce	230 g
1 (1.25 ounce) packet taco seasoning	35 g
1 (9-inch) frozen piecrust	23 cm
1 cup shredded cheddar cheese	115 g

- Preheat oven to 350° (175° C). In large skillet, brown and cook ground beef until no longer pink. Stir in corn, tomato sauce and taco seasoning. Keep warm.
- Place piecrust in pie pan and bake for 5 minutes. Remove from oven and spoon ground beef mixture onto piecrust, spreading evenly. Sprinkle cheese over top and bake for another 20 minutes or until filling is bubbly. Let stand for 5 minutes before slicing.

Potato-Beef Bake

1 pound ground beef	455 g
1 (10 ounce) can sloppy Joe sauce	280 g
1 (10 ounce) can fiesta nacho cheese soup	280 g
1 (32 ounce) package frozen hash-brown potatoes, thawed	1 kg

- In skillet, cook beef over medium heat until no longer pink and drain. Add sloppy Joe sauce and fiesta nacho cheese soup.
- Place hash browns in greased 9 x 13-inch (23 x 33 cm) baking dish. Top with beef mixture. Cover and bake at 400° (205° C) for 25 minutes. Uncover and bake for 10 minutes longer.

Southern Taco Pie

1 pound lean ground beef	455 g
1 large bell pepper, seeded, chopped	
2 jalapeno peppers, seeded, chopped	
1 (15 ounce) can Mexican stewed tomatoes	425 g
1 tablespoon chili powder	15 ml
1 (8 ounce) package corn muffin mix	230 g
1 egg	
⅓ cup milk	75 ml
1 (8 ounce) package shredded sharp cheddar cheese	230 g

Continued on following page

Continued from previous page

- Brown ground beef, bell pepper and jalapeno peppers in large skillet with a little oil; drain. Stir in tomatoes, chili powder, ½ cup (125 ml) water and a little salt to taste. Cover and cook on medium heat for about 10 minutes or until most liquid is absorbed, but mixture is not dry.
- Pour into greased 9 x 13-inch (23 x 33 cm) baking pan and sprinkle with cheese. Combine muffin mix, egg and milk and pour over meat mixture.
- Bake for 20 minutes or until corn muffin mix is light brown.

Casserole Supper

1 pound lean ground beef	455 g
¼ cup rice	45 g
1 (10 ounce) can French onion soup	280 g
1 (3 ounce) can french-fried onions	85 g

- Brown ground beef, drain and place in buttered 7 x 11-inch (18 x 28 cm) baking dish. Add rice, onion soup and ½ cup (125 ml) water. Cover and bake at 325° (165° C) for 40 minutes. Sprinkle onions over top and bake uncovered for 10 minutes.

Beef Patties and Mushroom Gravy

1 pound lean ground beef	455 g
¼ cup chili sauce	70 g
1 egg	
¾ cup crushed corn flakes	25 g
Canola oil	
2 (10 ounce) cans cream of mushroom soup	2 (280 g)

- In bowl, combine ground beef, chili sauce, egg, crushed corn flakes and salt and pepper to taste, mixing well. Shape into 4 patties, about ¾-inch (1.8 cm) thick.
- Place patties in skillet with a tiny bit of oil; on high heat, brown each patty on both sides. Reduce heat, cover and simmer for 10 to 15 minutes.
- Stir in soup with ½ cup (125 ml) water, mixing well. Spoon gravy over patties and let simmer for about 10 minutes. This gravy is great served over mashed potatoes or hot biscuits.

Beef Patties in Creamy Onion Sauce

1½ pounds lean ground beef	680 g
⅓ cup salsa	90 g
⅓ cup butter cracker crumbs	20 g
1 (10 ounce) can cream of onion soup	280 g
Noodles, cooked	

- Combine beef, salsa and cracker crumbs and form into 5 to 6 patties. Brown in skillet and reduce heat. Add ¼ cup (60 ml) water and simmer for 15 minutes. In saucepan, combine onion soup and ½ cup (125 ml) water or milk, heat and mix. Pour over beef patties. Serve over hot, cooked noodles.

Mexican Casserole

1 (13 ounce) bag tortilla chips, divided	370 g
2 pounds lean ground beef	910 g
1 (10 ounce) can Mexican stewed tomatoes	280 g
1 (8 ounce) package shredded Mexican 4-cheese blend	230 g

- Partially crush half bag chips and place in bottom of buttered 9 x 13-inch (23 x 33 cm) baking dish. Brown ground beef and drain.
- Add stewed tomatoes and cheese and mix well. Sprinkle finely crushed chips over casserole.
- Bake uncovered at 375° (190° C) for 30 minutes.

Speedy Steak Strombolis

1 (2 pound) package frozen pizza dough, thawed	910 g
⅔ cup hot salsa, divided	175 g
½ pound sliced roast beef	230 g
1 (8 ounce) package shredded cheddar cheese	230 g

- Preheat oven to 425° (220° C). On floured work surface, roll out half dough into 10 x 14-inch (25 x 36 cm) rectangle baking dish.
- Spread half salsa over dough, leaving ½-inch (1.2 cm) border. Cover with half sliced roast beef and half cheese. Starting at long side, roll jellyroll style, pinching ends together. Place on greased baking sheet. Repeat with remaining ingredients for second roll. Bake for 20 minutes or until light brown. Let cool for about 20 minutes and slice to serve.

Steak with Horseradish Sauce

1 (2 pound) 1-inch thick sirloin steak	910 g/2.5 cm
1 (8 ounce) carton sour cream	230 g
¼ cup horseradish	60 g

● Preheat broiler. Pat steak dry and sprinkle liberally with salt and pepper. Broil steak on rack about 3 inches (8 cm) from heat for 5 minutes. Let stand 5 minutes before slicing. In bowl, combine sour cream, horseradish and a little salt and pepper, mixing well. Serve with sirloin steak.

Beef and Broccoli

1 pound beef sirloin steak	455 g
1 onion, chopped	
Olive oil	
1 (10 ounce) can cream of broccoli soup	280 g
1 (10 ounce) package frozen chopped broccoli, thawed	280 g

● Slice beef across grain into very thin strips. In large skillet, brown steak strips and onion in a little oil and stir several times. Reduce heat and simmer for 10 minutes. Stir in soup and broccoli and heat. Serve over noodles.

Steak for Supper

1 pound round steak, cut in strips	455 g
1 (14 ounce) can beef broth	395 g
3 tablespoons cornstarch	25 g
1 tablespoon soy sauce	15 ml
1 red bell pepper, julienned	
1 green bell pepper, julienned	

● In large skillet brown steak strips; reduce heat, add ⅓ cup (75 ml) water, cover and simmer until liquid evaporates. Combine beef broth, cornstarch and soy sauce and pour over steak strips. Add bell peppers, stirring until mixture boils and thickens. Serve over rice.

Skillet Steak and Veggies

1 pound boneless sirloin steak, cut in strips	455 g
Olive oil	
2 (15 ounce) cans Italian stewed tomatoes	2 (425 g)
1 (16 ounce) package frozen Italian green beans, thawed	455 g
1 (8 ounce) carton sour cream	230 g
Egg noodles, cooked	

- Place sirloin strips in large skillet with a little oil. Cook on high heat for about 10 minutes. Add stewed tomatoes and green beans, bring to boiling, lower heat and cook for 10 minutes.

- Just before serving, fold in sour cream. Serve over egg noodles.

Easy Salisbury Steak

1¼ pounds lean ground beef	570 g
½ cup flour	60 g
1 egg	
1 (10 ounce) can beef gravy	280 g
Rice or noodles, cooked	

- In large bowl, combine beef, flour and egg. Add a little salt and pepper and mix well. Shape into 5 patties and place in shallow 7 x 11-inch (18 x 28 cm) baking dish.

- Bake uncovered at 350° (175° C) for 20 minutes and drain off any fat. Pour beef gravy over patties. Bake another 20 minutes. Serve with rice or noodles.

Thai Beef, Noodles and Veggies

2 (4.4 ounce) packages Thai sesame noodles	2 (125 g)
1 pound sirloin steak, cut in strips	455 g
1 (16 ounce) package frozen stir-fry vegetables, thawed	455 g
½ cup chopped peanuts	85 g

- Cook noodles according to package directions, remove from heat and cover. Season sirloin strips with a little salt and pepper.

Continued on following page

Continued from previous page

- Brown half sirloin strips in a little oil in skillet and cook for about 2 minutes. Remove from skillet and drain. Add remaining sirloin strips, brown in skillet with a little oil and cook for about 2 minutes.
- In same skillet place vegetables and ½ cup (125 ml) water, cover and cook 5 minutes or until tender-crisp. Remove from heat, add steak strips and toss to mix. To serve, sprinkle with chopped peanuts.

Skillet Sirloin

2 teaspoons olive oil	10 ml
2 teaspoons minced garlic	10 ml
½ teaspoon cayenne	2 ml
2 tablespoons soy sauce	30 ml
2 tablespoons honey	45 g
1 pound beef sirloin, thinly sliced	455 g

- Combine oil, garlic, cayenne pepper, soy sauce and honey and place in plastic freezer bag. Add sliced beef, seal and shake; refrigerate for 25 minutes.
- Place beef mixture in large greased skillet over medium-high heat and cook 5 to 6 minutes or until desired doneness, but do not over-cook. Serve over rice.

Pepper Steak

1 (1¼ pound) sirloin steak, cut into strips	570 g
1 (16 ounce) package frozen bell pepper and onion strips, thawed	455 g
1 (16 ounce) package cubed Mexican processed cheese	455 g
Rice, cooked	

- Sprinkle steak with a little salt. Cook steak strips in large sprayed skillet for about 10 minutes or until no longer pink. Remove steak from skillet and set aside.
- Stir in vegetables and ½ cup (125 ml) water. Simmer vegetables about 5 minutes until all liquid cooks out.
- Add cheese. Stir over low heat until cheese melts. Stir in steak and serve over rice.

Ginger Grilled Steak

1½ pound flank-steak	680 g
¼ cup low-sodium soy sauce	60 ml
¼ cup sugar	50 g
¼ cup ketchup	70 g
3 tablespoons cider vinegar	45 ml
1 tablespoon bottled ground fresh ginger	15 ml
¼ teaspoon cayenne	1 ml

- Place flank-steak in a large resealable bag and pour soy sauce over steak. Seal but move steak around getting soy sauce over all of steak.
- In bowl, combine sugar, ketchup, vinegar, ginger and cayenne pepper. Place steak on hot grill and cook about 5 minutes on each side, basting several times during cooking. Cut steak diagonally across grain; drizzle with remaining sauce mixture.

Grilled Steak with Garlic-Mustard Sauce

⅓ cup apple juice	75 ml
2 tablespoons dijon-style mustard	30 g
1 tablespoon minced garlic	15 ml
4 (1-inch) thick boneless beef top strip steaks	4 (2.5 cm)

- Combine apple juice, mustard, garlic and 1 teaspoon (5 ml) pepper in bowl, and mix well. Remove and set aside ¼ cup (60 ml) sauce for basting. Brush steaks with remaining sauce.
- Grill steaks on grill over medium hot coals. Grill about for 15 to 18 minutes or until desired doneness; turn occasionally.
- During last 8 to 10 minutes of grilling, baste steaks with the ¼ cup (60 ml) sauce set aside for basting.

Barbecued Pizza

1 (12-inch) pizza crust	32 cm
1 (12 ounce) package Mexican style shredded cheese, divided	340 g
1 pound shredded barbecued beef	455 g
1 (4 ounce) sliced ripe olives, drained	115 g

- Preheat oven to 400° (205° C). Place pizza crust on baking sheet and sprinkle with half cheese. Spread the shredded barbecued beef over top of cheese and sprinkle remaining cheese over top. Arrange olives over top of pizza.
- Bake 5 to 10 minutes or until hot and bubbly.

Texas Chili Pie

2 (20 ounce) cans chili without beans	2 (570 g)
1 (13 ounce) package small corn chips	370 g
1 onion, chopped	
1 (16 ounce) package shredded cheddar cheese	455 g

- Heat chili in saucepan. In 9 x 13-inch (23 x 33 cm) baking dish, layer corn chips, chili, onion and cheese one-third at a time. Repeat layers with cheese on top. Bake at 325° (165° C) for 20 minutes or until cheese bubbles.

Topnotch Hot Dogs

10 (8-inch) flour tortillas	10 (20 cm)
10 beef hot dogs	
1 (15 ounce) can chili with beans, slightly heated	425 g
1 (16 ounce) jar thick-and-chunky salsa	455 g
1 (8 ounce) package Mexican-style shredded cheese	230 g

- Preheat oven to 325° (165° C). Grease a 9 x 13-inch (23 x 33 cm) baking dish. Soften tortillas as directed on package.
- Place 1 hot dog and about 3 tablespoons (50 g) chili on each tortilla and roll tortillas. Place seam-side down on baking dish. Pour salsa over tortillas. Cover with foil and bake for 25 minutes. Remove from oven, uncover and sprinkle cheese over tortillas. Return to oven for 5 minutes.

Chihuahua Dogs

1 (10 ounce) can chili hot dog sauce	280 g

1 (10 count) package frankfurters
10 taco shells
Shredded cheddar cheese

- Place hot dog sauce in saucepan. Place frank in each taco shell. Top with heated chili sauce and cheese. Place in microwave and heat for 30 seconds or until frankfurters warm.

Winter Chili Supper

1 (40 ounce) can chili with beans	1.1 kg
1 (7 ounce) can diced green chilies	200 g
1 bunch green onions, sliced	
1 (8 ounce) package shredded Mexican 4-cheese blend	230 g
2½ cups crushed ranch-flavored tortilla chips, divided	220 g

- Preheat oven to 350° (175° C). Combine chili, green chilies, onions, cheese and 2 cups (175 g) crushed chips. Transfer to greased 3-quart (3 L) baking dish and bake 20 minutes.
- Remove from oven and sprinkle remaining chips over top of casserole and continue baking another 10 minutes.

Corny Chili and Beans

2 (15 ounce) cans chili with beans	2 (425 g)
1 (15 ounce) can Mexican-style stewed tomatoes	425 g
1 (11 ounce) can Mexicorn®, drained	310 g
2 diced ripe avocados	

- Combine chili, tomatoes and corn in microwave-safe bowl. Cover loosely and cook on HIGH in microwave for about 4 minutes. Stir in diced avocados and serve hot.

Pan-Fried Liver and Onions

Calf liver
Flour
Canola oil
2 large onions

● Slice calf liver in ¼-inch (.6 cm) thick slices. Season slices with salt and dredge with flour in shallow bowl. Brown both sides in small amount of oil in heavy skillet. Slice onions and separate into rings. Place rings on top of liver, cover and simmer for 20 minutes.

Quick-Friday-Night-Game Supper

2 (15 ounce) cans chili without beans	2 (425 g)
2 (15 ounce) cans pinto beans	2 (425 g)
2 (15 ounce) cans beef tamales	2 (425 g)
1 (8 ounce) package shredded Mexican 4-cheese blend, divided	230 g

● Preheat oven to 350° (175° C). In greased 9 x 13-inch (23 x 33 cm) baking pan, spoon both cans chili in pan and spread out with back of large spoon. Spread beans over chili. Remove wrappers from tamales and spread over beans. Sprinkle about ½ cup (55 g) cheese over top, cover and bake for 30 minutes. Sprinkle remaining cheese over top of casserole and bake for 5 minutes.

Zippy Tomato Sauce for Meat Loaf

1 (8 ounce) can tomato sauce	230 g
3 tablespoons brown sugar	40 g
1 tablespoon vinegar	15 ml
1 tablespoon Worcestershire sauce	15 ml

● In saucepan, combine all ingredients and heat, stirring constantly until mixture is thoroughly hot. Mixture may be spooned over meatloaf last 10 minutes of cooking time or spooned over each serving.

White Barbecue Sauce for Brisket

1½ cups mayonnaise	335 g
¼ cup white wine vinegar	60 ml
1 tablespoon Creole mustard	15 ml
1 tablespoon horseradish	15 ml
1 tablespoon minced garlic	15 ml
1 teaspoon sugar	5 ml

- In bowl, combine all barbecue ingredients and use as a marinade for the brisket or use it for basting the brisket. Bake or grill as you normally would when cooking a brisket.

Tortellini-Ham Supper

2 (9 ounce) packages fresh tortellini	2 (255 g)
1 (16 ounce) package frozen green peas, thawed	455 g
1 (16 ounce) jar alfredo sauce	455 g
2 - 3 cups cubed ham	280 - 420 g

- Cook tortellini according to package directions. Add green peas about 5 minutes before tortellini are done and drain. In saucepan, combine alfredo sauce and ham; heat until thoroughly hot. Toss with tortellini and peas. Serve immediately.

Supper-in-a-Dish

2 (9 ounce) packages instant rice-in-a-bag	2 (255 g)
1½ cups cubed, cooked ham	210 g
1½ cups shredded cheddar cheese	170 g
1 (8 ounce) can green peas, drained	230 g

- Prepare rice according to package directions. In large bowl, combine rice, ham, cheese and peas. Pour into 3-quart (3 L) baking dish and bake at 350° (175° C) for 15 to 20 minutes.

Mustard Ham

1 (1-inch) center slice of cooked ham	2.5 cm
2 teaspoons of dry mustard	10 ml
⅓ cup honey	115 g
⅓ cup cooking wine	75 ml

- Rub ham slice with 1 teaspoon (5 ml) mustard for each side. Place in shallow baking pan. Combine honey and wine; pour over ham. Bake uncovered at 350° (175° C) for 30 minutes.

Cherry Best Ham

1 (½-inch/1.2 cm) center-cut ham slice	
⅔ cup cherry preserves	215 g
½ teaspoon ground cinnamon	2 ml
⅓ cup chopped walnuts	45 g

- Preheat oven to 325° (165° C). Place ham slice in 9 x 13-inch (23 x 33 cm) glass baking dish. Spread preserves over ham and sprinkle cinnamon over preserves. Top with chopped walnuts. Bake uncovered for 20 minutes.

The Perfect Potato

4 large baking potato, baked	
¼ cup (½ stick) butter	60 g
¼ cup sour cream	60 g
1 cup finely chopped ham (leftover or deli)	140 g
1 (10 ounce) package frozen broccoli florets, coarsely chopped	280 g
1 cup shredded sharp cheddar cheese	115 g

- Preheat oven to 400° (205° C). Slit potatoes down center, but not through to bottom. For each potato, use 1 tablespoon (15 ml) each of butter and sour cream. With fork, work in ¼ cup (35 g) ham, one-fourth broccoli and ¼ cup (30 g) cheese. Place potatoes on baking sheet and heat for 10 minutes.

Peach-Pineapple Baked Ham

4 tablespoons dijon-style mustard, divided	60 g
1 (3 - 4) pound boneless smoked ham	1.4 - 1.8 kg
1 cup peach preserves	320 g
1 cup pineapple preserves	320 g

- Preheat oven to 325° (165° C). Spread 2 tablespoons (30 g) mustard on ham. Place ham in prepared, shallow baking pan and bake for 20 minutes. Combine remaining 2 tablespoons (30 g) mustard and both preserves and heat microwave oven for 20 seconds. Pour over ham and bake for another 20 minutes.

Sweet Potato Ham

1 (16 ounce) ½-inch thick, center cut fully cooked ham slice	455 g (1.2 cm)
1 (15 ounce) can sweet potatoes, drained	425 g
½ cup packed brown sugar	110 g
⅓ cup chopped pecans	35 g

- Cut outer edge of ham fat at 1-inch (2.5 cm) intervals to prevent curling, but do not cut into ham. Place on 10-inch (25 cm) glass pie pan and broil with top 5 inches (13 cm) from heat for 5 minutes.
- Mash each piece of sweet potato in bowl with fork just once (not totally mashed) and add brown sugar, a little salt and chopped pecans; mix well. Spoon mixture over ham slice and cook at 350° (175° C) for 15 minutes.

Fruit-Covered Ham Slice

2 (15 ounce) cans fruit cocktail with juice	2 (425 g)
½ cup packed brown sugar	110 g
2 tablespoons cornstarch	15 g
1 (½-inch/1.2 cm) thick center-cut ham slice	

- Combine fruit cocktail, brown sugar and cornstarch and mix well. Cook about 15 minutes on medium heat, stirring frequently, until sauce thickens.
- Place ham slice in large non-stick skillet on medium heat. Cook about 5 minutes or just until ham thoroughly heats.
- Spoon fruit sauce over ham.

Stove-Top Ham Supper

1 (12 ounce) package spiral pasta	340 g
3 tablespoons butter, cut in slices	45 g
2 - 3 cups cooked, cubed ham (leftover or deli)	280 - 420 g
1 teaspoon minced garlic	5 ml
1 (10 ounce) package frozen green peas	280 g
½ cup sour cream	120 g
1 (8 ounce) package shredded cheddar cheese, divided	230 g

- Preheat oven to 375° (190° C). Cook pasta in large saucepan, according to package directions, drain, while still hot, stir in butter. Add ham, garlic and 1 teaspoon (5 ml) seasoned salt.

- Cook peas in microwave according to package directions and stir, undrained, into pasta-ham mixture. Stir in sour cream and half cheese, mix until well blended. Spoon into buttered 3-quart (3 l) baking dish. Bake 15 minutes or just until bubbly around edges. Sprinkle remaining cheese on top and let cheese melt.

Honey-Ham Slice

⅓ cup orange juice	75 ml
⅓ cup honey	115 g
1 teaspoon prepared mustard	5 ml
1 (1-inch) thick slice fully cooked ham	2.5 cm

- Preheat broiler. Combine orange juice, honey and mustard in saucepan and cook slowly for 10 minutes, stir occasionally. Place ham in broiling pan about 3 inches (8 cm) from heat. Brush with orange glaze. Broil for 8 minutes. Turn ham slice over. Brush with glaze again and broil for another 6 to 8 minutes.

Ham Quesadillas

2 cups shredded (leftover or deli) ham	280 g
½ cup chunky salsa	130 g
2 teaspoons chili powder	10 ml
¾ cup whole kernel corn	125 g
1 (8 ounce) package shredded Mexican 4-cheese blend	230 g
8 large whole-wheat tortillas	

- In large bowl, combine shredded ham, salsa, chili powder and corn. Spread mixture over 4 tortillas to within ½ inch (1.2 cm) of edge and sprinkle cheese on top.
- Top with remaining tortillas and cook (1 at a time) on medium-high heat, in large non-stick skillet for about 5 minutes, turning after 2 minutes or until light golden brown. Cut in wedges and serve with pinto beans and guacamole.

Cran-Apple Ham

1 cup apple juice, divided	250 ml
1 tablespoon cornstarch	15 ml
1 cup whole cranberry sauce	280 g
1 center-cut (½-inch) thick ham slice	1.2 cm

- In medium saucepan over low heat, combine ¼ cup (60 ml) apple juice and cornstarch and stir until cornstarch is smooth. Add remaining apple juice. With medium heat, bring to boil and cook, stirring constantly, until mixture clears and thickens.
- Stir in cranberry sauce and heat for 2 to 3 minutes, stirring often.
- Place ham slice in shallow baking pan. Spread sauce over ham slice, bake at 350° (175° C) for 25 minutes and baste ham with sauce 2 to 3 times.

Broiled Ham with Sweet Potatoes

1 (½-inch thick) fully cooked, center-cut ham slice	1.2 cm
1 (15 ounce) can sweet potatoes, drained	425 g
⅔ cup packed brown sugar	145 g
2 tablespoons melted butter	30 g
1 teaspoon ground cinnamon	5 ml

- Slit edges of fat on ham slice at 1-inch (2.5 cm) intervals to prevent curling. Place ham on broiler pan and broil for about 5 minutes.
- Spoon sweet potatoes into shallow dish and mash with fork and stir in brown sugar, butter and cinnamon. Spoon sweet potato mixture over ham and place under broiler. Broil for about 5 minutes or until sweet potatoes are hot and beginning to brown.

Mac 'nCheese Casserole

4 eggs	
1½ cups milk	375 ml
12 ounces macaroni, cooked	340 g
1 (8 ounce) package shredded cheddar cheese	230 g
2 cups deli (or leftover) ham, cubed	280 g
¾ cup seasoned breadcrumbs	90 g

- Preheat oven to 350° (175° C). In large bowl, lightly beat eggs and milk with salt and pepper to taste. Stir in macaroni, cheese and ham. Spoon into buttered 7 x 11-inch (18 x 28 cm) baking dish and bake uncovered for 30 minutes.

Ham and Sweet Potatoes

3 tablespoons dijon-style mustard, divided	45 g
1 (3 - 4 pound) boneless smoked ham	1.4 - 1.8 kg
½ cup packed brown sugar	110 g
1 (29 ounce) can sweet potatoes, drained or 4 unpeeled, cooked sweet potatoes, quartered	805 g

- Preheat oven at 350° (175° C). Spread 2 tablespoons (30 g) mustard on ham. Place ham in sprayed shallow baking pan and bake for 20 minutes. Combine remaining mustard with brown sugar and spread over ham. Add sweet potatoes, baste ham with sauce and bake for 15 minutes.

A Different Macaroni

1 cup shell macaroni	105 g
½ cup heavy cream	125 ml
8 ounces shredded gorgonzola cheese	230 g
1 (10 ounce) package frozen green peas, thawed	280 g
2 cups cubed ham (deli or leftover)	280 g

- Cook macaroni according to package directions and drain. Stir in cream and cheese, stirring until cheese melts. Fold in peas and ham and cook on low heat, stirring constantly, until mixture is hot.

Ham and Veggies

1 (16 ounce) package frozen mixed vegetables	455 g
2 (10 ounce) cans cream of celery soup	2 (280 g)
2 cups cubed, cooked ham	280 g
½ teaspoon dried basil	2 ml
1 (22 ounce) package frozen buttermilk biscuits	625 g

- Cook vegetables according to package directions. Add soup, ham and basil. Bake biscuits according to package directions. Cut in half and spoon vegetable-ham mixture over biscuits.

Ham and Vegetable Supper

1½ cups corkscrew macaroni	160 g
1 (16 ounce) package frozen broccoli, cauliflower and carrots	455 g
1 (10 ounce) can broccoli cheese soup	280 g
1 (3 ounce) package cream cheese with chives, softened	85 g
¾ cup milk	175 ml
1 (8 ounce) package cubed processed cheese	230 g
1 tablespoon dijon-style mustard	15 ml
2 cups cooked, cubed ham	280 g

- In large saucepan, cook macaroni according to package directions. For last 5 minutes of cooking time, bring back to boiling, add vegetables and cook remaining 5 minutes. Drain in colander.
- In same saucepan, combine soup, cream cheese, milk, cheese and mustard over low heat, stirring until cream cheese melts. Gently stir in ham, macaroni-vegetable mixture and salt and pepper to taste, heat stirring often. Transfer to 3-quart (3 L) serving dish.

Hot Spiced Cherries for Baked Ham

1 (15 ounce) can pitted red sour cherries	425 g
1 (15 ounce) can crushed pineapple	425 g
2 tablespoons cornstarch	15 g
½ cup sugar	100 g
½ teaspoon allspice	2 ml

- Drain cherries and pineapple, reserving juices; set aside cherries and pineapple.
- In saucepan, combine cornstarch, sugar and allspice. Over medium heat, add reserved juices, stirring constantly and cook until mixture is thick and clear. Stir in cherries and pineapple and serve with baked ham.

Sweet-and-Sour Glaze
for Ham or Wieners

1 (6 ounce) jar yellow mustard	170 g
1 (12 ounce) jar grape or plum jelly	340 g

- In saucepan, combine mustard and jelly and heat. Stir until mixture is smooth.

Baked Pork Chops

¾ cup ketchup	205 g
¾ cup packed brown sugar	165 g
¼ cup lemon juice	60 ml
4 butter-flied pork chops	

- Combine ketchup, ½ cup (125 ml) water, brown sugar and lemon juice. Place pork chops in 7 x 11-inch (18 x 28 cm) buttered baking dish and pour sauce over pork chops.
- Bake covered at 350° (175° C) for 30 minutes. Uncover and continue cooking another 10 minutes.

Yee-Ha Pork Chops

1 (1 ounce) packet taco seasoning	30 g
4 (½-inch) boneless pork loin chops	4 (1.2 cm)
1 tablespoon canola oil	15 ml
Salsa	

- Rub taco seasoning over pork chops. In skillet, brown pork chops in oil over medium heat.
- Add 2 tablespoons (30 ml) water, turn heat to low and simmer pork chops for about 35 minutes. (Add water if needed.) Spoon salsa over pork chops to serve.

Stuffed Pork Chops

4 (1-inch) thick boneless center-cut pork chops	4 (2.5 cm)
2 slices rye bread, diced	
⅓ cup chopped onion	55 g
⅓ cup chopped celery	35 g
⅓ cup dried apples, diced	30 g
⅓ cup chicken broth	75 ml
½ teaspoon dried thyme	2 ml

- Preheat oven to 400° (205° C). Make 1-inch (2.5 cm) wide slit on side of each chop and insert knife blade to other side, but not through pork chop. Sweep knife back and forth and carefully cut pocket opening larger.
- In bowl, combine rye bread pieces, onion, celery, apples, broth and thyme and mix well. Stuff chops with stuffing mixture and press to use all stuffing mixture in pork chops.
- Place chops in heavy skillet with a little oil and saute each chop about 3 minutes on each side. Transfer to non-stick baking dish and bake uncovered for 15 minutes.

Sweet and Savory Pork Chops

4 - 6 (1-inch) thick boneless pork chops, trimmed	4 - 6 (2.5 cm)
½ cup grape, apple or plum jelly	160 g
½ cup chili sauce or hot ketchup	135 g

- Brown pork chops and season to taste with salt and pepper. Transfer browned pork chops to shallow baking dish, cover and place in oven and bake at 325° (165° C) for 15 minutes. Combine jelly and chili sauce or ketchup and spread over pork chops. Cook for 10 minutes, baste with sauce and cook another 15 minutes more or until pork chops are tender.

Spicy Pork Chops

4 - 6 pork chops
1 large onion
1 bell pepper
1 (10 ounce) can diced tomatoes and green chilies   280 g

- Brown pork chops in skillet with a little oil. Spray baking dish with non-stick spray. Place chops in dish. Cut onion and bell pepper into large chunks and place on chops. Pour tomato and green chilies over chops and sprinkle with 1 teaspoon (5 ml) salt over casserole. Bake covered at 350° (175° C) for 30 minutes.

Smoky Grilled Pork Chops

1 cup mayonnaise (not light)	225 g
2 tablespoons lime juice	30 ml
1 teaspoon ground cilantro	5 ml
1 teaspoon chili powder	5 ml
2 teaspoons minced garlic	10 ml
8 (1-inch) thick bone-in, pork chops	8 (2.5 cm)

- Combine mayonnaise, lime juice, cilantro, chili powder and garlic and mix. Set aside ½ cup (125 ml). Grill or broil pork chops 6 minutes on each side and brush with ½ cup (125 ml) sauce. Serve with remaining sauce on the side.

Skillet Pork Chops

⅔ cup biscuit mix	80 g
½ cup crushed saltine crackers	30 g
1 egg	
6 boneless (½-inch) thick pork chops	6 (1.2 cm)

- In shallow bowl, combine baking mix, crushed crackers and a generous amount of salt and pepper. In another shallow bowl, beat egg with 2 tablespoons (30 ml) water. Heat skillet with small amount of oil. Dip each pork chop in egg mixture and then in cracker mixture. Place in heated skillet and cook 8 to 10 minutes on each side.

Glazed-Grilled Pork Chops

1 cup mayonnaise	225 g
2 tablespoons lime juice	30 ml
2 tablespoons chopped fresh cilantro	30 ml
1 teaspoon chili powder	5 ml
8 (½-inch) thick pork chops	8 (1.2 cm)

- Combine mayonnaise, lime juice, cilantro and chili powder and blend well. Use ½ cup (125 ml) to brush over pork chops while grilling. Serve remaining glaze on the side.

Tangy Pork Chops

4 - 6 pork chops	
¼ cup Worcestershire sauce	60 ml
¼ cup ketchup	70 g
½ cup honey	170 g

- In skillet, brown pork chops. Place in shallow baking dish. Combine Worcestershire, ketchup and honey. Pour over pork chops. Cover and bake at 325° (165° C) for 20 minutes; uncover and bake another 15 minutes.

Saucy Pork Chops

4 (½-inch) thick pork chops	4 (1.2 cm)
1 tablespoon canola oil	15 ml
1 (10 ounce) can cream of onion soup	280 g
2 tablespoons soy sauce	30 ml

- In skillet, brown pork chops in oil and cook chops for about 15 minutes and drain. Remove chops from skillet. Add soup and soy sauce. Heat to boil. Return chops to skillet. Reduce heat to low. Cover and simmer about 20 minutes.

"Giddy-Up" Pork Chops

6 boneless pork chops	
½ cup salsa	130 g
½ cup honey or packed brown sugar	170 g/110 g
1 teaspoon soy sauce	5 ml

- Brown pork chops in ovenproof pan. Combine salsa, honey or brown sugar and soy sauce and heat for 20 to 30 seconds in microwave. Pour salsa mixture over pork chops, cover and bake at 350° (175° C) for about 35 minutes or until pork chops are tender.

Potato-Pork Chops

6 boneless loin pork chops	
1 (14 ounce) can chicken broth	395 g
2 (1 ounce) packet dry onion gravy mix	2 (30 g)
6 red potatoes, thickly sliced	

- Season pork chops with a little pepper and brown in large skillet with a little oil. Combine chicken broth, gravy mix and ¾ cup (175 ml) water. Add potatoes to skillet with pork chops and cover with gravy mixture. Heat to a boil, reduce heat, cover and simmer for 35 minutes or until pork chops and potatoes are tender.

Pork Chops with Black Bean Salsa

2 teaspoons chili powder	10 ml
2 tablespoons vegetable oil	30 ml
6 thin-cut, boneless pork chops	
1 (15 ounce) can black beans, rinsed, drained	425 g
1 (24 ounce) refrigerated citrus fruit, drained	680 g
1 ripe avocado, sliced	
⅔ cup Italian salad dressing	150 ml

- Combine chili powder and ½ teaspoon (2 ml) salt. Rub oil over pork chops, sprinkle chili powder mixture over chops and rub into meat. Place in skillet over medium heat and cook pork chops about 5 minutes on both sides.

- For salsa, combine beans, fruit and avocado and toss with salad dressing. Serve with pork chops.

Parmesan Covered Pork Chops

½ cup grated parmesan cheese	50 g
⅔ cup Italian seasoned dried breadcrumbs	80 g
1 egg	
4 - 5 thin-cut pork chops	

- Combine cheese and dried breadcrumbs in shallow bowl. Beat egg with 1 teaspoon (5 ml) water on shallow plate.
- Dip each pork chop in beaten egg then into breadcrumb mixture.
- Cook over medium-high heat in skillet with a little oil for about 5 minutes on each side or until golden brown.

Curried-Orange Pork Chops

¾ teaspoon curry powder, divided	4 ml
½ teaspoon paprika	2 ml
4 (½-inch) thick center-cut boneless pork chops	4 (1.2 cm)
Hot, cooked couscous	
½ cup orange marmalade	160 g
1 heaping teaspoon horseradish	5 ml
1 teaspoon balsamic vinegar	5 ml
⅛ teaspoon cayenne pepper	.5 ml

- Combine ¼ teaspoon (1 ml) curry powder, paprika and ½ teaspoon (2 ml) salt and sprinkle over pork chops. Place chops in skillet on medium-high heat and cook 5 minutes on each side. Transfer chops to plate.
- In same skillet, combine remaining ½ teaspoon (2 ml) curry powder, marmalade, horseradish, vinegar and cayenne pepper. Cook this mixture for 1 minute and scrape pan to loosen browned bits in skillet.
- Spoon sauce over pork chops. Serve over couscous.

Pork-Potato Chop

6 boneless or loin pork chops	
1 (14 ounce) can chicken broth	395 g
2 (1 ounce) packets dry onion gravy mix	2 (30 g)
4 red potatoes, sliced	

- Brown pork chops in large skillet. Combine chicken broth and gravy mix. Place potatoes with pork chops and pour gravy mixture over pork chops and potatoes. Heat to boiling, cover and simmer about 35 minutes or until pork chops and potatoes are fork-tender.

Pork Chops with Ginger-Soy Sauce

Sauce:

¾ cup chili sauce	205 g
2 teaspoons minced garlic	10 ml
1 tablespoon minced fresh ginger	15 ml
2 tablespoons Worcestershire sauce	30 ml

Pork Chops:

1 large egg, beaten	
¾ cup seasoned breadcrumbs	90 g
2 tablespoons canola oil	30 ml
4 (¾-inch) thick boneless pork chops	4 (1.8 cm)

- In small bowl, combine all sauce ingredients and set aside for flavors to blend. Place egg with 1 tablespoon (15 ml) water, in shallow bowl. Place breadcrumbs in another shallow bowl. In skillet on medium heat, pour in oil.

- Dip each chop in beaten egg first, dredge in breadcrumbs and coat well. Cook in skillet about 5 minutes on each side. Serve with ginger-soy sauce.

Chops and Stuffing

1 (6 ounce) box savory herb stuffing mix	170 g
6 center-cut pork chops	
3 onions, halved	

- Make stuffing according to package directions and set aside.

- Fry pork chops in skillet with little oil. Brown chops on both sides and place in greased 9 x 13-inch (23 x 33 cm) baking dish.

- Divide stuffing and onions among pork chops and mound on top of each. Cover and bake at 350° (175° C) for about 30 minutes.

Pork Chops in Cream Gravy

4 (¼-inch) thick pork chops	4 (.6 cm)
Flour	
2¼ cups milk	560 ml
Noodles, cooked	

- Dip chops in flour with a little salt and pepper. Brown pork chops on both sides in a little oil. Remove chops from skillet.
- Add about 2 tablespoons (15 g) flour to skillet, brown lightly and stir in a little salt and pepper. Slowly stir in milk to make gravy. Return chops to skillet with gravy. Cover and simmer on low burner for about 35 minutes. Serve over noodles.

Pork Chop Supper

1 (18 ounce) package smoked pork chops	510 g
1 (12 ounce) jar pork gravy	240 g
¼ cup milk	60 ml
1 (12 ounce) package very small new potatoes	340 g

- Brown pork chops in large skillet with a little oil. Pour gravy and milk (or water) into skillet and stir mixture around chops until mixed well. Add new potatoes around chops and gravy. Cover and simmer on medium heat for about 20 minutes.

Mexicali Pork Chops

1 (1 ounce) packet taco seasoning	30 g
4 (½-inch) thick boneless pork loin chops	4 (1.2 cm)
1 tablespoon canola oil	15 ml
Salsa	

- Rub taco seasoning over pork chops. In skillet, brown pork chops in oil over medium heat. Add 2 tablespoons (30 ml) water, turn heat to low, cover and simmer pork chops for 35 minutes. Add to more water if needed. Spoon salsa over pork chops.

Crunchy Pork Chops

1 cup crushed saltine crackers	60 g
¼ cup biscuit mix	30 g
¾ teaspoon seasoned salt	4 ml
1 egg, beaten	
5 - 6 boneless ½-inch thick pork chops	1.2 cm

- In shallow bowl, combine crushed crackers, biscuit mix and seasoned salt. In second shallow bowl, combine beaten egg and 2 tablespoons (30 ml) water.
- Dip pork chops into egg mixture and dredge in cracker mixture. Heat a little oil in heavy skillet and cook pork chops about 15 minutes, turning once.

Apple Pork Chops

4 butterflied pork chops	
2 apples, peeled, cored, halved	
2 teaspoons butter	10 ml
2 tablespoons brown sugar	30 g

- Place pork chops in non-stick sprayed shallow baking dish. Season with salt and pepper. Cover and bake at 350° (175° C) for 30 minutes.
- Place apple halves on top of pork chops. Add a little butter and a little brown sugar on each apple. Bake for another 10 minutes.

Pineapple Salsa for Pork Chops

1 (20 ounce) can pineapple tidbits, drained	570 g
¼ cup balsamic vinegar	60 ml
⅓ cup maple syrup	75 ml
2 tablespoons Asian sesame oil	30 ml

- In saucepan, combine all ingredients. Bring mixture to a boil, lower heat and simmer for 5 minutes. Serve with grilled pork chops.

Pork Chops and Fried Rice

4 - 6 boneless pork chops	
1 (11 ounce) box fried rice mix	310 g
⅓ cup frozen peas	50 g
3 green onions with tops, sliced	

- Dry pork chops and brown over medium heat in preheated, prepared large skillet. Add ¼ cup (60 ml) water and simmer until tender, adding water if needed.
- Remove pork chops from skillet and keep warm. In medium bowl, mix fried rice and ½ cup (125 ml) water. Add fried rice to skillet and heat for 10 minutes.
- Add peas and green onions to rice and cook for an additional 5 minutes or until peas are tender-crisp.

Rosemary Pork Tenderloin

¼ cup finely chopped fresh rosemary	10 g
2 teaspoons minced garlic	10 ml
2 (about 1 pound each) pork tenderloins	2 (455 g)

- Preheat oven to 450° (230° C).
- In small bowl, combine rosemary and minced garlic, mixing well.
- Make several deep slits in tenderloin and rub rosemary-garlic mixture into tenderloin. Sprinkle liberally with salt and pepper and place on greased baking pan. Bake uncovered for 20 minutes. Let stand for 10 minutes before slicing.

Spicy Glazed Pork Tenderloin

½ cup orange juice	125 ml
¼ cup lime juice	60 ml
½ cup packed brown sugar	110 g
1 teaspoon ground cumin	5 ml
1 teaspoon cayenne	5 ml
2 (1 pound) pork tenderloins	2 (455 g)

- In a small bowl, combine orange juice, lime juice, brown sugar, cumin and cayenne.

Continued on following page

Continued from previous page

- Pat tenderloins dry with paper towels and season with salt and pepper. In large skillet over medium-high heat, place a little oil. Cook tenderloins, turning until browned on all sides, about 9 to 10 minutes total. Reduce heat to medium and add orange juice mixture and cook, rolling tenderloins to coat, until mixture is thick and syrupy, about 10 minutes
- Transfer to cutting board and cover tenderloins with foil and let stand for 10 minutes before slicing crosswise into ½-inch (1.2 cm) slices. Arrange on serving plate and pour glaze over slices.

Pork Picante

1 pound pork tenderloin, cubed	455 g
2 tablespoons taco seasoning	30 ml
1 cup chunky salsa	265 g
⅓ cup peach preserves	105 g
Rice, cooked	

- Toss pork with taco seasoning and brown with a little oil in skillet. Stir in salsa and preserves. Bring to a boil.
- Lower heat and simmer 30 minutes. Pour over rice.

Rub for Pork Tenderloins

1 teaspoon chili powder	5 ml
1 teaspoon ground cumin	5 ml
1 teaspoon Italian seasoning	5 ml
1 teaspoon garlic powder	5 ml
1 tablespoon olive oil	15 ml
1 package (about 2 pounds) 2 pork tenderloins	910 g

- Combine all seasonings plus 1 teaspoon (5 ml) salt and stir in oil. Rub on both tenderloins.
- Preheat oven to 425° (220° C). Place tenderloins on foil-lined sprayed baking pan. Roast for 25 minutes or until meat thermometer in tenderloins registers 160° (70° C). Let stand for 5 minutes before slicing.

Pork and Veggie Stir-Fry

2 (12 ounce) whole pork tenderloins, thinly sliced	2 (340 g)
2 tablespoons peeled, grated fresh ginger	30 ml
1 (10 ounce) package frozen snow peas	280 g
2 small zucchini, cut lengthwise in half and sliced	
1 bunch green onions, cut in 3-inch pieces	8 cm
1 (10 ounce) can chicken broth	280 g
2 tablespoons teriyaki sauce	30 ml
1 tablespoon cornstarch	15 ml

- In large skillet with a little oil over medium-high heat, stir-fry pork slices and ginger just until pork loses its pink color. Transfer to serving bowl and keep warm.
- In same skillet with a little more oil, cook snow peas, zucchini and onions until tender-crisp.
- In small bowl, combine broth, teriyaki sauce and cornstarch, mixing well. Pour into skillet with vegetables and heat to boiling; boil, stir constantly, until sauce thickens. Return pork to skillet, stir to coat with sauce and heat thoroughly.

Grilled Pork Tenderloin with Rice

2 (about 1 pound each) pork tenderloins	2 (455 g)
1 tablespoon canola oil	15 ml
2 tablespoons jerk seasoning	30 ml
1 (6 ounce) package chicken-flavored rice	170 g
1 (15 ounce) can black beans, rinsed, drained	425 g
½ cup roasted red bell pepper, sliced	130 g
2 tablespoons chopped cilantro	30 mil

- Rub tenderloins with oil and sprinkle with jerk seasoning. Grill over medium-high heat for about 25 minutes, browning on both sides until meat thermometer inserted in center registers 160° (70° C).
- Cook rice according to package directions and add beans, bell pepper, cilantro and salt and pepper to taste. Spoon on serving platter. Slice tenderloin and arrange on top of rice-bean mixture.

Ravioli and Tomatoes

1 (9 ounce) package sausage-filled ravioli	255 g
1 (15 ounce) can Italian-stewed tomatoes	425 g
2 (4 ounce) cans sliced mushrooms	2 (115 g)
1 (5 ounce) package grated parmesan cheese	140 g

- Cook ravioli according to package directions and drain well. Stir in stewed tomatoes and mushrooms; bring to a boil. Reduce heat to low and simmer for 5 minutes. Sprinkle cheese on each serving.

Italian Sausage and Ravioli

1 pound sweet Italian pork sausage, casing removed	455 g
1 (26 ounce) jar extra chunky mushroom and green pepper spaghetti sauce	735 g
1 (24 ounce) package frozen cheese-filled ravioli, cooked, drained	680 g

- In roasting pan over medium heat, cook sausage according to package directions or until brown and no longer pink and stir to separate meat. Stir in spaghetti sauce. Heat to boiling. Add ravioli and heat through, stirring occasionally. Pour into serving dish and sprinkle with parmesan cheese.

Sausage Casserole

1 pound pork sausage	455 g
2 (15 ounce) cans pork and beans	2 (425 g)
1 (15 ounce) can Mexican-style stewed tomatoes	425 g
1 (6 ounce) package corn muffin mix	170 g

- Brown sausage and drain fat. Add beans and tomatoes, blend and bring to a boil. Pour into 3-quart (3 L) greased baking dish. Prepare muffin mix according to package directions. Drop by spoonfuls over meat and bean mixture. Bake at 400° (205° C) for 30 minutes or until top browns.

Colorful Sausage Supper

4 tablespoons olive oil, divided	60 ml
1 pound cooked Polish sausage, cut into ¼-inch slices	455 g/.6 cm
1 red bell pepper, julienned	
3 small zucchini, sliced	
3 small yellow squash, sliced	
1 (16 ounce) package penne pasta	455 g
1 (26 ounce) jar spaghetti sauce, heated	737 g

- In large skillet with 2 tablespoons (30 ml) oil, saute sausage, bell pepper, zucchini and squash until vegetables are tender-crisp.
- Cook pasta according to package directions, drain and stir in remaining oil; add salt and pepper to taste. Spoon into large serving bowl and spread heated spaghetti sauce over pasta. Using slotted spoon, top with sausage-vegetable mixture.

Sausage-Bean Casserole Supper

1 pound pork sausage	455 g
2 (15 ounce) cans pork and beans	2 (425 g)
1 (15 ounce) can Mexican-style stewed tomatoes	2 (425 g)
1 (8 ounce) package corn muffin mix	230 g
1 egg	
⅓ cup milk	75 ml

- Preheat oven to 350° (175° C). Brown sausage in large skillet and drain. Add beans and stewed tomatoes; stir and bring to a boil. Pour into sprayed 3-quart (3 L) baking dish.
- Prepare muffin mix with egg and milk according to package directions. Drop by teaspoonfuls over meat-bean mixture and bake 25 minutes or until top is light brown.

Sausage Stuffed Bell Peppers

6 large green bell peppers	
1 pound pork sausage	455 g
1 (8 ounce) can tomato sauce	230 g
1 onion, finely chopped	
1 cup instant rice	95 g

- Preheat oven to 325° (165° C). Slice peppers lengthwise in half through stem and scrape out centers.
- In bowl, combine sausage, tomato sauce, onion and rice, mixing well. Stuff pepper halves evenly with stuffing mixture and place in greased, shallow baking dish. Cover and bake for 25 minutes; uncover and bake for 10 minutes.

Simple Sauce for Sassy Ribs

2 racks baby back ribs, cut into individual ribs

Sauce:

¼ cup hoisin sauce	65 g
¼ cup wine vinegar	60 ml
2 tablespoons soy sauce	30 ml
⅓ cup apricot preserves	105 g

- Preheat broiler to high and line large shallow baking pan with foil. Place ribs in pan, meaty side down, close together but not touching.
- In small bowl, combine all sauce ingredients, mixing well. Spoon one-third of sauce over ribs and broil for 10 minutes 6 inches (15 cm) from broiler. Spoon additional one-third sauce over ribs and broil for an additional 6 minutes. Broil another 3 minutes or until ribs are crispy and done. Spoon on remaining sauce before serving.

Skillet Shrimp Scampi

2 teaspoons olive oil	10 ml
2 pounds uncooked shrimp, peeled, veined	910 g
⅔ cup herb-garlic marinade with lemon juice	150 ml
¼ cup finely chopped green onions with tops	25 g
Hot, cooked rice	

- Heat oil in large non-stick skillet. Add shrimp and marinade and cook, stirring often, until shrimp turns pink.
- Stir in green onions, Serve over rice.

Shrimp Supper

1½ pounds cooked, peeled shrimp	680 g
1 small head lettuce, shredded	
1 (14 ounce) jar artichokes, quartered, drained	395 g
2 avocados, peeled, sliced	
1 (8 ounce) bottle creamy ranch dressing	235 ml

- Combine all ingredients and serve with dressing.

Shrimp Newburg

1 (10 ounce) can condensed cream of shrimp soup	280 g
1 teaspoon seafood seasoning	5 ml
1 (1 pound) package frozen cooked salad shrimp, thawed	455 g
Hot, cooked rice	

- In saucepan, combine soup, ¼ cup (60 ml) water and seafood seasoning and bring to boil. Reduce heat and stir in shrimp. Heat thoroughly. Serve over rice.

Thai Peanut Noodles

1 (5.5 ounce) box Thai stir-fry rice noodles with seasoning packet	155 g
1 pound peeled, veined shrimp	455 g
1 (10 ounce) package frozen broccoli florets, thawed	280 g
½ cup peanuts	75 g

- Boil 3 cups (750 ml) water in saucepan and stir in noodles. Turn heat off and soak noodles about 5 minutes. Drain and rinse in cold water. Saute shrimp and broccoli in skillet with a little oil for about 8 minutes or just until shrimp turns pink.
- Add softened noodles, seasoning packet and peanuts.

Shrimp Florentine

2 (10 ounce) boxes frozen creamed spinach, thawed	2 (280 g)
1 (12 ounce) package penne pasta	340 g
2 tablespoons olive oil	30 ml
1 pound peeled, cleaned large shrimp	455 g
¼ cup grated parmesan cheese	25 g

- Cook spinach according to package directions. Cook pasta according to package directions. In large skillet, over medium-high heat, place oil, a little black pepper and shrimp; cook 3 minutes or until shrimp is thoroughly cooked.
- Add cooked spinach, pasta and parmesan cheese, gently tossing. If pasta is too dry, gradually add 1 tablespoon (15 ml) of hot water. Spoon into serving bowl and serve hot.

Shrimp Cooked in Beer

2 (12 ounce) cans beer	2 (355 ml)
3 tablespoons pickling spice	45 ml
Lemon slices	
2 pounds shrimp	910 g

- In large saucepan or stew pot, pour beer in pot and turn on high heat.
- Add pickling spice, lemon slices and ½ teaspoon (2 ml) salt. When mixture is steaming, add shrimp and stir well. Make sure there is enough liquid to cover or almost cover shrimp.
- Cook just until shrimp turns pink, remove from pot and drain.

Shrimp and Rice Casserole

2 cups instant rice	190g
1½ pounds frozen cooked shrimp	680 g
1 (10 ounce) carton alfredo sauce	280 g
1 (4 ounce) can diced pimentos, drained	115 g
4 green onions with tops, chopped	
1 (8 ounce) package shredded cheddar cheese, divided	230 g

- In saucepan, cook rice according to package directions and place in sprayed 9 x 13-inch (23 x 33 cm) baking dish. Thaw shrimp in colander under cold running water, drain well and remove tails. Set aside.
- In saucepan on medium heat, combine alfredo sauce, pimentos and green onions. Stir in shrimp and spoon mixture over rice. Cover with about half cheese and bake about 15 minutes. Sprinkle remaining cheese on top and bake for 5 minutes.

Shrimp and Chicken Curry

2 (10 ounce) cans cream of chicken soup	2 (280 g)
⅓ cup milk	75 ml
1½ teaspoons curry powder	7 ml
1 (12 ounce) can chicken breast, drained	340 g
2 (6 ounce) cans shrimp, drained	2 (170 g)
Rice, cooked	

- In saucepan, heat soup, milk and curry powder. Stir in chicken pieces and shrimp. Heat, stirring constantly, until mixture is thoroughly hot. Serve over rice.

Pan-Seared Shrimp Ancho

3 - 4 ancho chilies
6 - 8 cloves garlic, minced
1½ cups extra virgin olive oil   375 ml
2 pounds fresh shrimp, shelled, veined   910 g

- Clean ancho chilies well with dry cloth, heat for several minutes in lightly oiled
  skillet and soak in hot water for about 30 minutes. Dry chilies, remove stems
  and seeds and slice in long, thin strips. Place in large cast-iron or heavy skillet
  with garlic and about ¼ to ½ cup (60 to 125 ml) hot oil. Cook about
  1 to 2 minutes. Add shrimp and cook until they turn pink. Season with salt
  and pepper.

Creamed Shrimp over Rice

3 (10 ounce) cans cream of shrimp soup   3 (280 g)
1 pint sour cream   480 g
1½ teaspoons curry powder   7 ml
2 (5 ounce) cans veined shrimp   2 (140 g)
Rice, cooked

- Combine all ingredients in top of double boiler. Heat, stirring constantly, but
  do not boil. Serve over rice.

Grilled Garlic Shrimp

¼ cup (½ stick) butter   60 g
1 heaping teaspoon minced garlic   5 ml
1 teaspoon dried parsley   5 ml
¼ cup dry white wine   60 ml
1 pound medium fresh or frozen shrimp, peeled, veined   455 g

- For sauce, in saucepan combine butter, garlic, parsley and wine, adding about
  ½ teaspoon (2 ml) black pepper. Cook mixture about 1 minute and set aside.
- Thread shrimp onto metal skewers and grill on uncovered grill directly over
  medium-hot coals for about 12 minutes or until pink. Brush shrimp frequently
  with sauce.

Florentine Shrimp and Pasta

2 (9 ounce) frozen boil-in-bag creamed spinach	2 (255 g)
1 (12 ounce) package penne pasta	340 g
¼ cup heavy cream	60 ml
1 teaspoon Cajun seasoning	5 ml
2 tablespoons olive oil	30 ml
1 pound peeled, medium shrimp	455 g

- Bring large pot of water to boil and add spinach pouches; cook according to package directions.
- In another large saucepan, cook pasta according to package directions; drain and add cream and Cajun seasoning, mixing until well blended.
- In skillet with olive oil, cook shrimp about 3 minutes or until thoroughly cooked (but not over-cooked). Cut spinach pouches and add to pasta; stir in shrimp and transfer to serving dish.

Shrimp Scampi

½ cup (1 stick) butter	115 g
3 cloves garlic, pressed	
¼ cup lemon juice	60 ml
Hot sauce	
2 pounds raw shrimp, peeled	910 g

- Melt butter, saute garlic and add lemon juice and a few dashes of hot sauce. Arrange shrimp in single layer in shallow pan, pour garlic-butter over shrimp and salt lightly.
- Broil 2 minutes, turn shrimp and broil 2 more minutes.
- Reserve garlic butter and serve separately.

Broiled Lemon-Garlic Shrimp

1 pound shrimp, peeled, veined	455 g
1 teaspoon garlic salt	5 ml
2 tablespoons lemon juice and butter	30 ml
2 tablespoons butter	30 g

- Place shrimp in shallow baking pan.
- Sprinkle with garlic salt and lemon juice and dot with butter.
- Broil on one side for 3 minutes. Turn and broil 3 minutes more.

Beer-Batter Shrimp

1 (12 ounce) can beer	355 ml
1 cup flour	120 g
2 teaspoons garlic powder	10 ml
1 pound shrimp, peeled, veined	455 g

- Make batter by mixing beer, flour and garlic powder and stir to creamy consistency. Dip shrimp into batter and deep-fry in hot oil.

Orange Roughy with Peppers

1 pound orange roughy	455 g
Olive oil	
1 onion, sliced	
2 red bell peppers, julienned	
1 teaspoon dried thyme leaves	5 ml

- Cut fish into 4 serving pieces. Heat a little oil in skillet. Layer onion and bell peppers in skillet. Sprinkle with half thyme and pepper. Place fish over peppers and sprinkle with remaining thyme and a little pepper. Turn burner on high until fish is hot enough to begin cooking. Lower heat, cover for 15 minutes or until fish flakes easily.

Seafood Delight

1 (6 ounce) can shrimp, drained	170 g
1 (6 ounce) can crabmeat, drained, flaked	170 g
1 (10 ounce) can corn or potato chowder	280 g
2 - 3 cups seasoned breadcrumbs, divided	240 - 360 g

- Preheat oven at 350° (175° C). Mix shrimp, crabmeat, chowder and ⅓ cup (40 g) breadcrumbs. Place mixture in prepared 1½-quart (1.5 L) baking dish. Sprinkle with remaining breadcrumbs. Bake for 30 minutes or until casserole bubbles and breadcrumbs brown lightly.

Chipper Fish

2 pounds sole or orange roughy	910 g
½ cup Caesar salad dressing	125 ml
1 cup crushed potato chips	55 g
½ cup shredded cheddar cheese	55 g

- Dip fish in dressing. Place in greased baking dish. Combine chips and cheese; sprinkle over fish. Bake at 375° (190° C) for 25 minutes.

Baked Orange Roughy

1 egg, beaten	
¼ cup milk	60 ml
1½ cups cracker crumbs	90 g
⅓ cup grated parmesan cheese	35 g
4 large orange roughy fillets	

- Preheat oven to 425° (220° C). In shallow bowl, beat together egg and milk. In another shallow, combine cracker crumbs and parmesan cheese.
- Dip fillets in egg mixture, then dredge both sides of fillets in crumb mixture, pressing to use all the crumb mixture. Place in greased 9 x 13-inch (23 x 33 cm) baking pan. Bake, uncovered for 15 to 20 minutes or until fish flakes easily with fork.

Extra-Special Fried Fish

1 (16 ounce) package frozen, cooked batter-dipped fried fish	455 g
¾ cup chili sauce	205 g
1 bunch fresh green onions, chopped	
1 cup shredded cheddar cheese	115 g

- Preheat oven to 325° (165° C). Arrange fish in greased 9 x 13-inch (23 x 33 cm) glass baking dish and heat about 20 minutes or just until fish heats thoroughly. Heat chili sauce in saucepan and spoon over each piece of fish. Top with chopped green onions and cheddar cheese.

Sunday Best Fried Fish

1 (16 ounce) package frozen, cooked, batter-dipped fried fish	455 g
1 cup spaghetti sauce	250 g
2 teaspoons Italian seasoning	10 ml
1 cup shredded mozzarella cheese	115 g

- Heat fish according to package directions. While fish is heating, combine spaghetti sauce and Italian seasoning and heat. When fish heats thoroughly, place each piece on serving plate and spoon spaghetti mixture over fish. Sprinkle cheese on top.

Snappy Catfish

4 teaspoons paprika	20 ml
1 teaspoon cayenne	5 ml
2 teaspoons dried oregano	10 ml
3 tablespoons oil	45 ml
8 catfish fillets	

- In small bowl, combine paprika, cayenne, oregano and 1 teaspoon (5 ml) salt. Line fillets on baking sheet, lined with non-stick foil and coat each fillet with oil. Rub spice-mixture evenly over both sides of fish. Broil 5 minutes on each side.

Fish and Chips

1 cup mayonnaise	225 g
1 lime	
3 - 4 fish fillets, rinsed, dried	
1½ cups crushed corn chips	130 g

- Preheat oven to 425° (220° C). Mix mayonnaise and 2 tablespoons (30 ml) lime juice. Spread on both sides of fish fillets. Place crushed corn chips on wax paper and dredge both sides of fish in chips. Shake off excess chips. Place fillets on foil-covered baking sheet and bake for 15 minutes or until fish flakes.

Pan Fried Flounder

¼ teaspoon cayenne	1 ml
⅔ cup flour	80 g
¼ cup olive oil	60 ml
6 - 8 small flounder fillets	
¾ cup tartar sauce	175 g
⅓ cup ketchup	90 g

- In shallow bowl, combine 1 tablespoon (15 ml) salt, cayenne pepper, ¼ teaspoon (1 ml) black pepper and flour. Heat oil over high heat in large skillet and dredge each fillet in flour-seasoning mixture and place in skillet (in batches) and fry about 3 minutes on each side, depending on thickness of fillets. Drain on paper towels. Combine tartar sauce, ketchup and ½ teaspoon (2 ml) salt and serve with fried flounder.

Lemon Dill Fish

½ cup mayonnaise	110 g
2 tablespoons lemon juice	30 ml
½ teaspoon lemon peel	2 ml
1 teaspoon dillweed	5 ml
1 pound cod or flounder fillets	455 g

- Combine mayonnaise, lemon juice, peel and dillweed until they blend well. Place fish on greased grill or broiler rack. Brush with half sauce. Grill or broil 5 to 8 minutes, turn and brush with remaining sauce. Continue grilling or broiling 5 to 8 minutes or until fish flakes easily with fork.

Crispy Flounder

⅓ cup mayonnaise	75 g
1 pound flounder fillets	455 g
1 cup seasoned breadcrumbs	120 g
¼ cup grated parmesan cheese	25 g

- Place mayonnaise in small dish. Coat fish with mayonnaise and dip in crumbs to coat well.
- Arrange in shallow baking dish. Bake uncovered at 375° (190° C) for 25 minutes. Before serving, sprinkle with parmesan.

Flounder au Gratin

½ cup fine dry breadcrumbs	60 g
¼ cup grated parmesan cheese	25 g
1 pound flounder fillets	455 g
⅓ cup mayonnaise	75 g

- In shallow dish combine crumbs and cheese. Brush both sides of fish with mayonnaise. Coat with crumb mixture. Arrange in single layer in shallow pan. Bake at 375° (190° C) for 25 minutes or until fish flakes easily.

Baked Halibut

2 (1-inch) thick halibut steaks	2 (2.5 cm)
1 (8 ounce) carton sour cream	230 g
½ cup grated parmesan cheese	50 g
¾ teaspoon dillweed	4 ml

- Place halibut in greased 9 x 13-inch (23 x 33 cm) baking dish.

- Combine sour cream, parmesan cheese, dillweed and salt and pepper if desired. Spoon over halibut. Cover and bake at 325° (165° C) for 20 minutes. Uncover and sprinkle with paprika. Bake another 10 minutes or until fish flakes easily with fork.

Baked Halibut Fillets

4 fresh halibut fillets	
2 tablespoons lime juice	30 ml
1 (10 ounce) can diced tomatoes and green chilies	280 g
1 cup salsa	265 g
6 green olives, thinly sliced	
3 tablespoons butter, melted	45 g
Rice, cooked	

- Preheat oven to 350° (175° C). Place fillets on shallow plate and spoon lime juice over fillets. Let stand for 5 minutes.

- Place tomatoes and green chilies in 9 x 13-inch (23 x 33 cm) baking dish. Stir in salsa and olives and season with salt and pepper to taste. Place fillets on top of sauce and drizzle with melted butter. Bake for 15 minutes or until fish flakes easily with fork. Serve over rice, spooning sauce over each fillet.

Salmon Patties

1 (15 ounce) can pink salmon	425 g
1 egg	
½ cup cracker crumbs	30 g
1 teaspoon baking powder	5 ml
Canola oil	

- Drain liquid from salmon and set liquid aside. Remove bones and skin. Stir in egg and cracker crumbs with salmon.
- In small bowl, add baking powder to ¼ cup (60 ml) salmon liquid. Mixture will foam. After foaming, add to salmon mixture. Drop by teaspoons into hot oil in skillet. Brown lightly on both sides. Serve hot.

Lemon-Baked Fish

1 pound sole or halibut fillets	455 g
2 tablespoons (¼ stick) butter	30 g
1 teaspoon dried tarragon	5 ml
2 tablespoons lemon juice	30 ml

- Place fish fillets in greased, shallow pan with butter. Sprinkle with a little salt, pepper and a butter. Bake at 375° (190° C) for 8 to 10 minutes. Turn and bake another 6 minutes or until fish flakes. Melt butter with tarragon and lemon juice. Serve over fish.

Home-Fried Fish

1½ pounds haddock, sole or cod	680 g
1 egg beaten	
2 tablespoons milk	30 ml
2 cups corn flake crumbs	60 g

- Cut fish into serving-size pieces. Combine egg and milk. Dip fish in egg mixture and coat with corn flakes on both sides. Fry in a little oil in skillet until brown on both sides.

Ginger Salmon Steaks

¾ cup teriyaki marinade and sauce	175 ml
3 tablespoons brown sugar	40 g
1 teaspoon freshly peeled and grated ginger root	5 ml
4 salmon steaks	

- Combine teriyaki marinade, brown sugar and grated ginger and place in resealable bag; set aside ¼ cup (60 ml) of this mixture for later use. Place steaks in resealable bag and seal, pressing air out of bag. Turn bag over several times, coating well. Marinate 30 minutes.
- Grill salmon 5 inches (13 cm) from heat for 5 minutes on each side, brushing occasionally with reserved sauce.

Salmon and Green Beans

4 (6 ounce) salmon steaks	4 (170 g)
¼ cup soy sauce	60 ml
2 tablespoon lemon juice	30 ml
1 (10 ounce) package frozen whole green beans	280 g
Rice, cooked, buttered	

- Place a little oil in skillet over medium to high heat and add salmon steaks. Combine soy sauce and lemon juice and pour over steaks.
- Cover and cook about 5 minutes. Turn salmon and place green beans over salmon with 2 tablespoons (30 ml) water. Cover and steam 5 minutes or until beans are tender-crisp. Season green beans with a little salt and pepper and serve over rice.

Broiled Salmon Steaks

4 (1-inch) thick salmon steaks	4 (2.5 cm)
Garlic salt	
Worcestershire sauce	
¼ - ½ cup (½ - 1 stick) butter, melted	60 - 115 g

- Place salmon steaks on baking sheet and sprinkle both sides with garlic salt. Splash Worcestershire and butter on top of each steak and broil for 2 to 3 minutes. Turn steaks and splash Worcestershire and butter on top and broil for 3 minutes. (Fish will flake, but should not be dry inside.) Top with melted butter.

Alfredo Salmon and Noodles

3 cups medium egg noodles	115 g
1 (16 ounce) package frozen broccoli florets, thawed	455 g
1 cup alfredo sauce	245 g
1 (15 ounce) can salmon, drained, boned	425 g

- Cook noodles in large saucepan according to package directions. Add broccoli last 5 minutes of cooking time and drain. (Discard broccoli stems.) Stir in alfredo sauce and salmon and cook on low heat, stirring occasionally, until mixture heats through. Pour into serving bowl.

Tuna-Tomato Bowl

2 tablespoons olive oil	30 ml
1 teaspoon minced garlic	5 ml
¼ teaspoon cayenne	1 ml
2 teaspoons dried basil	10 ml
1 (15 ounce) can stewed tomatoes	425 g
1 (12 ounce) can water-packed tuna, drained	340 g
¾ cup pitted green olives, sliced	95 g
¼ cup capers, drained	30 g
1 cup pasta	75 g

- In saucepan, heat olive oil and add garlic, cayenne pepper and basil; cook on low heat for 2 minutes. Add tomatoes and bring to a boil, reduce heat and simmer 20 minutes.
- Cook pasta according to package directions and drain. In serving bowl, combine tuna, olives, capers, pasta and salt and pepper to taste. Stir in sauce and toss. Serve immediately.

Tuna Toast

1 (10 ounce) can cream of chicken soup	280 g
1 (6 ounce) can water-packed tuna, drained	170 g
2 slices thick Texas toast	
1 tomato, cubed	

- In saucepan, combine soup and tuna; stir to break up chunks of tuna. Brown Texas toast on both sides. Pour soup mixture over toast; sprinkle tomatoes over soup mixture. Serve immediately.

Tuna-Pasta Casserole

1 (8 ounce) package elbow macaroni	230 g
1 (8 ounce) package shredded processed cheese	230 g
1 (12 ounce) can tuna, drained	340 g
1 (10 ounce) can cream of celery soup	280 g
1 cup milk	250 ml

- Preheat oven to 350° (175° C). Cook macaroni according to package directions. Drain and stir in cheese until cheese melts. Stir in tuna, celery soup and milk and spoon into greased 7 x 11-inch (18 x 28 cm) baking dish. Cover and bake 30 minutes.

Tuna-Stuffed Tomatoes

4 large tomatoes	
2 (6 ounce) cans white meat tuna, drained	2 (170 g)
2 cups chopped celery	200 g
½ cup chopped cashews	90 g
1 small zucchini with peel, chopped	
½ - ⅔ cup mayonnaise	110 - 150 g

- Cut thin slice off top of each tomato, scoop out pulp and discard. Turn tomatoes over on paper towels to drain.
- Combine tuna, celery, cashews, zucchini, salt and pepper to taste and mix well. Add mayonnaise and blend. Add more mayonnaise if needed. Spoon mixture into hollowed-out tomatoes and refrigerate.

Short Order Fresh Tuna

4 (¾-inch thick) tuna steaks	4 (1.8 cm)
1 small onion, thinly sliced	
1 cup orange juice	250 ml
¼ teaspoon dried dillweed	1 ml
2 tablespoons butter	30 g

- Sprinkle both sides of tuna steaks with 1 teaspoon (5 ml) seasoned salt. Place in sprayed skillet. Cover and cook on medium heat for 6 to 8 minutes, turning once or until tuna is slightly pink in center. Remove tuna from skillet and keep warm.
- Add onion slices and cook 4 to 5 minutes and stir in orange juice, dillweed and butter. Continue cooking another 5 minutes or until sauce is slightly thickened. Serve sauce over tuna.

Tuna-Asparagus Pot Pie

1 (8 ounce) package crescent rolls, divided	230 g
1 (6 ounce) can solid white water-packed tuna, drained, flaked	170 g
1 (15 ounce) can cut asparagus, drained	425 g
1 cup shredded cheddar cheese	115 g

- Preheat oven to 375° (190° C). Form 7-inch (18 cm) square using 4 crescent rolls. Pinch edges together to seal.
- Place in 8 x 8-inch (20 x 20 cm) square, prepared baking pan. Spread tuna, then asparagus, followed by shredded cheese.
- Form remaining 4 crescent rolls into 1 square. Place on top of cheese. Bake 20 minutes or until top is brown and cheese bubbles.

Red Snapper with Salsa

6 (6 ounce) red snapper fillets	6 (170 g)
1 teaspoon ground cumin	5 ml
½ teaspoon cayenne	2 ml
½ cup chopped fresh cilantro	10 g
1 (15 ounce) can great northern beans, drained	425 g
1 (15 ounce) can Italian stewed tomatoes, drained	425 g
⅓ cup chopped green olives	45 g
1 teaspoon minced garlic	5 ml

- Dry snapper with paper towels and rub a little oil on both sides of snapper. Sprinkle with cumin, cayenne pepper and ½ teaspoon (2 ml) salt. Grill snapper about 5 minutes on each side or until fish flakes easily when tested with fork.
- Combine fresh cilantro, beans, tomatoes, olives and minced garlic, mixing well. Serve with each red snapper.

New Mexico Red Snapper

1 (8 ounce) can tomato sauce	230 g
1 (4 ounce) can diced green chilies	115 g
1 clove garlic, minced	
1 pound red snapper fillets	455 g

- In small bowl, mix tomato sauce, green chilies and garlic. Put snapper fillets on microwave-safe dish and brush tomato sauce mixture evenly over red snapper. Cover with plastic wrap. Microwave on HIGH about 3 minutes, rotate dish and microwave 2 minutes. Check snapper to see if it flakes easily. If not, microwave another 2 minutes and check if meat is flaky.

Broiled Red Snapper

2 tablespoons dijon-style mustard	30 g
¼ cup Italian dressing	60 ml
4 (6 ounce) red snapper fillets	4 (170 g)

- Preheat broiler. Combine mustard and Italian dressing in small bowl. Place snapper, skin side down on foil-lined baking pan that has been sprayed with cooking spray. Brush mustard-dressing mixture over fillets and broil 8 minutes or until snapper flakes easily when tested with fork.

Crab Mornay

2 (6 ounce) cans crabmeat, drained, flaked	2 (170 g)
1 cup cream of mushroom soup	250 g
½ cup shredded Swiss cheese	55 g
½ cup seasoned breadcrumbs	60 g

- Preheat oven to 350° (175° C).
- Combine crabmeat, soup and cheese. Pour into sprayed 1½-quart (1.5 L) baking dish and sprinkle with breadcrumbs. Bake uncovered for 30 minutes or until breadcrumbs brown.

Baked Oysters

1 cup oysters, drained, rinsed	160 g
2 cups cracker crumbs	120 g
¼ cup (½ stick) butter, melted	60 g
½ cup milk	125 ml

- Make alternate layers of oysters, cracker crumbs and butter in 7 x 11-inch (18 x 28 cm) baking dish. Pour warmed milk over layers and add lots of salt and pepper. Bake at 350° (175° C) for about 35 minutes.

Grilled Swordfish

4 (1-inch thick) pieces swordfish	4 (2.5 cm)
3 tablespoons olive oil	45 ml
½ teaspoon lemon pepper	

Sauce:

⅓ cup roasted red pepper	85 g
1 tablespoon dijon-style mustard	15 ml
3 tablespoons mayonnaise	40 g

- Rub swordfish with olive oil and sprinkle with ¾ teaspoon (4 ml) salt and lemon pepper. Grill over medium-high heat for about 10 minutes, turning once or until thoroughly cooked.
- For sauce, place all ingredients with ½ teaspoon (2 ml) pepper in blender; process until well blended. Serve over swordfish.

Marinade for Grilled Seafood

⅓ cup honey	115 g
¼ cup soy sauce	60 ml
¼ cup orange juice	60 ml
1 teaspoon cayenne	5 ml

- Combine honey, soy sauce, orange juice and cayenne, mixing well. Use as marinade for grilled or broiled seafood.

Restaurant-Style Tartar Sauce

1 quart mayonnaise	890 g
1½ cups dill pickle relish, well drained	370 g
½ cup very finely chopped onion	80 g
1 teaspoon lemon juice	5 ml
1 teaspoon dry mustard	5 ml

- In large bowl, combine all ingredients, mixing well. Store in refrigerator.

Tartar Sauce for Fried Fish

½ cup mayonnaise	110 g
2 tablespoons chopped sweet pickles	20 g
2 tablespoons finely chopped onion	20 g
1 teaspoon dried parsley	5 ml

- Combine mayonnaise, sweet pickles, onion and parsley and mix well. Serve with fish.

Red Sauce for Fried Fish or Shrimp

1 (10 ounce) bottle chili sauce	280 g
2 cups ketchup	810 g
¼ cup horseradish	60 g
3 tablespoons lemon juice	45 ml

- In bowl, whisk all ingredients together; cover and refrigerate until ready to serve.

Baked Rainbow Trout

1 pound trout fillets	455 g
3 tablespoons plus ¼ cup (7/8 stick) butter, divided	100 g
1 teaspoon tarragon	5 ml
2 teaspoons capers	10 ml
2 tablespoons lemon juice	30 ml

- Preheat oven to 375° (190° C).
- Place fish fillets with 3 tablespoons (45 g) butter in sprayed shallow pan and sprinkle with salt and pepper.
- Bake for about 6 to 8 minutes, turn and bake until fish flakes. (Do not overcook.)
- For sauce, melt ¼ cup (55 g) butter with tarragon, capers and lemon juice in saucepan and serve over warm fish. Serves 4 to 6.

Pistachio-Buttered Salmon

½ cup (1 stick) butter	115 g
8 - 10 leaves fresh basil, minced	
1 clove garlic, minced	
Lime juice	
¼ cup shelled pistachios	30 g
4 (6 ounce/1½ inches thick) skinless salmon fillets	4 (170 g/3.8 cm)
½ cup white wine	125 ml

- Preheat oven to 350° (175° C).
- Blend butter, basil, garlic, a little lime juice and pistachios in food processor until smooth and set aside or refrigerate until ready to use.
- Rinse and dry salmon fillets; place them in sprayed glass baking dish. Pour white wine over fillets and season with a little salt and pepper.
- Bake until slightly opaque, about 4 minutes. (Do not overcook.) Remove from oven and spread butter mixture over top. Continue baking until fillets are still slightly pink inside. Serves 4.

Howlin' Good Sweets

Desserts
Cakes
Pies & Cobblers
Cookies & Bars
Candy

Quick, Easy Chocolate Mousse

1 packet unflavored gelatin
½ cup light corn syrup   125 ml
1 (6 ounce) package semi-sweet chocolate chips   170 g
1 teaspoon vanilla   5 ml
1 pint heavy (whipping) cream, whipped   500 ml

- In saucepan sprinkle gelatin over ¼ cup (60 ml) water and let stand 2 minutes. Add corn syrup and over low heat, cook, stirring constantly for 5 minutes. Remove from heat and stir in chocolate chips and vanilla, stirring until smooth.
- Gently fold in chocolate mixture into whipped cream and spoon into individual serving bowls. Refrigerate.

Crave That Chocolate Sandwich

4 large slices bakery walnut or raisin bread
Butter, softened
3 - 4 ounces bittersweet chocolate bar, grated   85 - 115 g
Powdered sugar

- Lightly spread bread slices with butter. Top the unbuttered side of 2 slices evenly with the chocolate. Top with other slice, buttered side out. In a non-stick skillet, over medium-high heat, cook sandwiches until golden brown on both sides and chocolate is melted. Sprinkle with powdered sugar. Cut sandwiches in half or fourths and serve immediately.

Cranberry Pudding

1 (22 ounce) carton refrigerated tapioca pudding   624 g
¾ cup Craisins® (dried cranberries)   90 g
1 (8 ounce) can crushed pineapple, well drained   230 g

- In bowl, combine tapioca pudding, cranberries and pineapple, mixing well. Refrigerate for cranberries to blend into pudding.

Chocolate-Peanut Pizza

1 (18 ounce) roll refrigerated sugar cookie dough	510 g
⅔ cup peanut butter	190 g
1 (8 ounce) package peanut butter morsels	230 g
1 cup miniature candy-coated chocolate pieces	170 g
Hot fudge ice cream topping (optional)	

- Preheat oven to 350° (175° C). Spread dough evenly on bottom and up sides of greased 12-inch (32 cm) pizza pan. Bake on bottom rack for 20 minutes or until crust is golden brown. Cool for 15 minutes.
- Spread peanut butter evenly on top of cookie crust and sprinkle with morsels and chocolate pieces. Cut into wedges to serve. Drizzle top of each serving with hot fudge sauce.

Granny's Baked Custard

4 eggs, slightly beaten	
⅓ cup sugar	65 g
1 quart milk	945 ml
½ teaspoon vanilla	2 ml

- Preheat oven to 325° (165° C). In large bowl, combine all ingredients and stir until sugar is dissolved. Pour into small custard cups and place in pan containing ½-inch (1.2 cm) warm water. Bake for 25 to 30 minutes or until custard is firm.

Fresh Fruit with Orange Sauce

2 cups cut-up pineapple	310 g
2 cups cubed cantaloupe	355 g
2 cups strawberries, halved	305 g
2 cups green grapes	300 g
2 cups cut-up watermelon	310 g
2 cups blueberries	295 g

Orange Sauce:

1½ cups orange juice	375 ml
½ cup sugar	100 g
1 teaspoon vanilla	5 ml

- Combine all fruit in bowl with lid.
- Place orange juice, sugar and vanilla in jar with lid and shake until sugar dissolves. Pour over fruit, cover and refrigerate.

Cream Cheese Pastry

¼ cup (½ stick) butter, cut in small cubes	60 g
½ (8 ounce) package cream cheese, cut in small cubes	½ (230 g)
1 cup flour	120 g

- Preheat oven to 375° (190° C). Combine all ingredients and blend with pasty blender. With hands, knead and shape into ball, roll into round shape with rolling pin. Place in 9-inch (23 cm) pie pan. Bake 10 to 12 minutes or until lightly golden.

Fruit Cocktail

¾ cup sliced strawberries	125 g
¾ cup diced fresh pineapple	115 g
¾ cup sliced green or red seedless grapes	115 g
3 kiwis, peeled and diced	

Dressing:

2 tablespoons white rum	30 ml
2 tablespoons chopped fresh mint	30 ml
3 tablespoons sugar	40 g
1 teaspoon fresh lime juice	5 ml

- In bowl, combine strawberries, pineapple, grapes and kiwis.
- Combine dressing ingredients and pour over fruit, tossing occasionally, let stand 10 minutes until juicy and sugar dissolves.

Fruit Crispy

6 cups peeled, sliced apples	1.1 kg
3 tablespoon lemon juice	45 ml
½ cup flour	60 g
⅓ cup oats	25 g
⅓ cup packed brown sugar	75 g
1 teaspoon ground cinnamon	5 ml
¼ cup (½ stick) butter	60 g
⅓ cup chopped pecans	35g

- Preheat oven to 425° (220° C). Toss apple slices with lemon juice and place in buttered 7 x 11-inch (18 x 28 cm) baking dish. In bowl, combine flour, oats, brown sugar, cinnamon and a pinch of salt. Cut butter in with pastry blender and stir in pecans. Spoon over apples. Bake for 30 minutes until fruit bubbles and top is brown.

Grape Fluff

1 cup grape juice	250 ml
2 cups miniature marshmallows	90 g
2 tablespoons lemon juice	30 ml
1 (8 ounce) carton whipping cream	250 ml

- In saucepan heat grape juice to boiling. Add marshmallows and stir constantly until they melt. Add lemon juice and cool.
- Fold in whipped cream and spoon into individual serving dishes. Refrigerate.

Peanut Butter Sundae

1 cup light corn syrup	250 ml
1 cup crunchy peanut butter	290 g
¼ cup milk	60 ml
Ice cream or pound cake	

- In mixing bowl, stir corn syrup, peanut butter and milk until well blended. Serve over ice cream or pound cake. Refrigerate.

Honey-Rice Pudding Parfaits

12 cinnamon graham crackers, crushed	
1 (22 ounce) carton refrigerated rice pudding	625 g
½ cup honey	170 g
Fresh strawberries	

- Spoon about 2 heaping tablespoons (30 ml) crushed crackers in bottom of 5 sherbet or parfait glasses. In bowl, mix together rice pudding and honey and divide evenly into sherbet glasses.
- Sprinkle remaining crushed graham crackers over top of pudding and place 4 or 5 strawberries on top. Refrigerate.

Quick Company Apple Crisp

1 (8 ounce) carton whipping cream	250 ml
1 cup (2 sticks) butter	230 g
1½ cups packed brown sugar	330 g
⅓ cup light corn syrup	75 ml
1 (20 ounce) can pie apples (NOT pie filling)	570 g
1 (16 ounce) package crushed pecan shortbread cookies	455 g

- In saucepan, combine whipping cream, butter, brown sugar and corn syrup. Bring to a boil for 7 to 8 minutes, stirring several times. Reduce heat and cook about 3 minutes. Cool and transfer to storage jar with lid. (Sauce can be served warm or stored in refrigerator for later use, but warmed before use.)
- Place apples in individual serving bowls or sherbets and drizzle with caramel sauce and top with crushed cookies.

Strawberries in the Clouds

1 (8 ounce) package cream cheese, softened	230 g
1 tablespoon amaretto liqueur	15 ml
1 (16 ounce) box powdered sugar	455 g
1 (8 ounce) carton whipped topping, thawed	230 g

- Blend cream cheese and amaretto, beat until creamy and add powdered sugar. Gently fold in whipped topping.
- You can serve dollop of this creamy mixture over a bowl of sweetened strawberries or use as a dip for whole strawberries.

Spicy Cherry Topping

1 (20 ounce) can cherry pie filling	570 g
¼ cup sugar	50 g
¼ teaspoon ground cinnamon	1 ml
¼ teaspoon ground nutmeg	1 ml

- Place pie filling in saucepan and stir in sugar, cinnamon, nutmeg and ¼ cup (60 ml) water. Heat over medium heat, stirring several times until thoroughly hot. This topping is great served over pound cake, ice cream or creamy puddings.

Lemon Treat

1 (3 ounce) package lemon pie filling mix (not instant)	85 g
⅓ cup sugar	65 g
1 egg	
½ (8 ounce) carton whipped topping, thawed	½ (230 g)

- Mix pie filling, sugar and egg with ¼ cup (60 ml) water until smooth. Slowly add another 1¾ cups (425 ml) water.
- Cook, stirring constantly, over medium heat until mixture comes to full boil. Remove from heat and cool completely.
- Fold in whipped topping and spoon into individual dessert dishes. Top with fresh fruit.

Caramel-Apple Delight

3 (2 ounce) Snickers® candy bars, frozen	3 (60 g)
2 Granny Smith apples, chopped	
1 (12 ounce) carton whipped topping, thawed	340 g
1 (3 ounce) package instant vanilla pudding mix	85 g

- Smash frozen candy bars in wrappers with hammer. Mix all ingredients and refrigerate.

Spirit Sweet Fruit

2 cups peeled, cubed ripe mango	330 g
2 cups peeled, cubed kiwifruit	355 g
2 cups peeled, cubed fresh pineapple	310 g
½ cup sugar	100 g
¼ teaspoon ground cinnamon	1 ml
¼ cup white rum	60 ml
3 tablespoons lime juice	45 ml
¼ cup flaked coconut	20 g

- In large bowl, combine mango, kiwifruit and pineapple. Refrigerate until fruit is well chilled
- In saucepan, place sugar, cinnamon and ½ cup (125 ml) water; bring to a boil and cook 1 minute. Stir in rum and lime juice and cool completely. Pour syrup over fruit and gently toss. Sprinkle coconut on top.

Mother's Boiled Custard

½ cup sugar	100 g
4 eggs, slightly beaten	
1 gallon milk	3.6 L
2 teaspoons vanilla	10 ml

- In bowl, combine sugar, dash of salt and eggs and mix well.
- In double boiler, scald milk and add a little into egg mixture. Pour egg-milk mixture into double boiler and cook. Stir constantly until mixture is thick enough to coat spoon. Remove from heat and add vanilla. Refrigerate until ready to serve.

Sweet Crispies

1 (6 ounce) package semi-sweet chocolate chips	170 g
¾ cup crunchy peanut butter	215 g
6 cups Crispix® cereal	175 g
1½ cups powdered sugar	180 g

- In microwave-safe bowl, melt chocolate in microwave, stirring two times. Stir in peanut butter, mixing well. Gently stir in cereal, mixing until cereal is well coated. Place powdered sugar in large resealable bag and add cereal mixture. Seal and gently toss until cereal is well coated. Refrigerate in airtight container.

Divine Strawberries

1 quart fresh strawberries	715 g
1 (20 ounce) can pineapple chunks, well drained	570 g
2 bananas, sliced	
2 (18 ounce) cartons strawberry glaze	2 (510 g)

- Cut strawberries in bite size pieces. Add pineapple chunks and bananas. Fold in strawberry glaze and refrigerate.

Coffee Mallow

3 cups miniature marshmallows	135 g
½ cup hot, strong brewed coffee	125 ml
1 cup whipping cream, whipped	250 ml
½ teaspoon vanilla	2 ml

- In large saucepan, combine marshmallows and coffee. On low heat, stirring constantly, cook until marshmallows melt. Cool mixture. Fold in whipped cream and vanilla.
- Pour into individual sherbet dishes and refrigerate.

Dessert Fondue

1 (16 ounce) container coconut-pecan frosting mix	455 g
½ cup dry milk powder	35 g
¼ cup (½ stick) butter, cut in 1-inch slices	60 g/2.5 cm

- In saucepan, combine frosting mix, milk powder, butter and ¼ cup (60 ml) water. Heat, stirring constantly until butter melts and ingredients are well blended. Add about ½ cup (125 ml) water, just enough to make fondue dipping consistency. Keep warm over very low heat. For dippers, use apple chunks, banana chunks, angel food or pound cake chunks.

Caramel-Cinnamon Dessert

1 (4 ounce) package French vanilla instant pudding mix	115 g
3 cups milk	750 ml
1 (8 ounce) carton whipped topping, thawed	230 g
1 (14 ounce) box cinnamon graham crackers	395 g
1 (16 ounce) can caramel frosting	455 g

- Combine pudding and milk and mix well. Fold in whipped topping. Line bottom of 9 x 13-inch (23 x 33 cm) glass dish with whole graham crackers.
- Put half pudding mixture over crackers and top with second layer of crackers. Spread remaining pudding over top. Top with remaining crackers (2 or 3 crackers should be left). Add caramel frosting over last layer of graham crackers. Refrigerate.

Sweet Surrender

1 (14 ounce) can sweetened condensed milk	395 g
¼ cup lemon juice	60 ml
1 (20 ounce) can coconut pie filling, chilled	570 g
1 (15 ounce) can pineapple tidbits, drained, chilled	425 g
1 (15 ounce) fruit cocktail, drained, chilled	425 g
1 (8 ounce) carton whipped topping, thawed	230 g

- In large bowl, combine condensed milk and lemon juice. Stir in coconut pie filling, drained pineapple tidbits and drained fruit cocktail. Fold in whipped topping and refrigerate.

Apple Crescents

1 (8 ounce) can refrigerated crescent rolls	230 g
2 Granny Smith apples, peeled, quartered	
1 cup orange juice	250 ml
1¼ cups sugar	250 g
½ cup (1 stick) butter	115 g
1 teaspoon cinnamon	5 ml

- Preheat oven to 350° (175° C).
- Unroll crescent rolls and separate. Wrap each apple quarter with crescent roll. Place each apple crescent in greased 9 x 13-inch (23 x 33 cm) baking dish.
- In saucepan, combine orange juice, sugar, butter and cinnamon and bring to a boil. Pour over crescents and bake for 30 minutes or until golden and bubbly.

Winter Peach Dessert

1 (15 ounce) can sliced peaches	425 g
¼ cup grenadine syrup	60 ml
¼ cup sugar	50 g
1 cup crumbled coconut macaroon cookies	160 g

- Drain peaches, reserving ¼ cup (60 ml) liquid. In saucepan, combine peach slices, reserved liquid, grenadine syrup and sugar. Bring to a boil, reduce heat and simmer 6 minutes, turning peach slices to coat with syrup.
- Gently stir in crumbled macaroons over low heat until liquid is absorbed by macaroons. Serve warm in sherbert dishes.

Blueberry Fluff

1 (20 ounce) can blueberry pie filling	570 g
1 (20 ounce) can crushed pineapple, drained	570 g
1 (14 ounce) can sweetened, condensed milk	395 g
1 (8 ounce) carton whipped topping, thawed	230 g

- Mix pie filling, pineapple and condensed milk. Fold in whipped topping. Combine all ingredients and pour into parfait glasses. Refrigerate.

Chilled Fruit Medley

2 cups halved red grapes, chilled	300 g
2 cups cubed honeydew melon, chilled	355 g
1 (20 ounce) can pineapple tidbits, drained, chilled	570 g
1 large banana, sliced, chilled	
¾ cup peach preserves	240 g

- In salad bowl, combine grapes, melon, pineapple and banana. Add peach preserves and toss to coat all fruit. Refrigerate before serving.

Chocolate-Vanilla-Almond Parfait

1 (3 ounce) box instant chocolate pudding mix	85 g
1 (3 ounce) box instant vanilla pudding mix	85 g
4 cups milk	945 ml
2 cups slivered almonds	335 g

- Use 2 separate bowls to prepare each pudding with milk according to package directions. Cover tightly with plastic wrap and refrigerate.
- Place slivered almonds in dry skillet over medium heat. Stir until almonds brown evenly.
- In parfait glasses, first spoon in chocolate pudding, then vanilla pudding to top of glass. Garnish with almonds. Refrigerate.

Kid's Delight

¼ cup (½ stick) butter	60 g
1 (10 ounce) package marshmallows	280 g
6 cups cocoa rice cereal	155 g
½ cup miniature chocolate chips	85 g

- In large saucepan over low heat, melt butter and add marshmallows. Stirring constantly, mix until marshmallows melt. Remove from heat. Stir in rice cereal and chocolate chips. Spoon into sprayed 9 x 13-inch (23 x 33 cm) baking pan, using spatula to level cereal mixture. When cool, cut into squares to serve.

Pick Your Fruit–Here's the Dressing

This dressing is wonderful over a medley of fresh fruit.

½ cup mayonnaise	110 g
½ cup sour cream	120 g
½ cup powdered sugar	60 g
1 teaspoon lemon juice	5 ml
½ teaspoon ground cinnamon	2 ml

- In bowl, combine mayonnaise and sour cream and mix well; stir in powdered sugar, lemon juice and cinnamon to blend well.

Creamy Topping for Berries

4 ounces (½ of an 8 ounce package) cream cheese, softened	115 g/230 g
¼ cup honey	85 g
2 tablespoons orange juice	30 ml
¼ teaspoon ground cinnamon	1 ml

- With mixer, beat together cream cheese, honey, orange juice and cinnamon until creamy. Serve topping with an assortment of berries or fruit.

Pound Cake Deluxe

1 (10-inch) round bakery pound cake	25 cm
1 (20 ounce) can crushed pineapple	570 g
1 (5 ounce) package coconut instant pudding mix	140 g
1 (8 ounce) carton whipped topping, thawed	230 g

- Slice cake horizontally to make 3 layers.
- Mix pineapple, pudding mix and whipped topping; blend well. Spread on each layer and top of cake. Coconut may be sprinkled on top layer. Refrigerate.

Extreme Pound Cake

1 (9-inch round) bakery pound cake	23 cm
1 (20 ounce) can crushed pineapple with juice	570 g
1 (4 serving size) instant vanilla pudding or pie filling mix	
1 (8 ounce) carton whipped topping, thawed, divided	230 g

- Cut pound cake horizontally into 3 layers and place bottom layer on cake plate. In bowl, gently combine and mix crushed pineapple and pudding together. When well mixed, fold in half whipped topping.

Continued on following page

Continued from previous page

- Spread one-third pineapple mixture over top of bottom layer (not on sides). Place second layer on top and spread half remaining pineapple mixture. Top with third cake layer and remaining pineapple mixture. Top with remaining whipped topping. Refrigerate.

Pound Cake Supreme

1 round bakery pound cake	
1 (20 ounce) can apple pie filling	570 g
⅓ cup sugar	65 g
⅓ cup packed brown sugar	75 g
1 teaspoon ground cinnamon	5 ml
¾ cup finely chopped pecans	85 g

- Cut generous slices of pound cake (as many as you need) and place on individual dessert plates. In saucepan, combine apple pie filling, sugar, brown sugar, cinnamon and pecans and heat, stirring several times. Spoon over pound cake slices and serve warm.

Spiced-Up Pound Cake

1 (10 ounce) pound cake loaf, sliced	280 g
2 cups applesauce	510 g
½ cup sugar	100 g
½ teaspoon ground cinnamon	2 ml
½ teaspoon allspice	2 ml
¾ cup finely chopped pecans	85 g

- Place each slice of pound cake (as many as you need) on individual serving plate.
- Over medium-high heat, combine and heat applesauce, sugar, spices and pecans. Place heaping tablespoon (15 ml) applesauce mixture over pound cake slice.

O'Shaughnessy's Special

1 (10 ounce) pound cake loaf	280 g
1 (15 ounce) can crushed pineapple	425 g
1 (3.4 ounce) box pistachio pudding mix	100 g
1 (8 ounce) carton whipped topping, thawed	230 g

- Slice cake horizontally and make 3 layers. Combine pineapple and pudding mix and beat until mixture begins to thicken. Fold in whipped topping and blend well. Spread on each layer and on top. Refrigerate.

Delicious Lemon Sauce for Pound Cake

1 cup slaw dressing (from 16 ounce bottle)	250 ml/455 g
1 (8 ounce) package cream cheese, softened	230 g
¼ cup lemon juice	60 ml
¼ cup half-and-half cream	60 ml
1½ cups powdered sugar	180 g

- In mixer, beat together slaw dressing and cream cheese until creamy. Add lemon juice, cream and powdered sugar and continue beating until creamy. Spoon sauce over pieces of pound cake. It is also good over apple pie or spice cake.

Pecan Cake

1 (18 ounce) box butter pecan cake mix	510 g
½ cup (1 stick) butter, melted	60 g
1 egg	
1 cup chopped pecans	110 g
1 (8 ounce) package cream cheese, softened	230 g
2 eggs	
1 (1 pound) box powdered sugar	455 g

- Combine cake mix, ¾ cup (175 ml) water, butter and egg, mixing well. Stir in pecans. Pour into 9 x 13-inch (23 x 33 cm) baking dish.
- With mixer, combine cream cheese, eggs and powdered sugar. Pour over cake mixture. Bake at 350° (175° C) for 40 minutes. Test with toothpick to make sure cake is done.

Pink Lady Cake

1 (18 ounce) box strawberry cake mix	510 g
3 eggs	
1 teaspoon lemon extract	5 ml
1 (20 ounce) can strawberry pie filling	570 g

- In mixing bowl, beat cake mix, eggs and lemon extract together.
- Fold in pie filling. Pour in greased, floured 9 x 13-inch (23 x 33 cm) baking pan. Bake at 350° (175° C) for 30 to 35 minutes. Test with toothpick to make sure that cake is done.

Hawaiian Dream Cake

1 (18 ounce) yellow cake mix	510 g
4 eggs	
¾ cup oil	175 ml
½ (20 ounce) can crushed pineapple with ½ liquid	½ (570 g)

- With mixer, beat all ingredients for 4 minutes. Pour into greased, floured 9 x 13-inch (23 x 33 cm) baking pan. Bake at 350° (175° C) for 35 minutes or until cake tests done with toothpick.

Coconut-Pineapple Glaze for Hawaiian Dream Cake:

½ (20 ounce) can crushed pineapple with ½ liquid	½ (570 g)
½ cup (1 stick) butter	115 g
1 (16 ounce) box powdered sugar	455 g
1 (7 ounce) can flaked coconut	200 g

- Heat pineapple and butter and boil 1½ minutes. Add powdered sugar and coconut. Punch holes in cake with knife. Pour hot glaze over cake.

Lemon-Pineapple Cake

1 (18 ounce) box lemon cake mix	510 g
1 (20 ounce) can crushed pineapple	570 g
3 eggs	
⅓ cup oil	75 ml

- In mixing bowl, combine all ingredients. Blend on low speed to moisten and beat on medium for 2 minutes. Pour batter into greased, floured 9 x 13-inch (23 x 33 cm) baking pan.
- Bake at 350° (175° C) for 30 minutes. Test with toothpick to be sure cake is done. When cake is baking, start topping for cake. Cool for about 15 minutes.

Topping for Lemon-Pineapple Cake:

1 (14 ounce) can sweetened condensed milk	395 g
1 cup sour cream	240 g
¼ cup lemon juice	60 ml

- In medium bowl, combine all ingredients. Stir well to blend.
- Pour over warm cake. Refrigerate.

Quick Summer Cake

1 (16 ounce) frozen loaf pound cake	455 g
1 (8 ounce) carton whipping cream	250 ml
1 (20 ounce) can coconut pie filling	570 g
2 kiwifruit, peeled, halved, sliced	

- Split cake into three horizontal layers and place bottom layer on serving platter. With mixer, beat whipping cream until thickened and fold in coconut pie filling, mixing until well blended. Spread one-third mixture over bottom cake layer. Place second layer on top and spread half remaining cream mixture on top. Top with third layer and spread remaining cream mixture on top. Garnish with slices of kiwi. Refrigerate.

Miracle Cake

1 (18 ounce) lemon cake mix	510 g
3 eggs	
⅓ cup oil	75 ml
1 (20 ounce) can crushed pineapple	570 g

- In mixing bowl, combine all ingredients.
- Blend on low speed and beat on medium for 2 minutes.
- Pour batter into greased, floured 9 x 13-inch (23 x 33 cm) baking dish. Bake at 350° (175° C.) for 30 to 35 minutes until cake tests done with toothpick.

Topping for Miracle Cake:

1 (14 ounce) can sweetened condensed milk	395 g
¼ cup lemon juice	60 ml
1 (8 ounce) carton whipped topping, thawed	230 g

- Blend all ingredients and mix well. Spread over cake. Refrigerate.

All You Can Eat Chocolate Cake

1 (18 ounce) box chocolate cake mix	510 g
1 cup mayonnaise	225 g
3 eggs, slightly beaten	
1 teaspoon ground cinnamon	5 ml
1 (16 ounce) container chocolate frosting	

- Preheat oven to 350° (175° C).
- In mixing bowl, beat together cake mix, mayonnaise, eggs, cinnamon and 1 cup (250 ml) water. Pour into 2 (9-inch/23 cm) cake pans and bake as directed on cake mix box.
- Frost each layer with chocolate frosting.

Shortcakes for Fresh Berries

⅔ cup flour	80 g
¾ teaspoon baking powder	4 ml
2 heaping tablespoons shortening	40 g
3 tablespoons milk	45 ml
Sugar	
1½ cups mixed fresh berries	230 g
¾ cup sugar, divided	150 g
Whipped topping, thawed	

- Preheat oven to 400° (205° C). In bowl, combine flour, baking powder, a little salt and cut in shortening with fork. Stir in milk, just until moistened. Drop heaping ¼ cup (60 ml) batter about 2 inches (5 cm) apart on greased baking pan. Using wet glass bottom, flatten each circle and sprinkle on a little sugar. Bake for about 12 minutes.

- Sprinkle remaining sugar over berries. Split shortcakes in half; spoon berries on bottom half and replace tops. Garnish with whipped topping.

Strawberry Shortcakes

2½ cups biscuit mix	300 g
¼ cup sugar	50 g
3 tablespoons butter, softened	45 g
½ cup milk	125 ml
1 (8 ounce) carton whipped topping, thawed	230 g

Strawberry Glaze:

1 tablespoon cornstarch	15 ml
1 teaspoon almond extract	5 ml
¾ cup sugar	150 g
1 (16 ounce) container frozen strawberries, thawed	455 g

- Preheat oven to 350° (175° C). In mixing bowl, combine biscuit mix and sugar; cut in butter until mixture is crumbly. Add milk and stir just until soft dough forms. Drop heaping tablespoons of batter onto greased baking sheet. Bake for about 14 minutes until light brown.

- For strawberries, place cornstarch, almond extract, sugar and 2 tablespoons (30 ml) water in saucepan. Add strawberries and bring mixture to a boil, stirring constantly. Reduce heat, cook and stir until mixture thickens. Remover from heat and refrigerate.

- When ready to serve, split shortcakes in half, spoon about ½ cup (125 ml) strawberry mixture over each shortcake, top with an ample amount of whipped topping and place top half of shortcake on top.

Shortcakes for Strawberries or Raspberries

2½ cups plus 2 tablespoons flour	300 g/15 g
2½ teaspoons baking powder	7 ml
⅓ cup sugar	65 g
½ cup (1 stick) butter, softened, sliced	115 g
1 cup milk	250 ml

- Preheat oven to 400° (205° C). In bowl, combine flour, baking powder, sugar and butter. Stir and mix with fork until mixture resembles coarse meal.
- Add milk and mix until dough forms. Place dough on lightly floured surface and with lightly floured hands, pat dough into 4 x 6-inch (10 x 15 cm) rectangle. Cut dough into 8 squares and place on greased baking sheet.
- Bake for 30 minutes or until light golden. To serve, cut shortcakes in half and serve with sugared strawberries or raspberries and top with whipped topping.

Butter-Toffee Cake

1 (18 ounce) box butter pecan cake mix	510 g
1 cup almond toffee bits	170 g
1 cup chopped pecans	110 g
Powdered sugar	

- Mix cake mix according to package directions. Fold in toffee bits and pecans. Pour into greased, floured bundt cake pan. Bake at 350° (175° C) for 40 minutes or until toothpick inserted in center comes out clean. Allow cake to cool several minutes and remove cake from pan. Dust with sifted powdered sugar.

Apple Shortcakes

1 (7 ounce) package apple-cinnamon muffin mix	200 g
½ cup milk	125 ml
¼ cup sour cream	60 g
⅓ cup chopped pecans	35 g

Apple-Cinnamon Sauce:

1 (20 ounce) can apple pie filling	570 g
½ cup sugar	100 g
¼ cup raisins	40 g
¼ teaspoon ground cinnamon	1 ml

- Preheat oven to 425° (220° C).
- In bowl, combine muffin mix, milk, sour cream and pecans, stirring just until blended. Pour into greased and floured 9-inch (23 cm) cake pan and bake for 10 to 12 minutes or until toothpick inserted in center comes out clean. Cool completely and cut into squares.
- In saucepan over medium heat, combine pie filling, sugar, raisins, cinnamon and ¼ cup (60 ml) water. Stir until well blended and serve over shortcake squares.

Strawberry-Raspberry Shortcakes

Shortcakes:

2 cups biscuit mix	240 g
¼ cup cornmeal	40 g
½ cup plus 1 tablespoon sugar, divided	100 g/15 ml
1 (8 ounce) carton whipping cream	250 ml

Fruit:

2 pints strawberries, sliced	665 g
1 pint red raspberries	245 g
⅔ cup sugar	135 g
1 quart vanilla ice cream	945 ml

- Preheat oven to 400° (205° C). In bowl, combine baking mix, cornmeal and ½ cup (100 g) sugar. Stir in cream, mixing just until mixture is evenly moistened. Drop 8 mounds of dough 2-inches (5 cm) apart on ungreased baking sheet; sprinkle tops with scant tablespoon (15 ml) sugar. Bake about 15 minutes or until light brown. Remove to wire rack to cool.

Continued on following page

Continued from previous page

- While shortcakes are baking, combine strawberries, raspberries, sugar and 1 tablespoon (15 ml) water; leave at room temperature while shortcakes bake.
- To serve, carefully cut shortcakes horizontally in half with a serrated knife. Place bottom on each individual dessert plate. Top with scoop of ice cream, then spoon on berries and juice; then add shortcake tops.

Fudge Cake Squares

1 cup plus 2 tablespoons flour	120 g/15 g
3 tablespoons cocoa	15 g
1 cup sugar	200 g
½ teaspoon baking soda	2 ml
⅓ cup oil	75 ml
1 large egg	
1 teaspoon vanilla	5 ml

- Preheat oven to 350° (175° C).
- In large bowl, stir together flour, cocoa, sugar, baking soda and ½ teaspoon (2 ml) salt. Add ¾ cup (175 ml) water, oil, egg and vanilla and beat on low speed until well mixed. Then beat on medium speed another 2 minutes.
- Pour into sprayed 9-inch (23 cm) square baking pan and bake for 30 to 35 minutes or until toothpick inserted in center comes out clean; cool. Transfer cake to serving plate and cut into squares to serve.

White Chocolate-Almond Cake

1 (18 ounce) box white cake mix	510 g
4 egg whites	
¼ cup canola oil	60 ml
1 teaspoon almond extract	5 ml
1 cup chopped almonds	170 g
6 (1 ounce) squares white chocolate, melted	6 (30 g)
1 (16 ounce) container caramel frosting	455 g

- Preheat oven to 350° (175° C). In mixing bowl, combine cake mix, egg whites, oil, almond extract and 1½ cups (375 ml) water; beat until well blended.
- Stir in chopped almonds and melted white chocolate and pour into 2 (9-inch/23 cm) round cake pans. Bake 30 to 35 minutes or until toothpick inserted in center comes out clean.
- Spread each layer with half caramel frosting. Place second layer on top of first layer.

Coconut-Angel Cake

1 (14 ounce/10-inch) round angel food cake	396/25 cm
1 (20 ounce) can coconut pie filling	570 g
1 (12 ounce) carton whipped topping, thawed	340 g
3 tablespoons flaked coconut	15 g

- Cut angel food cake horizontally to make 3 layers.
- Combine coconut pie filling and whipped topping. Spread one-third mixture on first layer. Top with second layer.
- Spread one-third mixture on second layer and top with third layer. Spread remaining whipped topping mixture on top of cake. Sprinkle coconut on top of mixture. Refrigerate.

Fruit Cocktail Crepes

1 cup packed brown sugar	220 g
1 cup (2 sticks) butter, divided	230 g
3 (8-inch) packages flour tortillas	3 (20 cm)
4 (15 ounce) cans fruit cocktail, thoroughly drained	4 (425 g)

- Preheat oven at 325° (165° C). In small saucepan over low heat, stir constantly brown sugar and ⅓ cup (75 g) butter until sugar melts and mixes well.
- Melt remaining butter and brush flour tortillas on both sides. (If each tortilla is not soft enough to roll without breaking, heat 2 to 3 at a time wrapped in damp paper towel for 4 to 5 seconds in microwave oven.) For each crepe, place 2 teaspoons (10 ml) sugar mixture and 1 tablespoon (15 ml) drained fruit cocktail in middle of each tortilla.
- Roll each tortilla and place, seam-side down, in 7 x 11-inch (18 x 28 cm) baking pan. Spread remaining sugar mixture on top. Bake covered for 15 minutes or until sugar mixture bubbles.

Peanut Butter Pie

1 (8 ounce) package cream cheese, softened	230 g
1 cup sugar	200 g
1 cup peanut butter	290 g
1 teaspoon vanilla	5 ml
1 (8 ounce) carton whipping cream, whipped	250 ml
1 (9-inch) graham cracker piecrust	23 cm

- In mixing bowl, combine cream cheese, sugar, peanut butter and vanilla and beat until creamy. Fold in whipped cream and spoon into graham cracker piecrust and refrigerate.

Million-Dollar Pie

24 round, buttery crackers, crumbled	
1 cup chopped pecans	110 g
4 egg whites (absolutely no yolks at all)	
1 cup sugar	200 g

- Mix cracker crumbs with pecans. In separate mixing bowl, beat egg whites until stiff and slowly add sugar while still mixing.
- Gently fold crumbs and pecan mixture into egg whites. Pour into pie pan and bake at 350° (175° C) for 20 minutes. Cool.

Individual Apple Pies

2 tart baking apples	
⅔ cup sugar	135 g
¾ teaspoon ground cinnamon	4 ml
2 tablespoons flour	15 g
1 frozen piecrust (½ of 15 ounce package)	425 g

- Preheat oven to 425° (220° C). Peel, core and chop apples. In bowl, combine chopped apples, sugar, cinnamon and flour.
- Unroll piecrust flat and cut five circles and place each circle inside 5 spaces of muffin tin. Evenly divide apple mixture. Cut remaining piecrust into strips and place on top of apple mixture.
- Place about ⅓ cup (75 ml) water in extra muffin tin. Bake for 18 minutes or until bubbling and remove from tin when cool.

Apple Crumble

1 (20 ounce) can apple pie filling	570 g
½ cup packed brown sugar	110 g
½ teaspoon ground cinnamon	2 ml
½ teaspoon ground ginger	2 ml

- Preheat oven to 350° (175° C).
- In bowl, combine apple pie filling, brown sugar, cinnamon and ginger. Spoon into buttered 9-inch (23 cm) square baking dish.

Topping:

1 cup flour	120 g
¾ cup packed brown sugar	165 g
¼ teaspoon ground cinnamon	1 ml
¼ teaspoon ground ginger	1 ml
½ cup (1 stick) butter	115 g
⅓ cup slivered almonds	55 g

- In separate bowl, combine flour, brown sugar, cinnamon and ginger; cut in butter until mixture resembles coarse crumbs. Add almonds and sprinkle over apple mixture.
- Bake for 35 minutes or until filling is bubbly and topping is golden brown.

Holiday Pie

1 (8 ounce) package cream cheese, softened	230 g
1 (14 ounce) can sweetened condensed milk	395 g
1 (3.4 ounce) box instant vanilla pudding mix	100 g
1½ cups whipped topping, thawed	115 g
1 (9-inch) graham cracker piecrust	23 cm
Holiday candies, crumbled	

- With mixer, beat cream cheese until smooth. Gradually add sweetened condensed milk and beat until smooth.
- Add ¾ cup (175 ml) water and pudding mix and beat until smooth. Fold in whipped topping. Pour into piecrust. Top with crumbled holiday candies. Refrigerate.

Banana-Vanilla Pie

1 banana, sliced	
1 (9-inch) graham cracker piecrust	23 cm
2 cups cold milk	480 ml
⅓ cup sugar	80 ml
2 (4 serving size) packages vanilla instant pudding mix	
1 (8 ounce) carton French vanilla whipped topping, thawed, divided	230 g

- Place banana slices in graham cracker piecrust. Pour milk in medium bowl and add sugar and pudding mix; beat for about 2 minutes. Mixture will be thick. Fold in half of whipped topping and spoon into piecrust.
- Refrigerate before serving. Top each serving with dabs of remaining whipped topping.

Cherry Crisp

2 (20 ounce) cans cherry pie filling	2 (570 g)
1 (18 ounce) box white cake mix	510 g
½ cup (1 stick) butter	115 g
2 cups chopped pecans	220 g

- Pour pie filling into sprayed 9 x 13-inch (23 x 33 cm) baking dish. Sprinkle cake mix over top of filling. Dot with butter and cover with pecans. Bake uncovered at 350° (175° C) for 40 minutes.

Pound Cake Cobbler

1 (10 ounce) bakery pound cake loaf	280 g
1 (20 ounce) can pineapple pie filling	570 g
½ teaspoon almond extract	2 ml
¼ cup sliced, toasted almonds	40 g
3 tablespoons powdered sugar	25 g
1 (8 ounce) carton whipping cream, whipped	250 ml

- Cut cake into 1-inch cubes and place in a 7 x 11-inch (18 x 28 cm) glass baking dish. In bowl, combine pineapple pie filling, almond extract and ¼ cup (60 ml) water, mixing well. Spoon pie filling mixture over cake and microwave on HIGH for 2 to 3 minutes or until thoroughly hot.
- Stir powdered sugar into whipped cream. Spoon cobbler into individual sherbet glasses and top with whipped cream. Sprinkle almonds on top.

Cherry Cobbler

2 (20 ounce) cans cherry pie filling	2 (570 g)
1 (18 ounce) box white cake mix	510 g
¾ cup (1½ sticks) butter, melted	170 g
1 (4 ounce) package slivered almonds	115 g
Whipped topping, thawed	

- Spread pie filling in greased 9 x 13-inch (23 x 33 cm) baking pan. Sprinkle cake mix over cherries. Drizzle with melted butter over top. Sprinkle almonds over top.
- Bake at 350° (175° C) for 40 minutes. Top with whipped topping.

Blueberry Cobbler Deluxe

1 (20 ounce) can blueberry pie filling	570 g
½ cup sugar	100 g
1 tablespoon lemon juice	15 ml
1½ cups biscuit mix	180 g
¼ cup plus 1 tablespoon sugar	50 g/15 ml
¼ cup (1 stick) butter, divided	60 g
¾ cup sour cream	180 g

- Combine blueberry pie filling, sugar and lemon juice, stir to blend. Spoon into buttered 9-inch (23 cm) square baking dish.
- In large bowl, combine biscuit mix and ¼ cup (50 g) sugar; and cut in three-fourths butter until mixture is crumbly. Stir in sour cream, tossing with fork until mixture forms a ball.
- Roll out to fit top of baking dish and place pastry over filling. Melt remaining butter and brush over pastry. Sprinkle 1 tablespoon (15 ml) sugar over top.

Blueberry Bounce

1½ cups quick-cooking oats	120 g
2 cups packed brown sugar	440 g
1 (20 ounce) can blueberry pie filling	570 g
1 (18 ounce) box yellow cake mix	510 g
¾ cup chopped pecans	85 g
½ cup (1 stick) butter, melted	115 g

- Preheat oven to 350° (175° C). In medium bowl, combine oats and brown sugar and sprinkle half in sprayed 9 x 13-inch (23 x 33 cm) glass baking dish.
- Spoon blueberry pie filling over oat-sugar mixture and spread evenly, follow with cake mix, spread evenly. Combine pecans with remaining oat mixture and sprinkle over pie filling. Drizzle butter across top. Bake for 35 minutes.

Gingerbread Cookies

¾ cup (1½ sticks) butter, softened	170 g
2 egg yolks	
1 (18 ounce) spice cake mix	510 g
1 teaspoon ginger	5 ml

- In large bowl combine butter and egg yolks. Gradually blend in cake mix and ginger and mix well.
- Roll out to ⅛-inch (4 mm) thickness on lightly floured surface. Use gingerbread cookie cutter to cut out cookies and place 2 inches (5 cm) apart on cookie sheet. Bake at 375° (190° C) for about 8 minutes or until edges are slightly brown. Cool cookies before transferring to cookie jar.

Peanut Butter Cookies

1 cup sugar	200 g
¾ cup light corn syrup	175 ml
1 (16 ounce) jar crunchy peanut butter	455 g
4½ cups chow mein noodles	250 g

- In saucepan over medium heat, bring sugar and corn syrup to boil and stir in peanut butter. Remove from heat and stir in noodles. Drop by spoonfuls onto wax paper and allow to cool.

Lemon Cookies

½ cup (1 stick) butter, softened	115 g
1⅔ cup sugar	200 g
2 tablespoons lemon juice	30 ml
2 cups flour	240 g

- Cream butter, sugar and lemon juice and slowly stir in flour. Drop by teaspoons onto ungreased cookie sheet. Bake at 350° (175° C) for 14 to 15 minutes.

Devil's Food Cookies

1 (18 ounce) package devil's food cake mix	510 g
½ cup oil	125 ml
2 eggs	
¾ cup chopped pecans, optional	85 g

- Combine cake mix, oil and eggs in bowl and mix well.
- Drop by teaspoons onto non-stick cookie sheet. Bake at 350° (175° C) for 10 to 12 minutes. Cool and remove to wire rack.

Drop Cookies

1 cup (2 sticks) butter, softened	230 g
¾ cup cornstarch	95 g
⅓ cup powdered sugar	40 g
1 cup flour	120 g

- Mix butter, cornstarch, sugar and flour and mix well.
- Drop on cookie sheet in small balls and flatten slightly.
- Bake at 350° (175° C) for about 15 minutes but do not brown.

Frosting for Drop Cookies:

1 (3 ounce) package cream cheese, softened	85 g
1 teaspoon vanilla	5 ml
1 cup powdered sugar	120 g

- Blend all ingredients and mix well. Frost cool cookies.

Double-Chocolate Cookies

6 egg whites	
3 cups powdered sugar	360 g
¼ cup cocoa	20 g
3½ cups finely chopped pecans	390 g

- Beat egg whites until light and frothy. Fold sugar and cocoa into egg whites and beat lightly. Fold in pecans.
- Drop by teaspoons on lightly greased, floured cookie sheet.
- Bake at 325° (165° C) for about 20 minutes. Do not overbake; cool completely before removing from cookie sheet

Easy Peanut Butter Cookies

1⅔ cup powdered sugar	200 g
1 cup crunchy peanut butter	290 g
1 large egg	
1 teaspoon vanilla	5 ml

- Preheat oven to 325° (165° C). In bowl, combine powdered sugar, peanut butter, egg and vanilla, mixing well. Roll dough into 1-inch (2.5 cm) balls and place on greased baking sheet. Lightly press cookies with fork.
- Bake for 10 minutes and cool before storing.

Chinese Cookies

1 (6 ounce) package chocolate chips	170 g
1 (6 ounce) package butterscotch chips	170 g
1 cup salted peanuts	150 g
1 (3 ounce) can chow mein noodles	85 g

- In large saucepan, melt chocolate and butterscotch chips. Add peanuts and noodles and mix well.
- Drop by teaspoonfuls onto wax paper. Refrigerate just to harden.

Butterscotch Cookies

1 (12 ounce) and 1 (6 ounce) package butterscotch chips	340 g/170 g
2¼ cups chow mein noodles	125 g
½ cup chopped walnuts	65 g
¼ cup flaked coconut	20 g

- Melt butterscotch chips in double boiler. Add noodles, walnuts and coconut. Drop by tablespoonfuls onto wax paper.

Cheesecake Cookies

1 cup (2 sticks) butter, softened	230 g
2 (3 ounce) packages cream cheese, softened	2 (85 g)
2 cups sugar	400 g
2 cups flour	240 g

- Cream butter and cream cheese. Add sugar and beat until light and fluffy. Add flour and beat well.
- Drop by teaspoons onto cookie sheet and bake at 350° (175° C) for 12 to 15 minutes or until edges are golden.

Chocolate-Crunch Cookies

1 (18 ounce) package German chocolate cake mix with pudding	510 g
1 egg, slightly beaten	
½ cup (1 stick) butter, melted	115 g
1 cup crispy rice cereal	25 g

- Combine cake mix, egg and butter. Add cereal and stir until they blend. Shape dough into 1-inch (2.5 cm) balls. Place on lightly sprayed cookie sheet.
- Dip fork in flour and flatten cookies in crisscross pattern. Bake at 350° (175° C) for 10 to 12 minutes. Cool.

Butter Cookies

1 pound butter	455 g
¾ cup packed brown sugar	165 g
¾ cup sugar	150 g
4½ cups flour	540 g

- Preheat oven to 350° (175° C). Cream butter, brown sugar and sugar, slowly add flour and mix well. (Batter will be very thick.)
- Roll into small balls and place on ungreased cookie sheet. Bake for 15 minutes until only slightly brown.

Butter Cookie Special

1 (18 ounce) box butter cake mix	510 g
1 (3.4 ounce) package butterscotch instant pudding mix	100 g
1 cup canola oil	250 ml
1 egg, beaten	
1¼ cups chopped pecans	140 g

- Mix by hand cake mix, pudding mix, oil and egg. Beat thoroughly. Stir in pecans. With teaspoon place cookie dough on cookie sheet about 2 inches (5 cm) apart. Bake at 350° (175° C) for about 8 minutes.

Brown Sugar Cookies

¾ cup packed brown sugar	165 g
1 cup (2 sticks) butter, softened	230 g
1 egg yolk	
2 cups flour	240 g

- Cream sugar and butter until light and fluffy. Mix in egg yolk. Blend in flour. Refrigerate dough. Form dough into 1-inch (2.5 cm) balls, flatten and crisscross with fork on lightly greased baking sheet. Bake at 325° (165° C) for 10 to 12 minutes or until golden brown.

Macaroons

2 large egg whites	
3 tablespoons sugar	40 g
½ teaspoon vanilla	2 ml
½ teaspoon almond extract	2 ml
½ cup sweetened flaked coconut	45 g

- Preheat oven to 300° (150° C). Line large baking sheet with foil and spray with cooking spray and lightly dust with flour (shake off excess flour). In bowl, whisk together whites, sugar, vanilla, almond extract and a pinch of salt. Stir in coconut.

- Drop heaping tablespoons of mixture on prepared pan about 2 inches (5 cm) apart. Bake until tops are slightly brown in spots, about 18 minutes. Carefully lift foil with cookies from baking sheet and place on rack to cool. Peel macaroons off foil.

Coconut Macaroons

2 (7 ounce) packages flaked coconut	2 (200 g)
1 (14 ounce) can sweetened condensed milk	395 g
2 teaspoons vanilla	10 ml
½ teaspoon almond extract	2 ml

- In mixing bowl, combine coconut, condensed milk and extracts; mix well. Drop by rounded teaspoons onto foil-lined cookie sheet.

- Bake at 350° (175° C) for 8 to 10 minutes or until light brown around edges. Immediately remove from foil to prevent sticking. Store at room temperature.

Marshmallow Treats

¼ cup (½ stick) butter	60 g
4 cups miniature marshmallows	180 g
½ cup crunchy peanut butter	145 g
5 cups crispy rice cereal	130 g

- In saucepan, melt butter and add marshmallows. Stir until they melt and add peanut butter. Remove from heat. Add cereal and stir well. Press mixture into 9 x 13-inch (23 x 33 cm) pan. Cut in squares when cool.

Raisin Crunch

¾ cup light corn syrup	175 ml
1 cup sugar	200 g
1 cup crunchy peanut butter	290 g
1 (20 ounce) box raisin bran	570 g

● In saucepan combine corn syrup and sugar. Heat until sugar thoroughly dissolves. Remove from heat and stir in peanut butter. Place raisin bran in large container and pour sauce over top. Mix thoroughly. Pat mixture into 9 x 13-inch (23 x 33 cm) pan and cool completely in refrigerator. Cut into squares and store in airtight container.

Scotch Shortbread

½ cup (1 stick) unsalted butter, softened	115 g
⅓ cup sugar	65 g
1¼ cups flour	150 g
Powdered sugar	

● Cream butter and sugar until light and fluffy. Add flour and pinch of salt and mix well. Spread dough in 8-inch (20 cm) square pan. Bake at 325° (165° C) for 20 minutes or until light brown. Cool shortbread in pan, dust with powdered sugar and cut into squares.

Strawberry Crumbles

2¼ cups biscuit mix	270 g
1 cup oats	80 g
1 cup packed brown sugar	220 g
½ cup (1 stick) butter, softened	115 g
1 cup strawberry preserves	320 g

● Preheat oven to 375° (190° C). Mix together biscuit mix, oats and brown sugar. Cut in butter with a pastry blender, until mixture is crumbly.

● Press half this mixture in bottom of greased 9 x 9-inch (23 x 23 cm) baking pan. Spread strawberry preserves over crumbly mixture to within ¼-inch (.6 cm) of edges. Sprinkle remaining crumbly mixture over and gently press into fruit. Bake 30 minutes or until light brown. Cool and cut into bars to serve.

Walnut Bars

1⅔ cups graham cracker crumbs	175 g
1½ cups coarsely chopped walnuts	195 g
1 (14 ounce) can sweetened condensed milk	395 g
¼ cup flaked coconut, optional	20 g

- Place graham cracker crumbs and walnuts in bowl. Slowly add condensed milk, coconut and pinch of salt. Mixture will be very thick.
- Pack into sprayed 9-inch (23 cm) square pan. Pack mixture down with back of spoon. Bake at 350° (175° C) for 35 minutes. When cool cut into squares.

Toffee Bars

1½ cups (3 sticks) butter, softened	340 g
1¾ cups packed light brown sugar	385 g
2 teaspoons vanilla	10 ml
3 cups flour	360 g
1 (8 ounce) package chocolate chips	230 g

- Preheat oven to 350° (175° C).
- In mixing bowl, combine butter, brown sugar and vanilla; beat on medium speed for 3 minutes. Add flour and mix until completely blended and stir in chocolate chips.
- Place dough on a greased 9 x 13-inch (23 x 33 cm) baking pan and bake 25 minutes or until light brown. Cool slightly and cut into bars.

Snickers Brownies

1 (18 ounce) German chocolate cake mix	510 g
¾ cup (1½ sticks) butter, melted	170 g
½ cup evaporated milk	125 ml
4 (3 ounce) Snickers® candy bars	4 (85 g)

- Combine cake mix, butter and evaporated milk in large bowl. Beat on low speed until mixture blends well.
- Add half batter into greased, floured 9 x 13-inch (23 x 33 cm) baking pan. Bake at 350° (175° C) for 10 minutes.
- Remove from oven. Cut candy bars in ⅛-inch (4 mm) slices and place evenly over brownies. Drop remaining half of batter by spoonfuls over candy bars and spread as evenly as possible.
- Bake for 20 minutes longer. When cool, cut into bars.

Pecan Squares

1 (24 ounce) package almond bark	680 g
1 cup cinnamon chips	170 g
1 cup chopped pecans	110 g
8 cups frosted crispy rice cereal	320 g

- Melt almond bark and cinnamon chips in very large saucepan or roasting pan on low heat and stir constantly. After it melts, remove from heat and add pecans and frosted rice cereal. Mix well and stir into 9 x 13-inch (23 x 33 cm) pan. Pat down with back of spoon. Refrigerate. Cut into squares.

Honey-Nut Bars

⅓ cup (⅔ stick) butter	75 g
¼ cup cocoa	20 g
1 (10 ounce) package miniature marshmallows	280 g
6 cups Honey Nut Clusters® cereal	330 g

- Melt butter in large saucepan and stir in cocoa and marshmallows. Cook over low heat, stirring constantly, until marshmallows melt and mixture is smooth. Remove from heat and stir in cereal.
- Pour into sprayed 7 x 11-inch (18 x 28 cm) pan. With spatula, smooth mixture in pan. Cool completely and cut into bars.

Easy Blonde Brownies

1 (1 pound) box light brown sugar	455 g
4 eggs	
2 cups biscuit mix	240 g
2 cups chopped pecans	220 g

- Preheat oven to 350° (175° C). Using mixer, beat brown sugar, eggs and biscuit mix. Stir in pecans and pour into sprayed 9 x 13-inch (23 x 33 cm) baking pan. Bake for 35 minutes. Cool and cut into squares.

Date-Pecan Bars

Filling:

2 (8 ounce) boxes pitted dates, chopped	2 (230 g)
1½ cups orange juice	375 ml
¼ cup sugar	50 g
¼ teaspoon ground cinnamon	1 ml

Crust and Topping:

1½ cups flour	180 g
1½ cups oats	120 g
¾ cup packed brown sugar	165 g
1½ cups finely chopped pecans	165 g
1¼ cups (2½ sticks) cold butter, cut up	285 g

- In saucepan, combine dates, orange juice, sugar and cinnamon and bring to boiling; reduce heat and simmer, stirring several times, for 15 minutes until mixture thickens.
- Preheat oven to 350° (175° C). Place flour, oats, brown sugar and pecans in mixing bowl; cut in butter until mixture is crumbly.
- Transfer 2½ cups (625 ml) mixture to another bowl and set aside. Press remaining crumbs over bottom of sprayed 9 x 13-inch (23 x 33 cm) baking pan.
- Spoon filling over crust and spread up to ¼ inch (6 mm) from edge. Sprinkle set aside crust mixture over top of filling and bake for 35 minutes. Cool and cut into bars.

Chocolate-Cherry Bars

1 (18 ounce) devils food cake mix	510 g
1 (20 ounce) can cherry pie filling	570 g
2 eggs	
1 cup milk chocolate chips	170 g

- In large bowl, mix all ingredients by hand and blend well.
- Pour batter into greased, floured 9 x 13-inch (23 x 33 cm) baking dish.
- Bake at 350° (175° C) for 25 to 30 minutes or until cake tester comes out clean. Cool.

Continued on following page

Continued from previous page

Frosting for Chocolate Cherry Bars:

1 (3 ounce) square semi-sweet chocolate, melted	85 g
1 (3 ounce) package cream cheese, softened	85 g
½ teaspoon vanilla	2 ml
1½ cups powdered sugar	180 g

- In medium bowl beat chocolate, cream cheese and vanilla until smooth. Gradually beat in powdered sugar.
- Pour over cool chocolate-cherry bars.

Chocolate Chip-Cheese Bars

1 (18 ounce) package chocolate chip cookie dough	510 g
1 (8 ounce) package cream cheese, softened	230 g
½ cup sugar	100 g
1 egg	

- Cut cookie dough in half. For crust, press half dough onto bottom of sprayed 9-inch (23 cm) square baking pan or 7 x 11-inch (18 x 28 cm) baking pan.
- In mixing bowl, beat cream cheese, sugar and egg until smooth. Spread over crust. Crumble remaining dough over top.
- Bake at 350° (175° C) for 35 to 40 minutes or until toothpick inserted near center comes out clean. Cool on wire rack. Cut into bars. Refrigerate leftovers.

Chocolate Caramel Bars

1 (18 ounce) package chocolate chip cookie dough, divided	510 g
1 cup chopped walnuts, divided	130 g
1 (10 ounce) jar caramel ice cream topping	280 g

- Preheat oven to 350° (175° C).
- Press three-fourths cookie dough into greased 9 x 13-inch (23 x 33 cm) baking pan and bake for 10 minutes.
- Sprinkle half walnuts over cookie dough and drizzle caramel topping over walnuts. Top with teaspoonfuls of remaining dough and gently press into caramel topping.
- Top with remaining walnuts and bake for 16 minutes or until the edge of dough is set. Cool before cutting into bars.

Chocolate Cherry Squares

1 (4 ounce) package cook-and-serve chocolate pudding mix	115 g
1¾ cups milk	425 ml
¼ cup maraschino cherry juice	60 ml
1 (18 ounce) package chocolate cake mix	510 g
1 cup maraschino cherries, chopped	160 g
1 (6 ounce) package chocolate chips	170 g
1 cup chopped pecans	110 g

- Preheat oven to 350° (175° C). In saucepan, cook pudding mix, milk and cherry juice as directed on package.
- Stir pudding mixture into cake mix and cherries. Spread into 10 x 15-inch (25 x 38 cm) greased and floured baking pan. Sprinkle with chocolate chips and pecans and bake 30 minutes.

Apricot Bars

1¼ cups flour	150 g
¾ cup packed brown sugar	165 g
6 tablespoons (¾ stick) butter	85 g
¾ cup apricot preserves	240 g

- In mixing bowl, combine flour, brown sugar and butter and mix well. Place half mixture in 9-inch (23 cm) square baking pan. Spread apricot preserves over top of mixture. Add remaining flour mixture over top of dessert.
- Bake at 350° (175° C) for 30 minutes. Cut into squares.

Peanut Butter Balls

¾ cup light corn syrup	175 ml
2½ cups crunchy peanut butter	720 g
2¼ cups graham cracker crumbs	235 g
1¼ cups powdered sugar	150 g

- In bowl, combine corn syrup, peanut butter, cracker crumbs and powdered sugar and mix until smooth. Shape into 1-inch (2.5 cm) balls and place on wax paper lined baking sheet. Refrigerate for about 30 minutes.

Chocolate-Peanut Butter Crisps

1 (10 count) package 8-inch flour tortillas	20 cm
8 (1 ounce) squares semi-sweet chocolate, coarsely	
chopped or 8 ounces semi-sweet chocolate morsels	230 g
⅓ cup peanut butter or crunchy peanut butter	95 g
1 (14 ounce) can sweetened condensed milk	395 g

- Cut flour tortillas into 8 wedges and place on baking sheet. Bake at 350° (175° C) for 10 minutes and cool on rack.
- In heavy saucepan, melt chocolate over low heat, stirring constantly. Stir in peanut putter, sweetened condensed milk and 2 tablespoons (30 ml) water and heat through. (If sauce is too thick, add 1 teaspoon (5 ml) water at a time, until sauce smoothly drizzles on foil.)
- Drizzle warm chocolate sauce over wedges or serve immediately in chafing dish or fondue pot and dip crisp tortilla wedges.

Nutty Fudgies

1 (18 ounce) package fudge cake mix	510 g
1 (8 ounce) carton sour cream	230 g
⅔ cup peanut butter chips	115 g
½ cup chopped peanuts	85 g

- Beat cake mix and sour cream until mixture blends and is smooth. Stir in peanut butter chips and peanuts.
- Drop by teaspoonfuls onto sprayed cookie sheet. Bake at 350° (175° C) for 10 to 12 minutes. Remove from oven and cool.

Peanut Butter Crunchies

1 cup sugar	200 g
½ cup white corn syrup	125 ml
2 cups peanut butter	575 g
4 cups crispy rice cereal	105 g

- In saucepan, mix sugar and syrup and bring to a boil. Remove from stove and stir in peanut butter. Add crispy rice cereal and mix well. Drop by teaspoonfuls onto wax paper. Refrigerate.

Peanutty Cocoa Puffs

¾ cup light corn syrup	175 ml
1¼ cups sugar	250 g
1¼ cups crunchy peanut butter	360 g
4½ cups Cocoa Puffs® cereal	160 g

- In large saucepan bring syrup and sugar to rolling boil. Stir in peanut butter and mix well. Stir in cocoa puffs.
- Drop on wax paper by teaspoonfuls.

Porcupine Clusters

¼ cup corn syrup	60 ml
1 (12 ounce) package white chocolate morsels	340 g
2 cups chow mein noodles	110 g
¾ cup salted peanuts	110 g

- On low heat, melt corn syrup and white chocolate chips. Pour over noodles and peanuts and mix well. Drop by teaspoonfuls on wax paper. Refrigerate to harden. Store in airtight container.

Scotch Crunchies

½ cup crunchy peanut butter	145 g
1 (6 ounce) package butterscotch bits	170 g
2½ cups frosted flakes	105 g
½ cup peanuts	75 g

- Combine peanut butter and butterscotch bits in large saucepan and melt over low heat. Stir until butterscotch bits melt. Stir in cereal and peanuts. Drop by teaspoonfuls onto wax paper. Refrigerate. Store in airtight container.

Pumpkin Cupcakes

1 (18 ounce) package spice cake mix	510 g
1 (15 ounce) can pumpkin	425 g
3 eggs	
⅓ cup canola oil	75 ml

- With mixer, blend cake mix, pumpkin, eggs, oil and ⅓ cup (75 ml) water. Beat for 2 minutes. Pour batter into 24 paper-lined muffin cups and fill three-fourths full. Bake at 350° (175° C) for 18 to 20 minutes or until toothpick inserted in center comes out clean.

Caramel-Apple Cupcakes

1 (18 ounce) package carrot cake mix	510 g
3 cups chopped, peeled tart apples	375 g
1 (12 ounce) package butterscotch chips	340 g
1 cup finely chopped pecans	110 g

- Make cake mix according to package directions. Fold in apples. Fill 12 greased or paper-lined jumbo muffin cups three-fourths full. Bake at 350° (175° C) for 20 minutes or until toothpick comes out clean. In saucepan on very low heat melt butterscotch chips. Spread over cupcakes and sprinkle with chopped pecans.

Cracker Candy Bites

2¾ cups round buttery crackers, coarsely broken-up	160 g
¾ cup (1 ½ sticks) butter	170 g
2 cups packed brown sugar	440 g
1 (12 ounce) package milk chocolate chips	340 g

- Preheat oven to 350° (175° C) degrees. Place crackers in greased 9 x 13-inch (23 x 33 cm) baking dish.

- In saucepan, combine butter and brown sugar and bring to boiling. Boil 3 minutes, stirring constantly. Pour over crackers.

- Bake for 5 minutes and turn oven off. Sprinkle chocolate chips over cracker mixture. Return to oven and let stand for about 5 minutes or until chocolate melts. Remove from oven and spread chocolate evenly over cracker mixture. Cool, break into pieces.

Diamond Fudge

1 (6 ounce) package semi-sweet chocolate morsels	170 g
1 cup peanut butter	290 g
½ cup (1 stick) butter	115 g
1 cup powdered sugar	120 g

- Cook chocolate morsels, peanut butter and butter in saucepan over low heat, stirring constantly, just until mixture melts and is smooth. Remove from heat.
- Add powdered sugar and stir until smooth. Spoon into buttered 8-inch (20 cm) square pan and refrigerate until firm. Cut into squares.

Peanut Butter Fudge

1 (12 ounce) jar crunchy peanut butter	340 g
1 (12 ounce) package milk chocolate chips	340 g
1 (14 ounce) can sweetened condensed milk	395 g
1 cup chopped pecans	110 g

- In saucepan, combine peanut butter, chocolate chips and condensed milk. Heat on low, stirring constantly, until chocolate melts.
- Add pecans and mix well. Pour into 9 x 9-inch (23 x 23 cm) buttered dish.

Microwave Fudge

3 cups semi-sweet chocolate morsels	510 g
1 (14 ounce) can sweetened condensed milk	395 g
¼ cup (½ stick) butter, cut into pieces	60 g
1 cup chopped walnuts	130 g

- Combine chocolate morsels, condensed milk and butter in 2-quart (2 L) glass bowl. Microwave on MEDIUM 4 to 5 minutes, stirring at 1½-minute intervals.
- Stir in walnuts and pour into buttered 8-inch (20 cm) square dish. Refrigerate. Cut into squares.

Raisin Fudge

1 (12 ounce) package semi-sweet chocolate chips	340 g
1 cup crunchy peanut butter	290 g
3 cups miniature marshmallows	135 g
¾ cup raisins	120 g

- In saucepan melt chocolate chips and peanut butter over medium to low heat. Fold in marshmallows and raisins and stir until marshmallows melt. Pour into 7 x 11-inch (18 x 28 cm) pan. Refrigerate until firm. Cut into squares. Store where it is cool.

Easy, Fast Fudge

1 (14 ounce) can sweetened condensed milk	395 g
3 cups semi-sweet or milk chocolate chips	510 g
1 teaspoon vanilla extract	5 ml

- Combine milk, chocolate chips and pinch of salt in medium saucepan over medium-low heat. Stir constantly until chocolate is melted.
- Remove from heat and stir in vanilla.
- Spread in buttered 8 x 8-inch (20 x 20 cm) pan and let cool.

Hazel's Nutty Fudge

1 (12 ounce) package white chocolate chips	340 g
¾ cup hazelnut-cocoa spread	220 g
1½ cups chopped hazelnuts, divided	190 g
Coconut	

- In medium saucepan over low heat, melt white chocolate chips and add hazelnut spread. Cook and stir until mixture blends well. Remove from heat and stir in 1 cup (130 g) hazelnuts.
- Drop by teaspoons on wax paper. Garnish with remaining hazelnuts. Refrigerate.

Date Loaf Candy

3 cups sugar	600 g
1 cup milk	250 ml
1 (16 ounce) box chopped dates	455 g
1 cup chopped pecans	110 g

- Combine sugar and milk in large saucepan.
- Cook to soft-boil stage (234°/110° C on candy thermometer). Stir in dates. Cook to hard boil stage (260°/126° C), stirring constantly.
- Remove from heat, add pecans and mix well. Stir and cool until stiff. Pour mixture onto damp tea towel. Roll into log. Let stand until set. Remove tea towel and slice.

Dream Candy

2 (8 ounce) cartons whipping cream	2 (250 ml)
3 cups sugar	600 g
1 cup light corn syrup	250 ml
1 cup chopped pecans	110 g

- In saucepan, combine whipping cream, sugar and corn syrup. Cook to soft-ball stage. Stir and beat until candy cools.
- Add pecans and pour into 9-inch (23 cm) buttered pan.

No-Bake Chocolate Drops

1 (6 ounce) semi-sweet chocolate baking chips	170 g
½ cup crunchy peanut butter	145 g
1 (5 ounce) package chow mein noodles	140 g
1 cup salted, roasted peanuts	150 g

- In saucepan, combine baking chips and peanut butter and heat on low, stirring constantly until chocolate chips have melted.
- Add noodles and peanuts and stir until ingredients are evenly coated with chocolate. Drop by heaping teaspoonfuls onto wax paper. Refrigerate.

Tumbleweeds

1 (12 ounce) package butterscotch chips	340 g
¼ cup peanut butter	70 g
1 (12 ounce) can peanuts	340 g
1 (4 ounce) can shoe-string potatoes	115 g

- In saucepan on low heat, melt chips with peanut butter and mix well. Stir in peanuts and shoe-string potatoes. Drop by tablespoonfuls on wax paper. Store in airtight container.

Chocolate Toffee

1 cup sugar	200 g
1 cup (2 sticks) butter	230 g
1 (6 ounce) package chocolate chips	170 g
1 cup chopped pecans	110 g

- In heavy saucepan, combine sugar and butter. Cook until candy reaches hard-crack stage (300°/149° C). Pour onto greased baking sheet.
- Melt chocolate in double boiler and spread over toffee.
- Sprinkle with pecans and press pecans into chocolate.
- Refrigerate briefly to set chocolate. Break into pieces.

Pralines

1 (16 ounce) box light brown sugar	455 g
¾ cup evaporated milk	175 ml
1½ cups pecan pieces or halves	165 g
1½ teaspoons instant coffee or freeze-dried coffee granules	7 ml

- Mix all ingredients thoroughly in medium saucepan, cook slowly over low heat and stir constantly until mixture reaches soft-ball stage (234°/112° C). Remove from heat and set aside for 5 minutes.
- Beat with spoon until mixture is thick. Drop by teaspoonful onto greased foil. When cool and hard, peel foil from back and wrap each praline in plastic wrap.

Quick Pralines

1 (3 ounce) box butterscotch cook-and-serve pudding	85 g
1¼ cups sugar	250 g
½ cup evaporated milk	125 ml
2 cups pecan pieces	220 g

- In large saucepan, mix butterscotch pudding, sugar and milk.
- Bring to a boil, stirring constantly for 2 minutes.
- Add pecans and boil another 1½ minutes, stirring constantly.
- Remove from heat. Beat until candy begins to cool and drop by tablespoonfuls on wax paper.

Yummy Pralines

½ cup (1 stick) butter	115 g
1 (16 ounce) box light brown sugar	455 g
1 (8 ounce) carton whipping cream	230 g
2½ cups pecan halves	285 g

- In heavy saucepan, combine butter, brown sugar and cream.
- Cook until temperature comes to soft-ball stage (234°/112° C), about 20 minutes, stirring constantly. Remove from heat and set aside for 5 minutes.
- Fold in pecans and stir for several minutes until ingredients are glassy. With large spoon, drop onto wax paper and remove when cooled.

Index

Main Dishes

N

Nuts

Soups and Stews

Cookbooks Published by Cookbook Resources, LLC
Bringing Family and Friends to the Table

Easy Diabetic Recipes

The Best of Cooking with 3 Ingredients

The Ultimate Cooking with 4 Ingredients

Easy Cooking with 5 Ingredients

Gourmet Cooking with 5 Ingredients

4-Ingredient Recipes for 30-Minute Meals

Essential 3-4-5 Ingredient Recipes

The Best 1001 Short, Easy Recipes

1001 Slow Cooker Recipes

1001 Short, Easy, Inexpensive Recipes

1001 Fast Easy Recipes

1001 Community Recipes

Busy Woman's Quick & Easy Recipes

Busy Woman's Slow Cooker Recipes

Easy Slow Cooker Cookbook

Easy One-Dish Meals

Easy Potluck Recipes

Easy Casseroles

Easy Desserts

Sunday Night Suppers

Easy Church Suppers

365 Easy Meals

365 Easy Soups and Stews

365 Easy Vegetarian Recipes

365 Easy Casserole Recipes

365 Easy Chicken Recipes

365 Easy Soup Recipes

365 Easy One-Dish Recipes

365 Easy Pasta Recipes

365 Easy Slow Cooker Recipes

Quick Fixes with Cake Mixes

Kitchen Keepsakes & More Kitchen Keepsakes

Gifts for the Cookie Jar

All New Gifts for the Cookie Jar

Muffins In A Jar

The Big Bake Sale Cookbook

Classic Tex-Mex and Texas Cooking

Classic Southwest Cooking

Miss Sadie's Southern Cooking

Texas Longhorn Cookbook

Cookbook 25 Years

A Little Taste of Texas

A Little Taste of Texas II

Trophy Hunters' Wild Game Cookbook

Recipe Keeper

Leaving Home Cookbook and Survival Guide

Classic Pennsylvania Dutch Cooking

Simple Old-Fashioned Baking

Healthy Cooking with 4 Ingredients

Best-Loved Canadian Recipes

Best-Loved New England Recipes

Best-Loved Recipes from the Pacific Northwest

Best-Loved Southern Recipes

The California Cookbook

The Pennsylvania Cookbook

cookbook resources® LLC

www.cookbookresources.com

Your Ultimate Source for Easy Cookbooks

How to Order

1001 Fast Easy Recipes
and other cookbooks
published by Cookbook Resources LLC.

Visit our Web site to view
our entire collection of cookbooks:

www.cookbookresources.com

Your order will be processed
online with complete security.

Or call toll-free
1-866-229-2665
to place your order
or for additional information.